WITH

EXILE

AN AMERICAN'S ADVENTURES WITH
THE ARMY THAT CANNOT DIE

BY

FORTIER JONES

ILLUSTRATED WITH
PHOTOGRAPHS

1916

TO

THE MEMORY

OF

THE CHEECHAS OF SERBIA

THIS BOOK

IS REVERENTLY DEDICATED

"Grow old along with me!
The best is yet to be . . . "

TABLE OF CONTENTS

LIST OF ILLUSTRATIONS

LIST OF ILLUSTRATIONS

WITH SERBIA INTO EXILE

WITH SERBIA INTO EXILE

CHAPTER I

BATTLE LINES AT PEACE

I HAVE to thank a man on a Broadway express for the fact that at the close of September, 1915, I found myself in a remote valley of the Bosnian mountains. The preceding June this person, unknown to me, threw a day-old newspaper at my feet, and because it fell right side up, I became aware that men were wanted to do relief work in Serbia. In an hour I had become a part of the expedition, in a week I had been "filled full" of small-pox, typhus, and typhoid vaccines and serums. Three weeks more found me at Gibraltar enduring the searching, and not altogether amicable, examination of a young British officer, and within a month I was happily rowing with hotel-keepers in Saloniki, having just learned in the voyage across the Mediterranean that submarines were

3

at work in that region.   With a swiftness that left
little time for consideration the next few weeks
passed in camp organization at Nish, in praying
that our long-delayed automobiles would come, and
in getting acquainted with a country about which I
had found but little trustworthy information in
America.

Then because an English woman, Miss Sybil
Eden, with the intrepidity and clear-sightedness
which I later found characteristic of British women,
decided that relief must be carried where, on account of great transportation difficulties, it had
never been before, I spent six wonderful weeks
among the magnificent mountains of Bosnia at the
tiny village of Dobrun.

On a certain day near the end of this sojourn my
story of the great retreat properly begins.   I sat
chatting with a Serbian captain of engineers
beside a mountain stream six miles behind the
Drina River, where for almost a year two hostile
armies had sat face to face, watching intently but
fighting rarely.   It was a beautiful day, typical of
the Bosnian autumn.   The sunshine was delightfully warm and drowsy; the pines along the rugged
slopes above us showed dull green and restful,
while the chestnut-grove near which we sat show-

Miss Eden's Bosnian Expedition

Sir Ralph Paget is standing in the center. On his right are, successively, Mlle. Christitch, Miss Eden, and the author

ered hosts of saffron leaves into the clear stream at our feet. Overhead an almost purple sky was flecked with fluffy clouds that sailed lazily by. Peace filled the Dobrun valley, peace rested unnaturally, uncannily over the length and breadth of beautiful Serbia, and our talk had been of the preceding months of quiet, unbroken except for vague, disturbing rumors that were now taking more definite form and causing the captain grave concern.

On the other side of the little valley ran the narrow-gage railway which bridged the roadless gap between Vishegrad, on the Drina, and Vardishte, the frontier post between Serbia and Bosnia. It was down-grade all the way from Vardishte to Vishegrad, which was fortunate, for the Austrians had smashed all locomotives before they retreated, and Serbia had been unable to get any more over the mountains to this isolated little railway. As we talked, two large trucks thundered by loaded high with the round, one-kilogram loaves of bread that were baked at Vardishte, and thus sent down daily to the men in the Drina trenches. Ox-teams had laboriously to pull these trucks back again to the bakeries. A truck filled to a wonderful height with new-mown hay for the oxen at Vardishte now

stood on a siding to let the bread-train go by.   It
looked very queer being pulled along the railway
track like a farm-wagon by ten teams of huge oxen.
From the army blacksmith's shop near by came the
pleasant sound of ringing steel as the peasant
smiths fashioned shoes for the cavalry horses, and
the steady *rat-tat-tat* of hammers came from down
the river where the army engineers with the simplest
sort of tools were constructing a permanent bridge
to replace the one destroyed by the retreating
enemy.   Some refugee children, in filthy rags and
suffering from scurvy, splashed about in the creek,
shouting and laughing as if there were nothing in
all the world but sunshine and sparkling water.   It
was hard to think that less than six miles away, beyond two thin lines of trenches and a rushing river,
the sway of the great war lord began and stretched
unbroken to Berlin.

The evening before we had gone down to Vishegrad to see the trenches.   One always had to
choose the darkness for these visits, because the
Austrian guns from an impregnable position across
the river commanded all approaches to Vishegrad.
Only under cover of the night were we allowed to
venture in, although Serbian soldiers came and
went throughout the daylight hours by devious

paths known only to themselves. To get there one had to mount a hand car—"wagonette," the officers called it—take off the brake, and sit clear of the handles. Starting at a snail's pace, we soon gathered very creditable speed, and shot through tunnel after tunnel without lights, but whooping at the top of our voices to warn any unwary pedestrian who might be on the track.

Along the beautiful mountain gorge we sped, sometimes by the river-bank, sometimes hundreds of feet above the torrent, along walls of solid masonry built up from the bottom of the cañon. The stars came out, and a full moon was rising over the eastern mountains as we flashed through a last long tunnel and brought the car to a stop in a weed-grown railway yard. The commandant of the place and a group of officers welcomed us in subdued tones, and we set off down the rusty tracks toward the town. Thoughtlessly a companion stuck a cigarette into his mouth and struck a match. No sooner had it flashed than a large hand slid over his shoulder and crushed the flame, while an officer in polished French begged that monsieur would forgo smoking for a little while. Brief as the flash of light had been, this request was punctuated by the whiz of a rifle-bullet overhead and a distant report on the forbidding-looking slope on the opposite side of the river.

Stepping carefully, we came to the railway station, a large building that had just been completed before the war began, but now a pile of empty walls through many jagged holes in which the moonlight poured.

We came into what had been the town. In the moonlight it looked just like Pompeii. Whole portions of it had been pounded to ruins in successive bombardments, but now and then, due to the conformation of the terrain, patches of buildings had escaped uninjured, being out of range of the high-perched Austrian guns. There was deathly silence, which we dared not break except with guarded whispers, and distantly the rush of the Drina could be heard.

Beckoning me from the rest of the party, a former resident of Vishegrad, a druggist, led me up a side street and by a back court into a ruined apothecary shop. Here I could use my pocket flash-light to advantage. For months the shop had been unoccupied, yet there was a curious appearance of the proprietor having just stepped out. After demolishing the houses that adjoined it, a shell of large caliber had burst in the front entrance of the shop.

All the well-filled shelves at that end were blown
to splinters, and drugs and glass were scattered
over the place in a fine powder. But on the jagged
end of one of these shelves a large bottle of pink
pills stood jauntily, and below it hung a barometer
filled with purple liquid, absolutely untouched.
There was a glass case of tooth brushes standing in
the center, with debris piled two feet deep around it.
On the prescription-counter at my right a set of
druggist's scales stood, delicately balanced, some
unfinished prescription in one pan and weights in
the other. Hanging from the torn edge of the ceil-
ing a pulchrious maiden in strong flesh tints hailed
the rising sun, across the face of which the name of
a German shampoo was spread, while she luxuriously combed straw-colored locks of great abundance. I flashed the light here and there, revealing
these curious freaks of chance, and suddenly just
at my feet I saw something gleam white. I
stooped, and picked up a small handkerchief of
filmy lace, crumpled as if it had been tightly
gripped in a little hand. As I shook it out a faint
odor of violet perfume rose, bringing as nothing
else could the sense of tragic change between the
tense moments of Europe at that hour and those
far-off, happy days when youth and lace and violet

perfume went their careless way together through the streets of Vishegrad.

Emerging into the ruined, moonlit street, we found our party had disappeared, but just ahead were two of our soldiers. With these as guides, we stole with increasing care to a spot near the river-bank where some trees cast a black shade. From this vantage-point we could see clearly the ancient stone bridge about one hundred yards away. It is a beautiful bridge, more than five hundred years old, and consists of eleven arches, which evenly decrease in size from the middle one until they melt into solid masonry on each bank. The central arches were blown away at the beginning of hostilities, and in the moonlight the two remnants jutted out into the river like facsimiles of the famous pile at Avignon.

Later in the evening, when I dined at a sheltered house less than two hundred yards from the Austrian trenches, in a comfortable sitting-room, I smoked Austrian cigarettes and drank beer from Sarajevo while a companion played American rag-time on a grand piano. At the same time, I fancy, behind the Austrian trenches the officers were smoking Serbian cigarettes and drinking Serbian wine. For until a day or so previously there had been a truce lasting several weeks, and across the gap in the blown-up bridge the two hostile commanders had exchanged delicacies and greetings by means of an old tin pail hung on a rope. New troops had come to the other side, however, and the truce had ended as suddenly as it had begun. At the approach to the bridge a guard was always kept, and to shield the men, while changing this guard, a rough wall of corrugated iron had been constructed for about fifty yards from the end of a trench to the sheltered position on the bridge. Toward this barrier we now crept until we were leaning against it and could peep over at the river just below us, dimly across which we could see the earthworks of the Austrians, where we knew silent watchers were tirelessly waiting night and day, alert to kill some enemy. It gave one a peculiar feeling, that sense of myriads of human beings peeking at one another behind dirt banks with rifles poised and fingers on the triggers. It is the new warfare, the sort that this war has brought to high perfection.

My interest was such that I leaned too eagerly upon my sheltering sheet of iron. With what I am sure is the very loudest clangor I shall ever hear, it tumbled away from me, and fell into the river. The clash echoed and reëchoed through the silent town and up the valley. If I had pulled Schönbrunn crashing down about my ears, I could not have felt more conspicuous. Also I became aware that I was standing up there in the moonlight with nothing whatever between me and war, and I lost no time in placing the rest of the wall between that stern reality and myself. The opposite bank was as silent as before; not a rifle rang out. The soldiers in the trenches near by did not know what to make of it, but we soon had another piece of iron in the place of the one that had fallen. One of the sentries said he supposed it made such a dreadful row that the boys across the way thought some trick was being played on them.

Such tricks as this were more or less common. On one occasion, after two or three weeks of absolute quiet, a violent artillery and rifle engagement was precipitated when some Serbian wags tied tin cans to the tails of two dogs, and set them off down the trail in front of the Serbian trenches. The dogs kicked up a great noise for a couple of miles, and the Austrians, thinking an attempt to cross the river was in progress, rained shot and shell for hours along the two-mile front, while the Serbians sat snugly in their trenches. The dogs

A Bosnian refugee boy

Soldiers from the Drina trenches receiving their daily allowance
of bread

were unhurt. Also, if one was to believe report, the commandant at Vishegrad knew to a nicety what was going on in the enemy trenches. Every other night an Austrian officer of high rank was said to row across the river at a secluded spot and make a full report to the Serbians as to the number, nationality, and intention of the forces in his trenches. It is quite reasonable to believe this is true, and also that the Austrians were equally well informed as to what went on in Vishegrad.

After dining with the commandant, we were asked if we would like to see a "potato ball," which the soldiers and village maidens were holding at a small café in one of the islands of safety. Nothing could have been more bizarre than a ball, even a "potato ball," in that crumbling city, so we accepted the invitation with interest. Again we sneaked through the melancholy streets, making detours around huge holes that bursting shells had dug and piles of debris from fallen buildings. We entered a large, square room jammed full of people except for a clear space in the middle. Heavy black cloths draped all openings, so that no ray of light shone outside. Everything was shut tight, causing the air to grow vile, full of cigarette smoke and the odor of the dim kerosene lamps that lighted the place.   At one end of the room a jolly-looking, middle-aged woman bent over a stove, making Turkish coffee which she dispensed copiously.   On our entrance she came forward, secured us chairs, and smilingly brought us trays of her very excellent coffee.

The hubbub had stopped when the officers appeared with us, and I looked about on the silent, curious faces that peered at me.   They were mostly young soldiers and girls.   Among the latter I recognized some who had come to our relief station the day before destitute of food and clothing. Many of these young people, clinging tenaciously to the ruins of their homes, were the last remnants of families that the war had blotted out.   The soldiers had the mud of the trenches on their clothes, and on their faces the smiles of young fellows out for a night of it.   A little way across the river the enemy watched, or perhaps they, too, were dancing, for the width of a trench does not change human nature.   At a few words from the officers, the leading spirits overcame their diffidence and forced the old fiddler, who sat on the back of a chair, with his feet on the seat, to strike up a favorite dance. The boys fell into line, and, passing the group of girls, each chose a partner for the simple, crude, happy dance that followed. Plaintively pounding out the rhythm, the fiddler fiddled, perspiration poured from the gallant young soldiers, the maidens' faces flushed with the quickened dance, the atmosphere grew unbearably hot and heavy, and shrill, care-free laughter filled the room. So Pierrot danced his brief hours away in the stricken city.

In the small hours of morning we made our weary march back to Dobrun, for it was up-grade now, and easier to walk than to work the hand car.

Talking to the captain there on the river-bank, I remarked that this year of peace in war seemed strange to me. When first I came to Serbia in July I had heard a rumor of a great Teutonic drive through the country. Mackensen had massed half a million men along the Danube, it was said, and German troops were coming. The Austrian commander would lead, and the way to Constantinople up the Morava valley would be opened with Bulgaria's aid. But everywhere things were quiet. Along the Save and the Danube affairs might not be so sociable as at Vishegrad, but were just as peaceful. As I knew her last summer, Serbia was a land of pleasant places. There was still destitution among her refugees, but the traces of war were fast being obliterated. For a year she had been resting, merely toying with war, building up her army in every possible way after its wonderful victory against an invading force that outnumbered it three to one.

A few weeks earlier, at Semendria, now immortal in Serbian history, I had lunched in full sight of the Austrian guns. I recall the sleepy medieval street, the beautiful Danube, with vineyard-draped banks, yellow with sunshine, purple with grapes. I remember, with a feeling of unreality now, the charming, simple hospitality of the prefect as he came to greet us, perfectly attired in morning costume, and offered us a good lunch of the dishes of old Serbia, with excellent wine. I was motoring on an inspection tour with Mr. Walter Mallory, leader of the Columbia University Relief Expedition, and M. Todolich of the Interior Department, supervisor of Serbia's gendarmerie. These gendarmes, because of certain disabilities, could not serve in the regular army, but were drafted into the police force. When destruction fell on Belgrade, it found the trenches held mainly by these men who could not be real soldiers. They held those trenches for two horrible days while fire fell like snow on the city, held them until there were no trenches to hold, and those that were left fought the enemy through the streets of their beautiful little capital. From home to home they retreated until none was left to retreat, only piles of blue-coated bodies that with the thousands of dead civilians littered the streets. They knew 'they could not hold the city. It was merely a delaying action until the army could take up new positions, one of those rear-guard engagements so common in Belgium and France when the German army was sweeping on, in which the men who stayed behind faced sure defeat and certain death.

It was just about two months before this happened that we three, with a Serbian interpreter, left Nish at three o'clock one morning in the midst of a violent storm. There was a gale blowing, and rain was falling in solid sheets as our car pluckily splashed through mud above the axles on the road down the Morava valley to Alexinats. Motoring in Serbia is a strenuous occupation. If one makes forty or fifty miles a day, one has done well. Shortly out of Nish, one of our mud-guard supports snapped, and could not be mended. It meant that the whole guard had to come off, and that meant some one must "get out and get under" to unscrew the taps. For a mile we dragged along, looking for a dry place. There was no such thing in Serbia at the moment, I think, so at last I crawled under the car and did the job, lying in slush several inches deep which did not improve my appearance.   M. Todolich spoke not a word of English when we started, but, after a few blow-outs, carburetor troubles, etc., he had learned some.

"How is it now?" Mallory would frequently ask me, and my short "All right" seemed to amuse M. Todolich greatly.   Soon at each stop he was piping:

"How ees it naw, Guspodin Yones?   Awlright, eh?"

I knew next to nothing about the inner mysteries of an automobile, but am sure I impressed our Serbian guest with that "All right."   Soon he became exasperating as troubles increased and muddy disappearances under the car became more frequent.   "Awlright, awlright," he would peep over and over again, as if it were the greatest joke in the world.   Once, when I was at the wheel, we were starting down a very steep incline, and coming to a sharp "switchback," the brakes did not hold, and I had to take the hair-pin turn at an awful speed.   For a minute the car simply danced on its front wheels along the edge of a high cliff. Then I got past the curve and into the road again.

I glanced back, and saw "Nick," our interpreter, hanging far over toward the landward side, tongue sticking out and eyes staring; but M. Todolich was huddled unconcernedly in his corner, and flung out "Awlright" at me, as if I had n't scared us all to death.

After a while the rain stopped, and we made good time on the perfectly level road that runs along the broad floor of the Morava valley, which many ages ago served as an easy highway for the Third Crusade. For miles on each side stretched smooth fields of Indian corn, small grains, and magnificent truck-gardens. Despite the primitive methods of agriculture, the Morava valley, which runs almost the length of Serbia, is one great garden plot, and is as beautiful and fertile as the valley of the Loire, in France. Last summer, viewing this valley and its lesser counterparts along the Mlava, the Timok, and in the Stig country, the possibility of famine in such a rich land seemed too remote to consider. There were many workers in the fields, but all were women and children. It was they who gathered the ripened corn into the primitive ox-carts, reaped with scythes the waving wheat and rye, or plowed with wooden shares the rich, black loam. Women drove the farm stock along the highways, women filled the market-places in every village, and women for the most part waited upon us in the cafés. Almost the only men we saw were the lonely *cheechas* sparsely scattered along the railway to guard the bridges from the spies that lurked everywhere. We passed many prosperous villages in which, with the exception of the scarcity of men, life seemed to move on as prosaically as in times of peace. We stopped and looked over the large sugar mills at Chupriya, now silent on account of the war and the scarcity of labor, and we passed some of Serbia's best coal-mines. Finally, at dusk, we came to Polanka through a narrow road where the mud was so bad that we had to be hauled out.

The inns of Serbia are never luxurious and not always clean. The one we found at Polanka was no exception. Mallory and I shared a room on the ground floor. It had a single large window overlooking the sidewalk at a height of about seven feet. We retired early and, being worn out, slept soundly. I was awakened next morning by "Nick's" unmusical voice, saying, "Meester Yones, eet ees time to get up." A minute I lay in bed rubbing my eyes, trying to recall where I was, then I decided to take revenge on Mallory.

"Mallory," I shouted, "get up at once! Don't you know it's terribly late?"

But Mallory was already dressing. I cast a glance about the room, carelessly at first, then with an interest that quickly turned to anxiety.

"Mallory," I sternly demanded, "where *are* my clothes?" He looked up unconcernedly, took in the room at a glance, and shrugged his shoulders.

"Why, how should *I* know? I'm not your valet," he said. "Look behind the wash-stand or under your bed. The *rackiya* we had for dinner may have been stronger than I supposed."

Loath as I was to admit this insinuation, I looked, but with no success. Then I gradually remembered where I had placed them the night before, but I would not admit the horrible suspicion that arose.

"Mallory, if you do not produce my trousers at once, I'll cable the President. A man of your age should know that a sovereign American citizen cannot suffer these indignities in foreign lands without—" But my ultimatum was cut short by Nick, who thrust his ridiculous head in at the door.

"Meester Yones, the hotel maid wants to know eef thees ees yours," he happily interrogated, holding up a garment. "And, een addition, thees and thees and thees," and he held up in turn certain other garments, including my coat. "She says she found 'em scattered along for two hundred yards down the street outside your window. She says she hope you had nothing een your pockets, for there ees nothin een them now."

"This is not all, Nick," I screamed. "You have more, say you have more, or I am lost. Where are my trousers, Nick? Tell the maid to go down the street again, farther down the street, and see if she cannot find a pair of khaki trousers. Maybe they are hanging on a tree or on somebody's wall. They must be somewhere; they wouldn't fit any one but me."

"How ees everything? Awlright, eh?" M. Todolich drifted into the door, demurely, then stopped in amazement at the sight of me waving my incomplete costume about and entreating Nick.

The interpreter explained to him my situation, whereupon he grew greatly excited. What, an American Guspodin had his trousers stolen and that, too, when he was traveling with the chief of gendarmes. Outrageous! He would call the mayor at once, and order the gendarmes to make a thorough search of the town. No visitor from America should be able to say that he could not

safely leave his trousers wherever he wished in
Serbia. Then he shouted down the hall, and
brought to the scene of my humiliation the hotel
proprietor, his wife, his daughter, the maid, the
valet, and the cook, so that precipitately I sought
refuge under my sheets. He soundly berated the
hotel-keeper because he had not personally stood
guard over my trousers all night, made scathing
remarks about the citizens of Polanka, and not once
allowed himself a remark as to the mentality of
people who hung their clothes in open windows on
ground floors.

"Send for the mayor at once," he ordered, "and
all the gendarmes." This was too much. I saw
the *haute monde*, the *élite*, and the rank and file of
Polanka convoked around me trouserless. I
sensed the mayor's stupefaction at his city's deep
disgrace, and the gendarmes' merciless fury as
they made a house to house search for my khaki
trousers.

"Nick," I weakly implored, "please, Nick, persuade the old gentleman to let the matter stand.
Tell him I was going to throw them away. Tell
him it was my fault; probably the wind blew them
somewhere. Tell him anything you like, Nick, but
don't let him start a riot. I did n't lose my money,

so it does n't matter.   You must go to a shop right
away and get me a pair of soldier's trousers.   I
have always wanted some, anyway.   And, Nick,
clear this mob out of my room!"

Soon Nick's ever-ready tongue straightened matters out, and I had a brand-new pair of soldier's
trousers.   When I was dressed I walked the street
that had been bedecked with my wardrobe, and saw
a familiar-looking document fluttering in the gutter.   I raced for it, and with a sigh tucked it into
my pocket, for it bore the seal of the United States
and "requested" whomever it might concern to let
me freely pass.

From Polanka we had come next day for lunch
at Semendria, and after a pleasant chat with the
prefect and his son, a very likable young fellow
with happy manners, we took the road to Belgrade.
For fifteen or twenty kilometers the way ran on
the bank of the Danube, there being barely room
for a first-line trench between it and the river.
Three hundred yards away the Austrian trenches
were in plain sight across the river, though sometimes masked behind willow-trees.   Leaving Semendria by way of the old fruit-market, where
were for sale at very low prices unlimited quantities of white and purple grapes, huge plums, large

red apples, figs, pears, and fine peaches, we were at
once exposed to the fire of the enemy's cannon.
Only there was no fire. The guns were there, the
trenches, and the men, but unconcernedly we sailed
along for an hour, flaunting our car in their faces,
as it were, without calling forth as much as a rifle-
shot. This was disappointing, for we had been
told that they seldom let automobiles pass without
taking a pot-shot or two, and for the first time since
coming to Serbia we had seemed in a fair way for
a war thrill. The Serbian trench was deserted except for sentries at great intervals, but higher up in
the vineyards, on the other side of us, were more
trenches and, beyond these, dug-outs where the soldiers lived.

Now on another such day, two months later, suddenly a rain of shell began on that town and stretch
of road. It continued for forty-eight hours until
there was no town and no road and no trench.
Then across that quiet, beautiful river men put out
by fifties from the Austrian side in large, flat-bot-
tomed boats and, confident that nothing remained
alive on the other shell-torn shore, made a landing.
They were met by men who for two days had sat
crouched in dug-outs under an unparalleled fire.
The fighting that ensued was not war *de luxe,* with

all the brilliant, heartless mechanisms of modern war. It was with rifle and bayonet and bomb and knives and bare hands, and it raged for a long time, until finally the enemy was driven back across the river, leaving more than a thousand men behind. Only at Posharevats did they cross. The rear-guard at Semendria was nearly annihilated but it won the fight. An eye-witness, writing in the "Nineteenth Century," gives this description:

> There was no demoralization amongst the survivors in the river trenches. For that the Serbian temperament has to be thanked, which is perhaps after all only the temperament of any unspoiled population of agricultural peasants that live hard lives and have simple ideas. The effect of the bombardment had rolled off them like water off a duck's back, and they set to in the twilight and bombed and shot the landing parties off their side the river with great energy and application.

So that was what was hanging over the sunshiny piece of road that we so blithely sped along, while the two prosaic-looking battle-lines watched each other across the Danube—at peace.

In the late dusk we came to the heights behind Belgrade, and looked down on the lights of the city strung along the Save and the Danube, while just beyond the river the towers of Semlin gleamed in the waning light. London and Paris were dark

every evening last summer, but Belgrade, always
within range of the Austrian guns, was lit up as
usual.

With the exception of the section along the rivers
that had been bombarded during the first invasion,
and one hotel on the main street, which a shell had
demolished, Belgrade might have been the capital
of a nation at peace. The street cars were not running, but in such a little city no one missed them.
We ran up a very rough street and placed the car
in the yard of a private residence.   Then M. Todolich took us over to his home which, when the capital was removed to Nish, he had had to lock up and
leave like all the other government officials.   One
could see the pride of the home-loving Serb as he
showed us over the charming little villa built around
a palm-filled court where a small fountain played.
Belgrade being the only one of their cities which
the Serbs have had time and resources to make
modern, I found them all very proud of it, with an
almost personal affection for each of its urbane
conveniences.   With great enthusiasm monsieur
showed us the mysteries of his very up-to-date
lighting and heating apparatus.

"All the Serbian homes must be so some day
when peace comes to us," he said earnestly.   His

was typical of many homes in Belgrade before October 6.

In a fairly good hotel we spent the night. My window overlooked the Save, from the moonlit surface of which, as stark and melancholy as the ghostship of the "Ancient Mariner," jutted the great, black steel girders and tangled iron braces of the blown-up railway bridge. Now and then a dim light traveled slowly along the water on some tiny boat that, manned by English marines, was patroling the water-front of Semlin.

I was awake early next morning and, dressing hurriedly, went out into the brilliant August sunshine. The air was wonderfully clear and bracing. Newsboys cried along the streets, which many sweepers were busily at work cleaning. Nothing but peace in Belgrade! Searching out the automobile, I found a curious audience around it. There was Mitar, twelve years old, as straight as a young birch, with blue-black hair that fell in soft curls to his shoulders, and jetty eyes that peered with burning curiosity into every crevice of the motor, which he feared to touch. His beautiful body was tightly clothed in a dull-green jersey and white trousers that ended at the knees and left bare, sturdy legs very much bronzed. And there was his little brother, Dushan, age seven, with still longer hair, but a dark brown, large hazel eyes, pug nose, and freckled face, furnished with a toothless grin, for he was at that exciting age when one loses a tooth almost every day. He stood behind his big brother and admonished him not to touch the car. In the seat, bravest of the lot, saucy, impudent, naughty, sat Milka, age five, dressed in a blue wisp of cloth that left tiny throat and arms and legs bare to the summer sun. She had hold of the wheel, and was kicking at the foot-levers in wild delight, quite obviously driving that battered Ford at ten thousand miles a minute. But when suddenly she heard the step of the funny-looking American, one screech of laughter and fear, and Milka, like a flying-squirrel, was safe on the doorstep, demurely smiling. I tried to coax her back, but could not. Even when I lifted the hood, and Mitar danced about with excitement at sight of the dirty engine thus disclosed, and Dushan stood with eyes of wonder, Milka remained smiling at me, poised for flight. As I worked about the car, a woman came out of the house toward me. I heard her light step upon the paved court and looked up. She was dark, not very tall, but dignified and wonderfully graceful, as all Serbian women are. Smiling pleasantly, she offered me on a tray the inevitable *shlatko*. This is a time-honored custom in Serbia, and is observed very generally, though, of course, as Western ideas come in, the old customs go. When a guest comes to a Serbian home, the hostess—always the hostess in person—brings in a tray with preserved fruits. On it are spoons, and the order is for each guest to help himself to a spoonful of shlatko, place the spoon in a water-filled receptacle, and take a glass of water. Then Turkish coffee follows, and a liqueur, usually plum brandy, from the home-made store which every Serbian home keeps. It is a sort of good-fellowship pledge and charming in its simplicity. Now the lady of the house was observing the honored rights of the shlatko to this foreigner who late the evening before had deposited a very muddy automobile in her courtyard.

There was still a good half hour before M. Todolich would be ready, so I determined to take the children riding, my ulterior motive being to win over Milka. They had never been in an automobile before. We rolled the car out of the court, and started the engine. No sooner had the automobile appeared in the street than the neighborhood became alive with children, all running toward

us, the traces of half-finished breakfasts showing
on many of their faces.   I piled them all in, on top
of each other, in layers, and hung them about in the
tonneau.   Milka had deigned to come to the sidewalk, where I pretended not to notice her, but took
my seat at the wheel.   If you had never, never had
a ride in an automobile, and would like to very, very
much, and if you were to see one just about to go
away with everybody else in it and you left behind,
what would you do?

Milka did not set up a yell or smash anything.
No, at five she knew a better way than that.
Calmly, but very quickly, before the automobile
could possibly get away, she stepped upon the running-board, pushed two youngsters out of her way,
bobbed up between me and the wheel, climbed upon
my knee, and gave me, quite as if it had been for
love alone, a resounding kiss on the cheek.   I am
sure she might have had a thousand Fords if she
could have got in one such coup with the great Detroit manufacturer.   So on that cloudless August
morning we had a "joy ride" through the streets of
Belgrade, and the noise we made could, I know, be
heard in the enemy-lines.   This was only a few
short weeks before the sixth of October, 1915.

Of course war is war, but let us get a picture.

Suppose on a perfect day in Indian summer you sat in that tiny, flower-filled court with the hospitable mother; Mitar, the handsome; Dushan, the cautious; and Milka, the coquettish. As you romp with the children, you hear distantly a dull clap of thunder, just as if a summer shower were brewing. A second, a third clap, and you walk out to the entrance to scan the sky. It is deep blue and cloudless, but away over the northern part of the city, while you look, as if by magic, beautiful, shiny white cloudlets appear far up in the crystal sky, tiny, soft, fluffy things that look like a baby's powder-puff, and every time one appears a dull bit of thunder comes to you. For twelve months off and on you have seen this sight. You think of it as a periodic reminder that your nation and the one across the way are at war. You know that heretofore those powder-puffs have been directed at your own guns on the hills behind the city and at the intrenchments down by the river. But there are many things you do not know. You do not know, for instance, that Mackensen is just across the river now with a great Teutonic army outnumbering your own forces five or six to one. You do not know that for weeks the Austrian railways have been piling up mountains of potential powder-puffs

A Serbian peasant's home

A bridge built by the Romans at Ouchitze and still in perfect condition

behind Semlin, and bringing thousands of ponderous machines designed to throw said puffs not only at the forts and trenches, but at your flower-filled court and its counterparts throughout the city. You do not know that aëroplanes are parked by fifties beyond Semlin, and loaded to capacity with puffs that drop a long, long way and blossom in fire and death wherever they strike. You do not know that from a busy group of men in Berlin an order has gone out to take your city and your nation at any cost, and if you knew these things, it would now be too late. For as you look, in a few brief moments, the thunder-storm rolls up and covers the city, such a thunder-storm as nature, with all her vaunted strength, has never dared to manufacture. Mitar and Dushan and Milka stop their play. Worried, the woman comes out and stands with you. You say the firing is uncommonly heavy to-day, but it will mean nothing, and as you say this, you notice the powder-puffs on the slopes of the hills far short of the forts and over the town itself. High above you two of them suddenly appear, and the storm begins in your region, in the street in front of you, on the homes of your neighbors. With increasing rapidity the rain falls now, five to the minute, ten, fifteen, twenty, twenty-five, every sixty seconds, and every drop is from fifty pounds to a quarter of a ton of whirling steel, and in the hollow heart of each are new and strange explosives that, when they strike, shake the windows out of your house. Looking toward Semlin, you see the aëroplanes rising in fleets. Some are already over the city, directing the fire of the guns across the river, and others are dropping explosive bombs, incendiary bombs, and darts. In a dozen places already the city is blazing terribly. A thin, shrill, distant sound comes to you and the waiting woman, almost inaudible at first, but quivering like a high violin note. It rises swiftly in a crescendo, and you hear it now tearing down the street on your left, a deafening roar that yet is sharp, snarling, wailing. Two hundred yards away a three-story residence is lifted into the air, where it trembles like jelly, and drops, a heap of debris, into the street. Your friend lives there. His wife, his children, are there, or were, until that huge shell came. Milka, Dushan, and Mitar have come in time to see their playmates' home blown to atoms. Without waiting for anything, you and the quiet, frightened woman seize the children and start out of the city. As you come to the road that winds tortuously to the hills behind the town, you see that it is black with thousands and thousands of men and women dragging along screaming Mitars and Dushans and Milkas.   Hovering above this road, which winds interminably on the exposed hillside before it reaches the sheltering crest, flit enemy aëroplanes, and on the dark stream below they are dropping bombs.

There is no other road. You know you must pass along beneath those aëroplanes. You look at the woman and the children, and wonder who will pay the price. Oh, for a conveyance now! If only the American were here with his automobile, how greatly would he increase the children's chances! Carriages are passing, but you have no carriage. Railway-trains are still trying to leave the city, but there is literally no room to hang on the trains, and the line is exposed to heavy fire. Only slowly can you go with the children down the street already clogged with debris. Now in front you see a friend with his family, the mother and four children. They are in a coupé, drawn by good horses. How fortunate! The children recognize one another. Milka shouts a greeting. She is frightened, but of course does not realize the danger. Even as she is answered by her playmate in the carriage, all of you are stunned by a terrible

concussion, and there is no family or carriage or
horses any more. There is scarcely any trace of
them. The fierce hunger of a ten-inch shell sent
to wreck great forts is scarcely appeased by one
little family, and, to end its fury, blows a crater
many feet across in the street beyond. Along with
you Mitar has realized what is going on, and not the
least of the trouble that overwhelms you is to see
the knowledge of years drop in a minute on his
childish face when those comrades are murdered
before his eyes. If he gets out of this inferno and
lives a hundred years, he will never shake off that
moment. The shell has blown a crater in his soul,
and because he is a Serb, that crater will smoke
and smolder and blaze until the Southern Slav is
free from all which unloosed that shell or until he
himself is blown beyond the sway even of Teutonic
arms. He grasps his mother's hand and drags
her on.

Now you are in the outskirts of the city. No
word can be spoken because of the constant roar
of your own and the enemy's guns—a roar unfaltering and massive, such as in forty-eight hours
sixty thousand huge projectiles alone could spread
over the little city. On the road you pass frequently those irregular splotches of murder char-

acteristic of bomb-dropping. Here only one man
was blown to pieces by a precious bomb, yonder two
women and a child, farther along eight people, men,
women, and children, lie heaped. Here again only
a child was crippled, both feet or a hand gone. It
is hard to be accurate when sailing high in the air,
hard even for those fearless men who with shrapnel
bursting around their frail machines calmly drop
death upon women and children. I think they are
the bravest, perhaps, of all the fighting men, these
bomb-droppers in whatever uniform. For, it is
not easy to face death at any time, but to face it
while in the act of dropping murder on the bowed
heads of women, on the defenseless heads of sleeping, playing, or fleeing children, surely it requires
nerve to face death thus engaged.

Two loyal subjects of the Kaiser were dexter-
ously dropping bombs on Kragujevats one morning. They pitched some at the arsenal, which they
missed, and some at the English women's hospital
camp, which they hit, one bomb completely destroy-
ing all the unit's store of jam. A nurse was a few
feet away, unaware that anything was threatening
until orange marmalade showered her. Then she
and all her colleagues went out into the open to
watch the brave Germans. They were sailing

about nicely enough until a stray piece of shrapnel hit their gas-tank. Then the eagle became a meteor, which by the time it lighted in the middle of the camp was burned out. The two obedient subjects of the German emperor were incoherent bits of black toast, and the women came and picked souvenirs off the aëroplane. They showed them to me.

So you passed with the mother and children by these patches of horror that mark the trail of the newest warfare.

Or perhaps you lingered in the city until the second evening, when no one any longer dared to linger even in the scattered sheltered spots. Perhaps with the mother, Mitar, Dushan, and Milka, you came out at dusk of the second day, when the remnant of the population was leaving, when the enemy had effected their crossing, and hand-to-hand combat raged down by the river, when the guns were being dragged away to new positions, and the troops were falling hurriedly back. If you did, you left in a final spurt of the bombardment, and on the crest of the hills behind Belgrade you stopped to look back for the last time on that city. For the city that in future years you may come back to will have nothing in common with the

one you are leaving except location. Major El-
liot, of the British marines, stopped at this time to
look back. A few days later he told me what he
saw. There was a dump-heap, an ash-pile, several
miles in extent, lying along the Save and the Danube. In hundreds of spots great beds of live coals
glowed, in hundreds of others roaring flames leaped
high into the sky, and over the remaining dark
spaces of the heap, where as yet no conflagration
raged, aëroplanes, sailing about, were dropping
bombs that fell and burst in wide sprays of liquid
fire, sprinkling the city with terrible beauty.
Thirty or forty to the minute huge shells were
bursting in the town.

You may get away with the family, or you may
not. You and the mother may be killed, and Mitar
left to lead the younger ones. All three may be
blown to pieces, and only you two left with the
memory of it. More than seven thousand just like
you and yours, hundreds of Mitars with bright
dreams and curling hairs, hundreds of little,
freckled, pug-nosed Dushans, hundreds of dainty,
laughing Milkas, reddened the rough paving-stones
of Belgrade or smoldered beneath the glowing ruins
of homes such as M. Todolich had proudly shown
me.

We have supposed our picture, and every important detail of it is supposed from things that many eye-witnesses told me, among them Serbian officers of high rank, and Admiral Troubridge, Major Elliott, Colonel Phillips, and the British marines who helped in the defense. If still the details are wrong, there is one little fact that cannot escape attention: something has become of seven thousand civilians who on the sixth of October were in Belgrade. When I asked Admiral Troubridge if the estimate that this many had been killed was too high, he replied that it was certainly too low.

Innumerable such pictures as ours, I feel sure, God on high might have seen in Belgrade during those forty-eight hours. But perhaps God on high was not looking. It seems more than likely that He was too busy. Belgrade is tiny. In smiling lands to the west He had five hundred miles of thunder-storms to watch, many beautiful towns more important than Belgrade, where lived and died Mitars and Dushans and Milkas in numbers just as great. And on the other side of two old and charming countries, He had a thousand miles more of thunder to superintend, and farther to the east, where another nation flaunts a rival to His avowed only Son, He had certain other matters to oversee, a mil-

lion people massacred beside the soldiers on the battle-line.   Also over His wide, gray oceans there
were great ships with Milkas and Dushans and
Mitars on them, and their fathers and mothers.
He must witness the destruction of these, for surely,
like the rest of us, God loves the brave sailors.   So
a little forty-eight hour thunder-storm on the banks
of the "beautiful blue Danube" could not have
claimed very much of His attention.   As the ed-
itors say, He must be "full up on war stuff," and,
anyway, there are not enough of the Serbs to make
them so terribly important; like us, for instance.
Besides, people in the great world tell us war is
war.

After the fine morning ride with Mitar, Dushan,
and Milka, we left Belgrade, retraced our steps over
the peaceful road along the Danube, but at Semendria turned eastward and so, after nightfall, neared
Velico-Gradishte, also on the Danube, and nestled
in the very first foot-hills of the Carpathians.   Just
before sunset we had passed through Posharevats,
headquarters for the third Serbian army.   Shortly
beyond to the northward lies the famous Stig country, broad, level, and fertile as few lands are.   We
climbed a hill, from the top of which we overlooked
the wide valley ahead.   For many miles, until lost

in the deep blue of the distant Carpathians, the land was as smooth as a floor, and in the slanting rays of the sun a rich gold color was spread over all of it so unbrokenly and evenly that we could not imagine what it was.   Mallory and I guessed and guessed, but could not make it out.   Then we descended into it down a two-mile barren hill, and immediately the road became a narrow lane between solid walls of tasseling Indian corn, the wide-flung gold of which had puzzled us.   In no part of America have I seen corn superior to that of these fields, cultivated though they were by the most primitive methods. One of the things that brought Mr. Mallory there was to see to the transportation with his unit's automobiles of some three hundred thousand kilograms of corn which the Government had bought for the destitute in Macedonia.   The cars were to haul it to the railway station about twenty kilometers distant.   This corn was of the crop gathered two years previously.   That of the preceding year was stored untouched in the peasants' barns, and now we saw this wonderful crop almost ready to gather.   This shows how lack of transportation hampers everything in Serbia.   People in southern Serbia were on the point of starvation, while here was food

enough for the whole nation.   The Teutonic allies
have taken a rich country.

For two hours we ran at top-speed across this
level farm, and then, crossing a thin strip of woods,
came to a long tree-lined avenue, very similar to a
route nationale in France.   We were bounding
along this, our head-lights making plain the road,
when a mounted gendarme rode into the way ahead
and held up his hand.   He made us put out all
lights and sneak along very slowly, for we were now
under the enemy's guns again, and at this point
they were more disposed to pop at anything they
saw, particularly automobile-lights.   So we crept
into the little place, which was knocked to pieces almost as much as Vishegrad, had our supper, and
went to bed in houses where every crevice was carefully covered to conceal the light.

It was considered an act of foolhardiness and
daring to cross the public square of Velico-Gradishte in daylight.   The main street of the place
could be swept by gun-fire across the river at any
time.   So the few remaining citizens, and there
were more than one would think, took devious ways
down side streets to get from one place to another.
We stopped most of the next day, a very hot, still

day, in which it seemed very incongruous that we had to sneak about like thieves, and in the afternoon left, making a wide detour through the Stig country further to inspect the harvest.

Another trip which I made from Nish to Zajechar along the valley of the Timok further revealed to me the vast, potential resources of Serbia. We saw little of armies on this trip, because we were along the Bulgarian frontier, and it was then too early for Serbia to have heavy forces massed there. Everywhere the peasants pointed to the eastward and told us: "There lies the Bulgarian frontier. There it is, just on top that mountain. From here it is only half an hour's walk." They spoke of it as if it were a thing alive, which was being held back by them by main strength and awkwardness, and they spoke of it with awe. How well, in that peaceful summer, they realized what a move on the Bulgarian frontier would mean to them.

During this year of peace in war there was no anxiety on the part of the Serbs as to their Austrian frontiers. I spoke to scores of officers and soldiers, and not once was anything but confidence expressed. But their frontier to the east they almost without exception distrusted. I do not think that there was one Serbian in Serbia who did not firmly believe that Bulgaria would attack when fully prepared. It was a thing that called for no more discussion, a thing so patent to all observers of affairs in the Balkans that only allied diplomacy was too stupid to see. I know now that while I was talking to the captain about it, there in Bosnia, the English papers were full of an entente cordiale with Bulgaria, but also as we talked that afternoon an orderly rode up, handing his superior a note. The captain glanced at it and turned to me. "At last," he said in French. "The blue order has come. We must be ready to go in half an hour."

And this for me was the bell that rang up the curtain on what is without doubt one of the greatest tragedies our century will see. It came on a nation almost as much at peace as Belgium was, a country much larger than Belgium, with no good roads, with no France, no England to offer refuge, nothing but wild mountains devoid of food. It came not in the days of summer, when shelter is a habit and not a necessity, but at the beginning of the savage Balkan winter, when a roof very frequently means life, and it lasted not three or four weeks, but ten.

CHAPTER II

WHEN the long expected "blue order" came, it meant that Serbia was stripping her war frontiers of all reserves and most of her first-line troops. It meant that on the Drina only a skeleton army was left, while along the long frontiers of the Save and the Danube perhaps a hundred thousand men were spread, and all the others—Serbia's whole army numbered about three hundred and fifty thousand—were to be massed along the Bulgarian border to guard the nation's one hope—the single line of the Orient Railway from Saloniki to Belgrade. At about this time the English Parliament was being regaled with "the cordial feeling that always existed between England and Bulgaria."

The next morning I watched the garrison at Vardishte file over the Shargon Pass to Kremna, the chief post of the Drina division, while the fourth-line men, the cheechas, were sent down to Vishegrad to take the first-line places.

Of all the fresh, unhackneyed things that Serbia

offered abundantly to the Western visitor, perhaps
none is more indicative of the nation's real spirit,
certainly none is more picturesque and appealing,
than these cheechas of the army.   Cheecha means
"uncle," and in Serbia, where men age more swiftly
than anywhere else on earth, it is popularly applied
to men more than thirty.   But the cheechas of the
fourth line range from forty five to an indefinite
limit.   The Serb seems never too old to fight.

They had no uniforms, these patriarchs of the
army, and, marching by, presented a beggar's array
of tattered homespuns at once ludicrous and touching.   To see their grandfathers in dirty rags, un-
washed, half starved, blue with cold, drenched with
rain, many of them suffering with rheumatism,
scurvy, neuralgia, and in the last days of their nation's life dying by hundreds of wounds, cold, and
starvation, was one of the things the Serbs had to
bear.

It was the cheechas who first welcomed me to
Serbia.   I shall never forget my feelings when at
Ghevgheli, the border town between Greece and
Serbia, I looked out of the train window at my first
cheecha.   I wondered if this was the typical Serbian soldier, for he looked not a day under seventy,
despite the broad grin on his face when he saw the

party of American workers. It was midsummer and as hot as southern Italy, but the old fellow was dressed about as heavily as we would be for a blizzard. On his shoulders he had a thick woolen cape of brown homespun, attached to which was a peeked hood designed to slip over the head in wet weather, and which, when in place, added a monk-like touch to the rest of his outlandish costume. Underneath the cape he wore a sleeveless jacket of sheepskin, with the thick wool turned inside, and this in July. Beneath the jacket was a shirt of linen, home manufactured, and he wore long trousers that fitted skin tight about his calves and thighs but bagged like bloomers in the back. He had on thick woolen stockings, which he wore pulled over the trousers up to his knees, like golf hose, and which were resplendent with wide borders of brilliant colors. On his feet were the half-shoe, half-sandal arrangements known as *opanki*. His queer get-up made one forget how old and forlorn he must be, for despite his cheerful face, he could not have been but wretched with nothing in life before him except to guard that scorching railway track while his sons and grandsons died on the frontiers.

As I saw him standing there in the dust and heat, some dialect lines of Lanier's came to me:

A Chevelu and his dwelling

One of the numerous guards along the Orient Railway

What use am dis ole cotton stalk when life done picked my cotton?

But that was because I was ignorant of Serbia. Not by a long way had "Life done picked" those cheechas' "cotton." Nearly a million Germans, Austrians, and Bulgarians did it a few months later, but the harvest, thank God! was not all one-sided.

As the slow-moving train crept north into Serbia, our acquaintance with the cheechas grew. At every little bridge there were four of them, two at each end, living in tiny tepee-like shelters built of brush. At the stations companies of them were drawn up along the track, grotesque groups, nondescript and filthy, with rifles of many makes slung over their stooping shoulders. They never failed to salute us and cheer us, their enthusiasm being mingled with a charming naïve gratitude when we scattered American cigarettes among them.

While we were camping just outside Nish during the last weeks of July there were three ancient cheechas who passed our camp every afternoon at sunset on their way to sentry duty, and every morning just after sunrise they returned. We could never say anything to one another except "Dobra-vechie" ("Good evening") and "Dobra-utro"

("Good morning"), but a friendship sprang up between us, nevertheless. Month after month this was their occupation, oscillation between their filthy, vermin-infested abodes in Nish and that desolate hilltop where they watched through the starlit or stormy nights. They had beaten out a narrow, dusty path through the upland pastures, monotonously treading which, munching hunks of black bread and large green peppers, they symbolized the cheechas' existence.

Their childlike natures might lead one to suppose that as guards they would not be worth much, but this would be wrong. Most guard duty is simple. You stand up and watch a place, and when some one comes you challenge him. If his answer is satisfactory, good; if not, you cover him with your rifle and then march him in to your superior. If he disobeys, you shoot. Nothing is said about exemption. A sentry is no respecter of persons, and the simpler minded he is, the less of a respecter is he inclined to be.

One evening a man of our camp wandered to the precincts sacred to our three cheechas. He heard a loud "Stoy!" to which, instead of halting, he responded, "Americanske" and kept going. Another "Stoy!" brought the same result, and so a

third. Then out of the dimness loomed a hooded
figure, and with an obsolete rifle blazed away, above
the trespasser's head, of course, but not greatly
above it, a sort of "William Tell" calculation.
Swifter than the roebuck came our wanderer home,
down the dusty trail, hatless and breathless, wise in
the ways of cheechas.

Near Belgrade one night a gentleman of some
military consequence decided to inspect certain
trenches. Depending upon his uniform and well-
known name, he did not bother to get the password.

"And do you know," he told me, "two bally old
chaps from Macedonia who spoke no known language marched me a mile and a half to their captain, and it was all he could do to convince the stern
beggars that I had a right to my uniform and was
really the British military attaché."

When fighting was going on with the Bulgarians,
not very far from Nish last autumn, one of the
American Sanitary Commission, a hopelessly col-
lege-bred person, with strong laboratory instincts,
wandered alone and unaided about the environs
of the city, dreaming of hypothetical water-
supplies; and dreaming thus, he wandered into
realms he wot not of, and, what mattered more, into
the snug nest of two valiant cheechas set to guard

a road. Two days later inquiring government officials, set in motion by still more inquisitive friends, found him living the life and eating the food of the cheechas. They had orders not to leave that post, and they were determined that he should not until an officer had seen him.

Despite this inconvenient, unflinching devotion to the letter of the law, I found a softer side to the cheechas. One afternoon at Nish I climbed a steep and dusty trail up one of the neighboring hills which overlooks for thirty miles or more the broad sweep of the Morava. Accompanying me was a delightful, but really distressingly proper, English lady whom I had recently met. A rich Balkan sunset across the valley was well worth the climb, we thought, but to the gay old cheecha we found at the top it seemed incredible that any one not touched with divine madness would make that exertion just to see the sun go down. With ingenuous and embarrassing signs he made it known that duty held him there, but that we need not mind; and thereupon, with a wink as inconspicuous as the full moon, he turned his back upon us and so remained. We stood that back as long as it was humanly possible to stand it, and then rose to go; but he motioned us to stop, and running to a clump of bushes, he pulled

out a luscious melon,—all his supper, I am sure,—
and with as obvious a "Bless you, my children!" as I
ever saw, presented it to us.

They are made of a fine timber these cheechas.
With amazing endurance and wearing qualities,
nothing seems to shake them. On one of my trips
with M. Todolich we stopped for coffee in a little
village near Zajechar. Of course the only men in
the café were very old, too worn out even for Serbian military service. Several of these gathered
about our table to hear what news M. Todolich
could give, and one among them I specially noticed.
I am sure that Job in the last stages of his affliction
approached this old fellow in appearance. He had
had six sons, all of whom had been killed. His wife
had died shortly before, and just the previous week
a great flood on the river had completely destroyed
his home and livelihood, and had drowned his one
daughter-in-law with her two little sons. What
would you say to a man of seventy five who has
watched his life go by like that? M. Todolich tried
to say something, and I heard the cheecha reply
in a few Serbian words the meaning of which I
did not understand, nor how he could reply at
all in that level, uncomplaining, perfectly calm
tone.

"What did he say?" I asked the interpreter.

"He says, 'God's will be done.'" And that was all we heard him say.

At Dobrun four old cronies were detailed to be "hewers of wood and drawers of water" to our camp, and tirelessly they hewed and drew. When one considers the deep-rooted, constitutional aversion to work which is without doubt the Serbs' worst drawback, this industry on their part appears at its true value. A woman journalist, measuring with her profound gaze the length and breadth and depth of Serbia, and the hearts of its people, in a junket of a couple of weeks or so, has insinuated the ungratefulness and cupidity of the Serbs. Nothing could be further from the truth. For the smallest acts their gratitude overflows all bounds, and as for pride, no peasants of Europe can approach these lowly people in their dislike of dependence. An appealing desire to show us at least their sense of thankfulness actuated even these old codgers to do things which by nature they despised to do.

At first our Bosnian menage rotated about a refugee cook from Vishegrad, who, had she not been Serb, would certainly have been Irish. She was a leisurely soul who refused to let any exigency whatever make her hasten. On the first pay-day we

missed her, and, searching the camp, finally found
her in the cellar. Alas! she was a disciple of Omar,
and not to be awakened. So with the perfect courtesy that we never failed to encounter from Serbian
officers, the major at Vardishte sent us his own
cook, a cheecha, and by far the sleekest, best-fed,
most fortunate-looking cheecha I ever saw.

There was something undeniably Falstaffian in
his nature, and he affected a certain elaborate mock
dignity which made me give him at once the respect-
ful title of "Guspodin." "Guspodin Cook" we
called him, to his delight. He was soon referring
to himself as "Guspodin Couk." While unpacking a box of old clothing sent out by well-meaning
people from England or America, we came across,
amid ball-dresses and stiff-bosomed shirts, a battered top-hat. It was a perfect example of the hat
always seen askew on the swinging heads of stage
inebriates, but it took Guspodin Cook's eye.
Thereafter he was never seen without it, whether
peeling potatoes, carrying away garbage, or spin-
ning a yarn.

Only one thing on earth did he prefer to cooking,
and that was telling stories. Sitting about the
great fire which we always made of pine-logs after
supper, our American-Serb soldiers would get Gus-

podin Cook wound up and translate for us. I
could never rid myself of a sneaking suspicion
that our honorable chef had never seen a battle-
line; he was too good a cook.   But I had no proof
of this from his speeches.   His *chef-d'œuvre*, the
pièce de résistance, of his narrative larder, which he
always got off while sitting tailor fashion, his "Al
Jolson" hat cocked over one eye, went something
like this:

One day last winter, after we had run the Suabas out
of Serbia and I was stationed up here, I asked my captain to let me make a visit to my family at Valjevo.
He told me I could, so I started out to walk home.   I
got to Ouchitze in two days all right, and after resting
there a little while started out on the way to Valjevo.
The road runs over the tops of the mountains, a wild
country, and hardly anybody lives there.   Once in a
while I found traces of the fighting that had been done
the month before, but now the whole country was quiet,
and I met no one at all, not even any Serbian soldiers.
About the middle of the afternoon I heard a cannon go
off four or five kilometers away, and I heard something
terrible tear through the trees not far to my left.   I
could n't imagine what a cannon was doing there, with
no army within fifty kilometers and no fighting going on
at all.   While I was wondering, a big shell tore up the
road a few hundred meters ahead of me.   Then I knew
the Suabas had slipped back into Serbia, and I began
to run.   I heard a lot more shots, and I kept on going.

Wounded Cheechas being transported to a hospital

A Cheecha flashing army dispatches by means of a heliograph

In an hour I came to a village where there were some
gendarmes. I told them the Suabas were coming right
behind me, but they said that I was a liar. Then I said
for them to go back up the road on their horses and see.
But they made me go back with them.

We went to where the shot had hit the road, and while
we were standing around looking at it, we heard the
cannon again; but the shell did n't come our way this
time. We turned into a wood road that led in the direction from which the sound came. Soon we were nearly
knocked off our horses by another shot, which went off
right at us behind a lot of thick bushes on our left. We
stopped short to listen, but could n't hear anything.
The gendarmes were scared to death now, but I was all
right. I said, "Come on; let's go there and see who is
shooting up the country." They said it was mighty
strange. Suabas would n't be acting like that, and one
of 'em, Mitrag, said a battle had been fought about where
we were and a lot of good men killed and he did n't know
—maybe some of 'em had come back to life.

But I led up to the bushes, and we crawled to where
we could see a clear space behind. There was a Suaba
field-gun all right, with a lot of ammuniton piled up. A
good many empty shells were lying about, too; but there
was n't anybody—no Guspodin, I swear it; not a sign
of any Suaba or anybody around that place. The gendarmes lay there on their bellies, but I jumped up and ran
to the gun crying, "Long live Serbia." I put my hand
on the gun, but jerked it away mighty quick. It was
hot enough to boil soup on, almost. I picked up some of
the shells, and they were hot, too. Guspodin, I began
to shiver and jump about like a restless horse. Here was

a hot gun and hot shells, and no enemy in the country at all, and nobody around the gun; and, anyway, the shots had been scattered all over the country without any aim. It seemed almost as if something or other had come back to life and was shooting that gun just because it was in the habit of doing it. I was about ready to go back to those gendarmes when they began to yell, and started out through the brush like rabbits. "There they are! Get 'em! Get 'em!" they said, and would n't stop a minute to answer me. Then I decided the best thing for me was to get back to the horses, which I did.

In a few minutes the gendarmes came up, leading four boys about fifteen years old. They were clawing and biting and putting up a good fight. At last the gendarmes got them quiet and made 'em tell their story. They said they had found the gun and ammunition there not long after the Suabas went away. They supposed they had gone in such a hurry that there was n't time to break up the gun, and our soldiers had n't found it. They said they had been trying to make it go off for two weeks, but had just found out how that day. They did n't mean any harm; it was fun, and away out in the woods where they would n't hurt anybody, they said. That was enough; each one of us cut a long stick and took a boy for half a hour. Then we went off and reported the gun to the army.

With this final statement Guspodin Cook would always take off the top-hat, wipe the noble brow beneath, and place it tenderly on again slanted at the opposite angle.

He had a curious theory that by some strange sense children always detected when war would come. He could give numerous examples to prove his statement. One was that whenever the children all over the country were seized with a desire to play at war, real war was sure to come soon. He said that in July of 1914 all over Serbia he had never before seen the children playing soldier so much; and, lowering his voice, he told us that now he saw them at it again everywhere, so that "Something was coming soon." Heaven knows this prophecy at least was true.

Such were the cheechas whom, on that fine autumn morning, I watched go down to Vishegrad. Our four orderlies were with them, and also Guspodin Cook. His time had come at last. Serbia was now facing a period when no man able to stand alone could be spared from the battle-line. Cheecha always has been a term of deep respect and love among the Serbs, and rightly so; but after this war they will hold a ten times stronger lien on the affections of their country. Young troops, fresh and perfectly munitioned, were awaiting them in the enemy trenches on the Drina—troops that these old grandfathers could not hope to stop.

They knew what they were going into; they had

no illusions. Distributing among them thousands of cigarettes of which I had become possessed, I gathered from their words of thanks how much hope they had of ever coming back. "These will be all I 'll ever want," one gray-bearded scarecrow remarked to our interpreter when I gave him a hundred. He and the others seemed neither sorry nor glad. Somebody had to go. They were chosen, and there was an end to it. They were as completely wiped out as troops can be, dying almost to a man. And during the nightmare of the next ten weeks, wherever the fourth line had to bear the brunt, they distinguished themselves. Many episodes could be told, but the defense of Chachak is perhaps one of the most remarkable.

Chachak is on the narrow-gage Ouchitze branch of the Orient Railway. Not far to the south is Kraljevo. When the first great onslaught of the Bulgarians carried them by sheer weight of numbers to the environs of Nish, the capital was moved to Chachak, supposedly a temporarily safe retreat. But the Germans, as usual, did not fight according to their enemies' surmise. Risking most difficult roads, they suddenly threatened the new capital from the northwest, forcing the Government southward, first to Kraljevo, then to Rashka,

Mitrovitze, Prizrend, and Scutari. The cheechas
defended Chachak. Three times the Germans
wrested the town from them, and each time the
cheechas retook it. Only when four fifths of them
had been put out of action did the Germans finally
succeed in holding the place.

With rifles of every possible description, too
old for real soldiers, rejected by the first three
lines of defense, the cheechas of Chachak faced as
fine troops as Germany could muster, perfectly
equipped, splendidly provisioned, and feeling with
increasing assurance a whole nation crumbling before them. For the cheecha knows not only how
to thrive on half a pound of dry bread a day, and
nothing else; he knows how to lie against a tree or
turn himself into a stone, and with Serbia in her
death-grip, he only wished to die.

I believe the cheechas felt the loss of their country more keenly than any one else. Most of them
had lived through nearly all of her free history.
Unlike the educated Serb, they could not see a
bright political lining behind the present pall of
blackness. But I have yet to hear a complaint
from one of them. There was Dan, one of the orderlies who retreated with the English nurses. He
had been to America, and he had numerous fail-

ings, but no one could see him at that time without forgetting everything except his grief. The suffering he underwent, the cold and hunger, seemed to matter nothing to him; but by the hour at night he would squat by his smoldering fire and mumble:

"Whata I care 'bout myself? Whata I 'mount to? T'ree million people lost! Nuthin' else don't matter. T'ree million people—t'ree million—lost!"

All Serbs love to sing, and most of their songs have a mournful tinge. The more uncomfortable the Serb becomes, the louder and longer he sings. When, seven weeks after Chachak, I passed a company of the fourth line on top of the Montenegrin mountains, during days when there was absolutely no food for them, when they saw their comrades drop by the hundred, dead of starvation, cold, and exhaustion, when not one foot of Serbian soil was free, separated from their families in all probability forever, at the best for years, miserable, it seemed to me, beyond all human endurance, the cheechas were singing. I cannot forget that song. The fine sleet cut their faces, and formed grotesque icicles on their woolly beards. The mountain wind blew their voices to shreds—voices mechanical, dreary, hopeless, unlike any Serbians I had ever heard before. Not until I was right among them did I recognize the song, a popular one that had sprung up since the war, its content being that "the Suabas are building houses the Serbians shall live in; the Suabas are planting corn the Serbians shall eat; the Suabas are pressing wine the Serbians shall drink."

The irony was sharp, but when one has lived in hell for ten weeks and is freezing to death on a mountain-top, one hears no trivial sarcasms, but only the great irony of life. Or so the cheechas seemed to feel.

CHAPTER III

EVACUATION SCENES

TWO weeks after I saw the cheechas go down to Vishegrad I motored to Valjevo, where were the headquarters of the first Serbian army. This was the sixth of October, the day on which the Austrians and Germans crossed the Drina, the Save, and the Danube, and the bombardment of Belgrade was begun in earnest. Two days later, through confidential sources, I got news of the serious situation, but it was not until refugees began to pour in from the Save that the general public of Valjevo knew anything of the fate of their capital.

General Mishich was in command of the first Serbian army at Valjevo, while farther to the east the second army was centered at Mladenovats under General Stepanovich, and beyond the Morava, General Sturm had the headquarters of the third army at Posharevats. General Zivkovich, known throughout Serbia as the "Iron General," was in separate command of the defense of Belgrade. Soon after the fall of the capital the three armies began their retreat southward in parallel lines, the third army being driven more to the westward by the Bulgarians. After traversing about two thirds the length of Serbia, all three bent sharply westward toward the frontier between Prizrend and Ipek, and, after a conference of the three commanders at the latter place, made their marvelous, but heartbreaking, retreat through the Albanian and Montenegrin mountains. This is a brief general summary of what the official *communiqués* have to say. The hardship and suffering of both soldiers and civilians during these simple manœuvers a thousand books could not adequately describe.

While the fall of Belgrade created a serious situation at once, there was no immediate peril at Valjevo. One day at this time, with the prefect of the district, I motored some fifty kilometers due north to Obrenovats. There had been an incessant rain for two weeks, and the road was almost impassable even for the automobile we were using. It was a terrible ride, and we arrived at the Colonel's headquarters, only a few kilometers behind the trenches, wet, cold, and very hungry, the last being our greatest concern, for it seemed the most desolate spot imaginable, and we had brought no pro-

visions with us.   We could not continue to Obrenovats because it was being violently shelled.   Sitting on boxes around a rough pine table, we lunched
with the Colonel on—delicious Russian caviar and
French champagne!   I do not know how he worked
this miracle; I shall always wonder.

Twenty-four hours later, however, the Austrians were where we had lunched, and, indeed, a
great deal farther along, and we were evacuating
Valjevo.   Kragujevats was also preparing for
evacuation, the arsenals being emptied and the
munition factories smashed.

Both these places were large hospital centers,
and after the first few days of fighting both were
crowded with wounded.   Before I left Valjevo
the hospitals had been emptied of all but the most
desperate cases, and it required a very desperate
condition indeed to force the Serbian patients to
stay behind.   The period of dreary, continuous
rainfall continued, and it was into a sea of water
and mud that the wounded had to flee.   I stood on
a street corner opposite one of the largest hospitals
in Valjevo and watched the patients come out on
their way to the railway station.   I did not hear
about this; I saw it.   Nearly all the hobbling, ban-
daged, bloody, emaciated men were bareheaded.

Before they got ten feet from the door they were soaked to the skin. The bandages became soggy sponges, and wounds began to bleed afresh. There were foreheads, cheeks, arms, legs, and feet incased in cloths dank with watery blood, and soon filthy with the street slush. The worst of it was that not only did virtually all lack overcoats, but many were barefooted and in cotton pajamas.

They refused to stay and be captured. There were no more clothes for them, so they faced a journey in the pouring rain, no one knew where nor how long. Some could not walk alone, and these the stronger aided. This determination never to be prisoners was general throughout the hospitals of Serbia. That is why in the next two weeks the railway stations, the rest-houses of the Red Cross, and even the railway-yards were dotted with rigid forms of men who had breathed their last in soaked, bloody clothing, lying on vile floors or in the mud. Why were they not forced to remain in the hospitals? I do not know. I doubt if any power on earth could have kept them there. There is a certain sort of man who cannot be made to do a certain sort of thing. The Serb never believes he is going to die until he is dead, and the wounded Serbs wanted to fight again.

There were no vehicles to take them to the railway station, and when they arrived there it was not to get into comfortable hospital-trains, the few of these that Serbia had being utterly insufficient for the hordes of wounded. As long as the covered coaches lasted they poured into them, and then they boarded the open freight-trucks. I watched them get on like this at Valjevo, but it was not the last I saw of them and thousands like them.

Many nurses and doctors told me about the scenes at Kragujevats. This place was the headquarters for the huge Stobart mission as well as for other hospitals. It had comfortable accommodations for not more than three thousand patients. During the week of the Belgrade bombardment more than ten thousand came there. Most of them were pretty well shot to pieces. The wards were filled, the floor spaces were filled, the corridors were filled, tents were filled, and finally wounded men lay thick in the yards, awaiting their turn at the hasty care the cruelly overworked doctors and nurses could give. For a week or ten days this kept up, then evacuation began. The scenes of Valjevo were reënacted, but on a greater scale. Again the open trucks that were meant for coal and lumber were piled with horribly suffering men.

In telling of the harrowing finish of the work of these hospitals, which for the most part had been sent out from neutral or allied countries, it seems to me only just to pause a moment and give a little information, as accurately as I could gather it, about the work of Americans in Serbia, even though it does not tally with popular impressions in this country. I believe it is about as reliable as such information can be, and I unhesitatingly give my sources.

If anything besides natural conditions stopped the typhus in Serbia, it is to Russian money and Russian workers that more credit should go than to any other agency. America did something, but not very much, toward stamping out typhus. What she did do has been blatantly advertised in this country.

When in the last part of January, 1916, I returned to New York, a representative of one of our greatest American dailies came on board. The paper he represents has the reputation of employing only expert reporters, and "ship-news" men are supposed to be specially keen. He came up to the group of first cabin passengers—only nine of us in all—evidently intent on getting a "story." He was on a good trail. Besides several Americans who had seen the war inside out on many fronts, there was among us the chief surgeon of the Imperial Russian hospitals of Nish, Dr. S. Sargentich of Seattle. Dr. Sargentich probably knows more about what has been done for the relief of Serbia than any other man in America. Also he has many interesting personal experiences. Alone at Arangelovats for nearly a month, he faced a situation which was perhaps extreme even for that terrible epidemic, but which illustrates pretty well the general condition throughout the country. In his hospital there were nine hundred typhus patients and several hundred more in the town. He had started with fifty-seven unskilled soldiers as nurses and orderlies. All of them came down with typhus almost at once. He had had six assistant doctors; all got typhus, and one died. Finally the cooks, treasurer, commissary-man, and pharmacist came down. The doctor and four orderlies reigned supreme over this pleasant company. No aid could be sent to him. America had as yet scarcely realized that such a thing as typhus existed in Serbia.

Dr. Sargentich speaks all the Balkan languages as well as French, German, and Russian. Born in Dalmatia, in his youth he passed many years among the wild mountaineers of Montenegro and Albania, and he has an insight into the Balkans that few can match. He holds degrees from our best universities, and several times has received high decorations, particularly from Russia and Montenegro. The King of Italy and the King of Montenegro have repeatedly expressed their admiration for him and his work. He was in Serbia eighteen months, and, what sets him off from nearly all of the workers we sent over, he drew no salary. Dr. Sargentich had a story, even though it would have required a little persuasion to get it out of him.

The reporter faithfully took our names, being very careful to spell them correctly, and on the advice of one of the party turned to Dr. Sargentich.

"Let's see, er—er—you were in Serbia, Doctor? What did you find to do there?"

"I was interested in the Russian hospitals."

"Russian? *Russian,* did you say? How's that? Russians in Serbia—why, man, they're at war!"

Ceasing his questioning after a moment, which was well, he pulled out a kodak and took pictures.

Glancing over an index to American periodicals of the preceding year, I found such titles as these, "Sanitary Relief Work in Serbia," "American Relief in Serbia," "Serbia Saved by Americans." There are dozens of such articles advertising our work done there. Somewhere there may be a comparison of our work with the work of other nations, but if so, I have failed to find it. The English and French certainly have done their part in the relief of Serbia, but the Russians, being first on the ground and the only nation as far as I know to have any really important contingents at work during the height of the typhus epidemic, must serve as a comparison with us.

In the estimates that follow I have in both instances included workers of all description except those employed directly by the Serbian Government on a business basis. Perhaps a score of American doctors went out under this arrangement. Dr. Sargentich has furnished me with the Russian estimates, while the American figures are compiled from data found in the "Annual Report of the Bureau of Medical Service for 1915," Major Robert U. Patterson, Chief of Bureau, of the American Red Cross.

According to Dr. Sargentich, the typhus epidemic began in Serbia at Valjevo about December 20, 1914. By March 15, 1915, it was "thoroughly under control." So that about the time we were beginning to realize it, the epidemic was over.

In September, 1914, Russia sent up from Saloniki two doctors, two sanitary inspectors, and five nurses. On October 15, 1914, three doctors and twelve nurses arrived in Belgrade from America. By November 1, 1914, Russia had four doctors, ten nurses, and two sanitary inspectors, while America had the original three doctors and twelve nurses. By January 15, 1915, when the epidemic was well under way, America had seven doctors and twenty-four nurses, whereas Russia had sent in ten doctors, one hundred and ten nurses and orderlies, with equipment costing more than two hundred and fifty thousand dollars. The Russians had also built numerous hospital barracks, while the Americans used buildings furnished by the Serbian Government. This was the ratio of the two nations during the worst of the typhus; our seven doctors to their ten, our twenty-four nurses to their hundred and ten. The value of our equipment I could not learn, but it did not approach their quarter of a million dollars. Both forces were so pitifully insufficient to meet the need that it seems an impertinence even to enumerate them. Both groups lost some of their bravest, and both faced terrific risks, acting in the most heroic manner.

The relief workers of all nations who came after March ran virtually no danger from the disease, and the lurid accounts given after this date are mainly imaginary.   Most of the American workers came months after this date.   The first contingent of the American Sanitary Commission sailed from New York April 8, 1915, and the second on May 17.   It was well into June before they could begin any sort of work.   The Columbia University Relief Expedition sailed from New York on June 27, and was to return on September 15.   A month was required to reach Nish and organize.   The Frothingham unit is not included because of lack of data. It was not large.

When typhus was fast waning, by March 25, 1915, America still had only seven doctors and twenty-four nurses, although to the Russian force of ten doctors and one hundred and ten nurses had been added a very large unit, the exact number of which I could not learn.   This new unit was to prepare for the expected return of typhus in the autumn, much the same object that the American Sanitary Commission had but three months earlier on the ground and with equipment twenty times as valuable.   They spent two million dollars and built hospitals for four thousand patients, and this in addition to the quarter of a million dollars already expended. I am unable to give figures for the American expenditure. At the very greatest estimate for *all* American activities in Serbia it is far less than a million dollars. The Sanitary Commission began with appropriations of forty thousand. How much they later expended I do not know. They employed young sanitary engineers at two hundred and fifty dollars a month and all expenses. The Columbia Expedition represented an outlay of about thirty thousand dollars, every one connected with it being absolutely without salary.

The largest totals for the two nations at any time are: twenty-nine American doctors to forty-five Russian; seventy-four American nurses, sanitary inspectors, and chauffeurs to more than four hundred similar Russian workers. In addition, Russia built hospitals for four thousand patients and spent more than two and a half millions, while we spent less than a million and built no hospitals.

Obviously Serbia was not saved by Americans. The much-talked-of Sanitary Commission had only to do with the fifteen southern districts. The French and English took care of this sort of work in the rest of the country.

In Belgium, England has spent many times as much as America. Of course it was "her job" more than ours, but we hear so much of what we do! The English expenditures in Serbia have also been enormous. A little thought and a few figures thus readily show that our well-known relief workers are also good advertisers.

I do not wish to be misunderstood. I am not arguing that we ought or ought not to help Europe when there is so much needed at home. I am not arguing at all. I am merely trying to gage as accurately as possible what has actually been done, in order to furnish some sort of criterion by which to judge the oft-repeated sentiment that we are binding unfortunate nations to us by our stupendous generosity. The conviction that no nation at all has ever been or ever will be bound to another (at least to the extent of real aid in time of trouble) except by the natural ties of self-interest is a purely personal view. I give the facts as I found them.

But whatever the origin of the hospitals, they were now throwing their gruesome burdens upon the railways, which, when the enemy approached, dumped them out on the muddy roads that led into the wilderness, where they died. Traveling southward down the main line at this time, amid the wildest confusion of thousands of families rushing away with only what could be carried on their backs, and of vast military stores being moved with no time for proper organization, of congested tracks and inexperienced trainmen, and the thousand and one incidents of a wholesale hegira, the thing which impressed me most, and which still lingers in my mind, is that flood of mangled, maimed humanity.

The horror of it grew in extent and intensity as we passed from Valjevo to Mladenovats, Yagodina, Chupriya, and culminated at Krushevats in suffering soldiers multiplied ten thousand times. Krushevats was the sort of picture which, having once been seen, changes forever the aspect of life. If I were asked to give the death of Serbia in a few sentences, I should tell of a tearless woman beside the shreds of her little boy, struck down by an aëroplane bomb for "moral effect"; of old men and young men, old women and young women, boys and girls, starving hopelessly in a frozen wilderness; of the Serbian army groping and staggering into Scutari; and of the wounded at Krushevats. One does not get rid of such pictures. One goes on living with them long after the events themselves. They are seen in the bright shop windows and in the theaters.   All music speaks of them: if shallow, it mocks; if deep enough, it eulogizes or mourns. Sleep only makes them more vivid.   They are spread upon all that one writes or reads.   So I was startled when I read in the "New York Tribune" an account by Gordon Gordon-Smith, who trod for a while the same paths as myself.   He writes under the date of November 6.   I left Krushevats on the morning of November 3.   He saw the Krushevats horror three days later than I.   When I left, it was getting worse, more wounded coming in, greater congestion, less care.   When I last saw it, the economic life of Krushevats, its social life, its citizens, its garrison, its refugees were bowed down as seldom in the world's history humanity has been bowed down.   Everything belonging to the old normal life was gone.   Purple clouds of overwhelming woe had intervened, and Krushevats that day was a place new and very terrible.   Huge crowds were in the streets searching for food, for lost friends, for lost families.   The floors of every available building were covered thick with filthy, bloody men.

Something miraculous, something that changed the temper of Krushevats' mourning thousands, must have happened between November 3 and November 6. Gordon Gordon-Smith says something did—something that is all the more remarkable because it is not at all in accordance with any known national characteristic of the Serbs, but directly contradictory to all the evidence I have ever read about them and what I have seen of them in an experience which will, I believe, compare favorably in extent with his. Mr. Gordon-Smith, with true British directness, says that, on November 6, Krushevats got drunk. He does not say he saw one or a dozen or a thousand people drunk in the city. He does not leave us the comfort of thinking that he may be speaking of that irreducible quantity of care-free do-nothings, innocent or vicious, who are to be found in any crowd, and who without doubt would have speedily availed themselves of such an opportunity as he describes. No. Krushevats, facing greater horror than did Sodom, was like that gay ancient city, devoid of any redeeming inhabitant, and the spectacle was so gripping, unusual, strange, and picturesque, such good copy, in fact, that Mr. Gordon-Smith presents it with evident gusto to the English-reading world.

After describing a similar condition at Chichivats, he says:

When we reached Krushevats we found the town apparently in high festival. Everybody seemed in the best of humor and gaiety reigned everywhere.

We soon discovered the cause. The whole town, men, women, and children, had been drinking unlimited quantities of French champagne, a trainful of which was lying in the station.

Good God! When I reached Krushevats late in the afternoon I found the town apparently an unrelieved hell. We came in between two trains of at least fifty cars each. They were open cars, loaded with coal and boxes and—other things. As numerous as the stars, wounded and dead men lay on the coal-heaps or sprawled over the boxes. They had not been there for an hour or two hours; you could see that. They had been there for days and days. It was pouring rain when I came in, and had been for two weeks. Most of them looked like heaps of bloody old clothes that had been picked out of a gutter, and their only sign of life was crying for food, except now and then one "off his head" would rave and screech. Everybody seemed dead, insane, or in torment, and hell reigned everywhere.

We had been kept waiting near Krushevats for seven days before our train could be brought in. "We soon discovered the cause." The whole yard was crammed with just such trains as the two be-

We arrived at the Colonel's headquarters wet, cold, and very hungry

Refugee family from the frontier driving all their possessions through a street in Valjevo

tween which we were. The whole town was filled
with wounded and refugees. "Men, women, and
children had been drinking unlimited quantities of"
the bitterest agony human beings could know, and
trainfuls more of them, half-naked and soaked,
were dying in the station.

When our train stopped opposite one of those
coal-cars, I saw a man who had been lying humped
in a ball bestir himself. I thought he was a very
old man. I was doubly sorry for old men in those
circumstances. His body was worn, his movements
were listless, his profile was tortured and lined.
All his companions on the car were inert. I could
not tell if they were dead. It seemed queer that
this old soldier should be the only one inclined to
stir. Then he turned his full face toward me. He
was not old at all; twenty five at the most; he was
simply done for. He poked a man who lay near.
"Voda! voda!" he said huskily ("Water! water!").
The other sat up, and together they started to
crawl off the truck. I shouted at them that I
would bring some "voda"; they paid no heed, not
understanding. The old young man got to the
ground, going through strange contortions. His
companion wavered on the edge a moment, then
fell heavily and rolled under the truck, either sense-

less or dead. The other looked at him, started to bend over, then jerked up again with an exclamation of pain. There was something the matter with his chest. A dirty old shirt was tied around him in lieu of a bandage. Even as he cried the stained shirt became a warm red. He tried to climb between the trucks of our train to get to the station pump, I suppose. He got half-way, but fell back just as we came to him. Before the nurses could save him he bled to death. The man under the train was dead. They were not alone. We just happened to see this. I was told that men went carefully before the trains coming into Krushevats at night to be sure the tracks were not littered. Unpleasant things had happened several times. "We found the town apparently in high festival. Everybody seemed in the best of humor and gaiety reigned everywhere." Potent champagne that from the sunny vineyards of glorious France! Potent champagne which so could dilute the black Teutonic brew I saw Krushevats swallow!

I do not say that Mr. Gordon Gordon-Smith did not see Krushevats as he says he did. I was not there; he came three days after me. I do say that there is nothing at all to make me think his words are true, and what I have just described to make me think they are a damnable lie.

If exaggeration is used to make more readable a dry account of a pink tea or to tell more touchingly how somebody's mother slipped on a banana-peel, I do not quarrel with it.   If for the sake of a striking paragraph, it is used cynically to vilify a heroic people at the moment of their crucifixion, nothing gives me more satisfaction than to go far out of my way to brand it as stupid, cowardly, dishonest, and contemptible.

CHAPTER IV

GETTING AWAY

ON the nineteenth of October I left Valjevo with the "Christitch Mission." This mission had been founded early the preceding spring by Mlle. Anna Christitch of London, a member of the London "Daily Express" staff. Mlle. Christitch had come out to Valjevo in February, 1915, when the typhus epidemic, which began at Valjevo, was at its height. The misery of the refugees, the filthy cafés, the poor hospitals insufferably crowded with dying men, and the gruesome piles of unburied dead that increased too rapidly for interment, had made such an impression upon her that she returned to London and persuaded her paper to start a fund for the relief of the beautiful, but stricken, little city. Through the strong appeal of the cause itself and her own unusual talent as a lecturer and writer, a large sum was raised at once, and the "Daily Express Camp" was established at Valjevo.

Before the somewhat sudden advent of the

writer, this mission had differed from others in Serbia in that no mere man had any part in it. Eleven days before evacuation I descended upon it in a Ford, the tonneau of which had been fashioned, according to my own ideas of coach-building, from the packing-case that had brought it from far-away Detroit. The work with which I had been connected having been completed, I humbly petitioned Mme. Christitch, the mother of Mlle. Christitch, to take on one man at least, accompanied by an automobile. I imagine that the car, despite the tonneau I had made, won the victory, for I became an integral part of the mission, being in some hazy way connected with the storehouse of refugee supplies. An Austrian prisoner, named Franz, a Vienna cook, whom Mme. Christitch requisitioned for the mission household, followed me in breaking the decree against males. Besides Mme. and Mlle. Christitch, the mission had four nurses, Miss Magnussen of Christiania, Norway, and the Misses Helsby, Spooner, and Bunyan of London.

During the second week of October the military authorities three times warned Mlle. Christitch that Valjevo was seriously threatened and advised her to take the mission farther south.

With many thousand dollars' worth of relief-supplies in her storehouse, and with a great need for nurses in the hospitals, now overflowing with wounded, Mlle. Christitch would not heed these warnings, her course being heartily approved by the rest of us. Also she was prone to put down all such advice from the military authorities as due to over-solicitude on the part of Field-Marshal Mishich, who had known her from childhood. Even when the other mission, the "Scottish Women," was ordered to go, she made a dash for headquarters and came back triumphant, announcing that we could stay so long as the Field-Marshal himself remained.

But on Sunday morning, October 17, an ultimatum came, and I was enjoined to see to the packing of some thirty-five thousand dollars' worth of blankets, clothing, shoes, hospital-supplies, and food-stuffs within forty-eight hours. Much of this material Mlle. Christitch succeeded in distributing among soldiers just leaving for the front, but it required eighty-five ox-carts to transport the remainder to the station, where I saw it loaded on six large railway-trucks, the guardian of which I thenceforth became.

Our plan at the moment was simple. We were

to follow the orders of the military medical chief, and he had ordered us to Yagodina on the main line of the railway. This meant that at Mladenovats, twenty kilometers from which fierce fighting was going on, all our material would have to be shifted from the narrow-gage to the broad-gage cars, involving a loss of valuable time. But this material had been bought with public money, and Mlle. Christitch was not the kind to abandon it lightly. This motive governed her actions throughout the time I was with her, and finally resulted in the capture of her mother and herself.

It was late Tuesday afternoon when the eight of us, the four nurses, the Christitches, Franz and I splashed down to the depot through knee-deep mud under a heavy downpour. Our train was to leave at seven, but it did not go until nearly midnight. In the meantime we had the honor of making the very interesting acquaintance of the "Little Sergeant," the youngest officer, as well as the youngest soldier, in the Serbian army.

He is—or, now, perhaps was—a real sergeant. On his diminutive soldier's coat he wore three gold stars, and in lieu of a sword he carried an Austrian bayonet, and in lieu of a rifle a Russian cavalry carbine. A full-sized, well-filled cartridge-belt was slung over his shoulders, because it would easily have encircled his baby waist three times. He was ten years old, and had been in the service for "a long time." He had asked and obtained a leave to go home just before all the trouble began, and now he was answering the hurried summons sent out to all soldiers on leave to return to their regiments at once. His home was three days' walk from Valjevo, the nearest railway point, and he had walked the whole way alone; but he was late, and was afraid of exceeding the time allowed for soldiers to return. He said if he reached his station too late, he "would be shot as a deserter, and rightly so." Then his regiment "would be disgraced." He had no money, but did not need any. At the military stations he demanded his loaf of bread as a Serbske *vrenik,* and got it. As for sleeping, well, any café-owner would not refuse a Serbian soldier the hospitality of his floor.

Our train showed no signs of departing, so we took him into the town and gave him dinner at the hotel. He ate tremendously, but seriously, preoccupied, as a man would have been, and at times discussing military affairs. Despite all his efforts, we detected a slight limp, and found his small feet in a frightful condition. His *opanki* had not

"A *man* does not die a hundred times," said the Little Sergeant

Mme. Christitch distributing relief supplies at Valjevo

fitted well and were nearly worn out. Blisters and
stone-bruises were in great evidence. To his
boundless, but unexpressed, delight, we were able
to give him a new pair.

Every one plied him with questions, which he
answered slowly, taking great care as to his words.
Whom had he left at home? Why, his mother and
little sister, who was five years older than himself.
His father and brother were in the army. When
he went home on leave he was able to cut wood and
bring water, see to the prune-trees and feed the
pigs; but most of the time the women had to do this,
which was very bad. But what could one do?
His country was at war, and that meant that men
must fight. Soon, though, when his own regiment,
with which none other could compare, had admin-
istered a much-needed thrashing to the Suabas, he
would return home and help build up the farm.
Yes, his father was a soldier of the line in his regiment, the bravest man in the regiment. He himself had shot well, and had been cautious in the
trenches, and so had been promoted above his
father, who now, according to military discipline,
had to salute his son. But he never allowed this;
he always forestalled his father, and at the same
time conserved discipline by seizing the hand that

would have saluted and kissing it.   His regiment was somewhere near Semendria, but exactly where he did not care to say, because there were spies all about—this with a wary glance at me.

As we waited in the smoky little station, crowded with refugees, he stood as straight as an arrow before the seated ladies, refusing a seat.   He was a Serbske vrenik with a party of civilians who had been kind to him, and while men of that party had to stand, he would not sit.   Blisters and bruises might go whence they came, to the devil.   But as it grew late, an enemy he could not conquer attacked him.   He had risen at four that morning, and it was now ten at night.   With the tactfulness born of long years of diplomatic life in European capitals, Mme. Christitch quietly made room on the bench beside her, which a moment later the "Little Sergeant" unconsciously filled.   Almost at once his head sank to her lap, his hands sought hers, and a last, convincing, incontestable proof that he was a real Serbske vrenik was given: a snore, loud, resonant, manly, broke on the watching crowd.

Two hours later, when our train whistled, I gathered up a sergeant of the Serbian army, carbine, ammunition, sword, knapsack, and all, and carried him without resistance to the freight-truck in which

we were to travel, and laid him, covered with my
blankets, on a soft bale of clothing. I hope that
if ever in the distant future I shall so hold a boy
more closely akin to me, I can be as proud of my
burden as I was that night. Shortly before our
ways parted next day we asked him if he was not
afraid to go back to the trenches.

"A *man* does not die a hundred times," he replied
quietly.

I almost find myself hoping that in the horrible
carnage which occurred at Semendria a few days
later a bullet found the "Little Sergeant" after
some momentary victory, some gallant charge of
his beloved regiment. Life had been so simple for
him! His country was at war; she could not be
wrong; all true men must fight. And he had
known her only in glorious victory.

"*Sbogum, Americanske braat*" ("Good-by,
American brother"), he murmured when we separated.

We began that night a mode of living which for
fifteen days we pursued almost uninterruptedly.
For this length of time we lived, moved, and had
our very excited beings in a railway freight-truck.
We cooked there, dined there, and slept on piles
of soft bales. We took our recreation mainly by

making wild dashes to the station pumps for a drink or a "wash" between stops, or by counting the hundreds of refugees that piled in, hung on, and crowded around every train on every siding. After a trying delay at Mladenovats, during which the battle-line came appreciably nearer, we got on the main line, and succeeded in procuring enough trucks to leave one virtually empty for general uses and a sleeping-apartment for the ladies, while another, nearly full, afforded space for me, Franz, and Tichomir, a young soldier whom we had decided to take with us.

Franz and Tichomir were about the same age, and the fact that Tichomir's father, more than sixty five and not a soldier, had been taken from his home into Austria as a "hostage," and had there died from exposure, did not keep the two boys from becoming boon companions. They used to sit about by the hour, smoking my cigarettes and guying each other in a terrific jargon of German and Serbian. Tichomir was a fine sample of the young Serb, with a face that would have made most European princes look like farm-laborers, and which made it quite impossible to fall out of humor with him, although his aversion to anything savoring of work made it impossible to keep in humor with him, a trying combination! Franz, on the other hand, looked like the stupid, well-meaning cherub that he was. He had a voice like a German lullaby, with which he was always assuring *"Gnadige Frau Christitch"* that the Magyars were the *"Sehre schlectest Menschen am Welt,"* while privately he confided to me that he wanted only one thing on earth, which, put crudely, was to thumb his nose at the illustrious Emperor whose name he bore, and with the wife he had left behind in Austria to go to America for a new start. He did America the honor of thinking it the only country left worth living in, and altogether ingratiated himself into my affections to an alarming extent. Incidentally he ably upheld the best traditions of Vienna cookery, and had about as much business in a battleline as one of Titian's little angels would have in Tammany Hall. All in all, they were a horribly lazy, highly diverting pair. Very probably Tichomir has been killed, and Franz has starved to death.

We were not allowed to stay at Yagodina, but were ordered to Chupriya until further notice. Here several diverting things occurred, not least among them being that we slept in beds once more, the municipal hospital having opened its doors to us. Sleeping in that hard hospital bed has since become an event to me. I slept in it for the last time on the twenty-fifth of October, and with the exception of two nights a few days later, the next time that I slept in anything that even looked like a bed was on the nineteenth of December in Rome. The catalogue of my resting-places during this period comprises hill-tops, pastures, drink-shop floors, flooded corn-fields, snow-covered river-banks, hay-lofts, harems, Montenegrin and Albanian huts, Turkish cemeteries, the seasick deck of a seasick ship, pursued by five submarines, and the floor of a *wagon-lit*.

Late in the afternoon of the day we arrived at Chupriya, Mlle. Christitch and I were at the depot seeing to the shunting of our trucks, for permission had been granted to leave our material on them for a few days until we could decide what to do. The station itself, the yard about it, and the tracks were covered with thousands of homeless women and children. We were standing perhaps a hundred yards from the station building, talking, when we noticed people looking up, and detected the unmistakable hum of an aëroplane. It came out of the east, a tiny golden speck that caught the setting sun's rays and gleamed against the sky at an altitude of perhaps three thousand feet. But it was coming lower, as we could plainly see and hear. Many of the refugees were from Belgrade and Kragujevats, both of which had suffered severely from aëroplanes. These refugees immediately became panic-stricken, the women weeping, the children screaming. At such an altitude, when an aëroplane gets anywhere nearly straight overhead, it appears to be directly so, and you can no more run out from under it than you can get out from under a star. One can only stand and wait, grinning or glum, according to temperament and presentment.

The men in the machine, which was Austrian, could now be seen as tiny specks, and they appeared to be directly over us. We knew, of course, that they were aiming at the station, but that did not help the incontestable evidence of our eyes that they were straight over our heads, and bomb-droppers are not adept at throwing curves. It was our first raid. We saw the thing hang almost motionless for what seemed many minutes as it turned more to the south, and watching intently, we saw nothing, but heard a sharp whiz as of a cane whirled swiftly through the air, and then a deafening report came that stunned us a little. At the same time anti-air-craft guns began their fusillades. When the dust and smoke lifted, there were hundreds of women and children trembling with fear, and less than fifty feet from us what had been a little boy of twelve and an old soldier barely alive. Unhurt, the aëroplane sailed away into the sunset.

After four days at Chupriya, orders came to proceed to Krushevats, there to shift once more to the narrow-gage and go to Kraljevo, which had become the temporary abode of the Government. Ordinarily this journey would require four or five hours.   Ten days later we left the railway at Trestenik, a station not far from Kraljevo, having never come to our destination at all.   So great was the congestion in the railway-yard at Krushevats that for seven days we waited on a siding three miles outside the place before our train could be brought in.   This siding led to one of the largest powder factories in Serbia, and our train stood very near it.   Every day hostile aëroplanes came over, hovering like tiny flies far above the factory, which was going at full blast.   But at the four corners of the place anti-air-craft guns poked their ugly muzzles skyward, and the Austrian aviators dared not come low enough to drop bombs.

The highway ran past our car-door, giving us

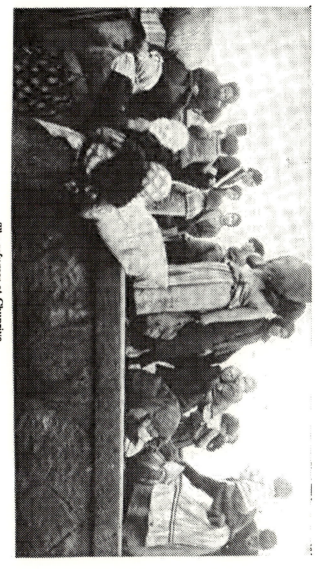

The refugees at Chupriya

Taken only fifteen minutes before the aeroplane raid that killed a little boy

endless glimpses into the life of the fleeing population, each a little drama in itself. One day six limousines came by, filled with men in silk hats and frock-coats. It was the cabinet fleeing from the Bulgarians before Nish. I saw Pashich, the greatest of Balkan statesmen, looking rather wearily, I thought, out of the window, old, worn, worried. These were the men who had had to face Austria's ultimatum, and who were now just beginning to face the consequences of their refusal to surrender the liberty of their nation.

After we had finally been taken into Krushevats, Mlle. Christitch and I were walking down the tracks into the town one day when we saw a new eight-cylinder American touring-car. In it we recognized Admiral Troubridge and Major Elliott, the British military attaché. They had just missed the train which was to take them on to Kraljevo and intended going on in an automobile. As we were talking, however, word came that the road was almost impassable, and the Serbian officer in attendance went to secure a special train for them. I remember my wonder that in such a bedlam of congestion a special train was still possible. They got out, and we walked up the tracks together. I had met Admiral Troubridge before.

He is a perfect picture of an admiral. His typically British face, ruddy complexion, and snow-white hair, combined with a certain easy-going, almost lackadaisical air, make him just like an admiral on the stage. Mme. Christitch had given me a highly interesting account of a conversation which she, her daughter, and the nurses had had with him at Chupriya, but which I did not hear.

The Admiral, then fresh from the bombardment of Belgrade, had assured them that the Serbs were making no resistance "worth speaking of." They were abandoning everything, he said, and were suing for peace, which, he assured the ladies, would be concluded within fifteen days. He said that the firing we heard was a mere pretense, that no serious fighting was going on since the fall of Belgrade. He did not tell whence came the thousands of wounded and dying which we had seen in Valjevo and right there in Krushevats, and which we were soon to hear about from the nurses at Kragujevats. These thousands excluded all those from the Bulgarian battle-line, about which, so far as I know, the Admiral did not express himself, and excluded the unparalleled (for the number engaged) slaughter that occurred at Zajechar and Pirot. He said that this peace, which was to come

in fifteen days, was the only thing left to Serbia;
he expressed it as his opinion, in very much
the same words that I use here, that the diplomacy
of England had been so stupid, so ignorant, so
criminally careless that the Serbs would be justified
in making a separate peace as a "slap in England's
face." He added that all the foregoing summer
he had been begging his Government to send out
reinforcements to him on the Danube. He also
told us that he understood the Germans were acting in a most conciliatory manner toward the Serbs
in an endeavor to placate them. The policy which
they had followed in Belgium had not been followed in Serbia, he said. These remarks by a
British admiral of wide note, commander-in-chief
of the only force which England sent to Serbia
until the final attack, seemed to have impressed the
ladies deeply. Made, as they were, to Mme.
Christitch, who has given thirty years of her life
to Serbia, and whose husband is a well-known
figure in Balkan diplomacy, and to her daughter,
who since 1912 has devoted most of her time to
her native country, they naturally were not soon
forgotten, and, I feel sure, that an hour after the
Admiral left I had a substantially verbatim report
of them.

Although I had not met Colonel Phillips before, I knew something of him. I had heard of him as governor of Scutari during the period of the formation of Albania as a kingdom, and as a man who knew the Balkans "like a book." He is most things the Admiral is not. He is tall, with no superfluous flesh, has a red face and sandy mustache. He is army all over, whereas the Admiral is navy all over, and could be at home only on a bridge—a stage bridge, perhaps, but still a bridge. Before coming to Serbia, Colonel Phillips had served for several months on General French's staff in France. The Admiral seemed to me always ineffably bored, the Colonel always irrationally irritated.

Standing on the railway-track, waiting for his train, Colonel Phillips talked to me. If he thought about the matter at all, he may have known in an uncertain manner that I was supposed to be an American who claimed to have been engaged in relief work, and who at the moment was traveling with the Christitch Mission. He could not have known more, and two hostile aëroplanes that shortly before had appeared just as the Crown Prince's train was starting—the train which the Colonel should have caught—testified an almost

Tichomir and some of his relatives

General Putnik, Serbia's oldest general and a popular hero

uncanny system of espionage on the part of the enemy. This seemingly did not worry Colonel Phillips, and, as for me, having the Admiral's remarks as a precedent, I was prepared for anything from a British officer in Serbia. To use a homely simile, the Colonel reminded me of nothing so much as the safety-valve of an overcharged boiler when suddenly released. I did not release it with skilful questioning. A wooden Indian could have interviewed the Colonel that morning. Already two weeks of the tremendous pressure of the retreat had blunted my journalistic tendencies; the Colonel awakened them from their supine slumber.

He opened the conversation with the brief remark that the Serbian General Staff were idiots, a statement which, considering such men as Putnik, Stepanovich, and Mishich, might, to say the least, be open to argument. Like the Admiral, he said that they were suing for peace, which would be made within a fortnight. He said that they had "completely lost their heads" and had "nothing even resembling an organized plan of campaign." They and the Serbian army were running away as fast as possible, according to him. He told me that "the French military attaché and myself, backed by our respective Governments, have submitted a plan of campaign to the Serbian General Staff, and so far they have refused to consider it." Those were his exact words.   Then apparently to prove the fitness of his plan, which was backed by England and France, he proceeded *to detail that plan to me, an utter stranger!*   It consisted in brief of abandoning all of northern Serbia at once and retreating south in a desperate attempt to hold the Orient Railway, an impossibility at the time we talked.   I never saw the French attaché, so have no way of deciding if what the Colonel said is true.

The Colonel then discussed briefly, much to my interest, the position of England in the war.   He said that up to the present England had saved herself all she could, and had attempted to organize her forces so perfectly that in the spring or early summer of 1916 she would be able to hurl a vast army against the western German lines at a time when Germany would be beginning to show exhaustion.

With scarcely a break in his speech, the Colonel turned his attention to the King of Montenegro, whom he taxed with certainly having a secret understanding with Austria.   He characterized his

Montenegrin majesty as a "knave and a rascal," and told me that he, Colonel Phillips, did not dare to go into Montenegro now for fear of his life because in past years he had so infuriated the King.

At this point it occurred to him to ask what I had been doing, and when I replied with a brief account of relief-work among the refugees of Bosnia, he made some observations on such work. He accused both his own countrymen and the Serbians with gross dishonesty in the administration of charitable funds, and, as for my refugees, they were n't due to the war at all, but had infested the mountains in that same state of starvation "for ten thousand years more or less."

Then, and then only, was I guilty of my first question. I mentioned something about the United States. With the courtesy and kindness which he had shown to me throughout, he begged to be excused from "discussing your country, as I would certainly hurt your feelings." Now, would not this make any normal American curious? I pressed the subject, saying that I thought I could stand it, as I was far away from home and might never see the old place again, anyway. I do not pretend to have understood his position in regard to America. The one concrete thing I could get at was that we were a nation of conscienceless dollar-snatchers, who refused to fight because it cost money, "in spite of the infinite debt of gratitude" we owed to England. Instead of helping her, he said, we were deliberately taught to hate her. He said he knew the United States "like a book," had traveled extensively North and South, and had found that in our schools we systematically "taught our children to hate England." I murmured I was Southern. He said that in the South we hated Englishmen as we did "niggers." I did not say yes and I did not say no to this. I remarked that there "were 'niggers' and 'niggers,'" and so, doubtless, when I had met more Englishmen, I should find they were not all the same sort.

Then, at the risk of displaying crass ignorance, I asked what our debt of gratitude to England might be. He thought a moment very studiously, and then remarked that we spoke the same language. I could not resist the temptation that came to me. "On the level," I asked, "what are you handing me?" But I had to translate for him.

Next, with fear and trembling, remembering his position as a member of General French's staff, I turned the steam on France. I received only two statements, and these were exceedingly enigmatic.

In their proper order they are, "France, like your own country, has thought only of money in this war," and, "As regards men, France is now exhausted." Let him who wishes to rush in, attempt a reconciliation of these two statements. Colonel Phillips made them; I report them here.

The Colonel confided to me that he and Admiral Troubridge "had been cruelly punished by being sent to Serbia" because they had too emphatically and openly criticized England's policy at the Dardanelles.

By this time the Colonel seemed a bit relieved, and boyishly told me of a lovely little prank of his. As matters of taste can never be argued, I shall leave each reader to form his own opinion without any admonition from me. The Colonel said that at last, when he was forced to leave Belgrade, just before the Germans were due to reach the house where he lived, he prepared a little welcome for them in his sitting-room. At the grand piano, which he had procured from some ruined home previously, he seated a skeleton, with grinning skull turned toward the door and the fleshless hands lying on the keys. He had draped the skeleton in a German uniform and had placed upon its head a German helmet.

When at last the special train which the Serbian Government had produced on thirty minutes' notice appeared to bear him away, the Colonel cordially shook my hand, saying he had enjoyed meeting and talking with me.

Thus spoke the British military attaché in Serbia, whose position entitled him to the confidence of the General Staff on whom the fate of a nation hung, to me an absolute stranger, when the country he had been sent out to aid was facing as awful a fate as any country ever faced, and was facing it alone either because of the weakness, stupidity, or treachery of her allies.

I report these two interviews because they were interesting to me and so, I think, will prove to others. I do not feel that there is any breach of confidence in this. The sentiments expressed by these two distinguished British officers were not expressed in confidence at all,—would to heaven they had been!—and, furthermore, were expressed by them to numbers of people on different occasions. They were the common talk among the English during the retreat. Certainly, I have little or no feeling toward these gentlemen one way or the other. In trying to write the story of Serbia, I cannot omit one of her major afflictions.

Finally, in the night, we were jerked out of
Krushevats. Jerked is the proper word, for at
this time the wide-spread congestion had called into
service many locomotive engineers who perhaps had
seen locomotives before, but were certainly not on
speaking terms with the fine arts of coupling and
switching. The terrible bumps we got were really
dangerous, especially in the men's car, where every
tremor threatened to bring down huge bales of
philanthropic shirts upon our heads. We heard of
one man who was standing with his head stuck out
of the door of a freight-truck when a sudden bump
slammed the sliding-door shut and decapitated him.
After that we kept our heads inside, preferring the
threatening shirts.

At Stalach we were delayed several hours for
some unknown reason, but had a most sociable time
receiving in our "villa box-car" several distinguished guests; for Stalach is the junction of the
line from Nish with the Kraljevo line, and at this
moment was crowded with the Serbian *haute
monde*. That well known soldier, Captain Petronijevich, who had been detailed by his Government
as Sir Ralph Paget's attendant, came to our menage
filled with some gleeful secret. He sat about on
packing-cases, and made witty remarks with a dis-

tinctly gloating air that mystified us until, like a
magician, he produced three cans of pâté de foie
gras.   His triumph did not last long.   From behind a pile of baggage I drew two wonderful roast
ducks that Franz, with great skill and loving care
had done to a turn on our tiny little stove.   So luxury ran riot at Stalach.

Sir Ralph's "country place" was down the track
about a hundred yards.   Numerous army-blankets
and rugs strewn about gave it a wild Oriental air
worthy of Essad Pasha, but Sir Ralph had no
stove.   Altogether our car had the honors of the
day.

Just as we were leaving Stalach a young officer
leaped into our truck.   He was gloriously clean,
flashing, magnificent.   I am sorry to have lost his
name.   He was responsible for all that part of the
railway, a terrific task at this time.   He could give
news, and became so engrossed with the ladies that
he did not notice the bumps which told us we were
starting.   When he did "come to," we were making
good time a mile out of Stalach, and he had to be
back in Stalach.   I swung open the door, and he,
producing a pocket flash-light, stood in the opening
a moment searching the ground below.   There was
a continuous ditch, filled to the brim with black

Misses Helsby, Spooner, and Magnussen in the author's car, shortly before they were forced to evacuate Valjevo, leaving the automobile behind

water. Only an instant he paused, then disappeared into the night, and a loud splash was the last we ever heard of him.

That night our train was stopped at Trestenik, for Kraljevo had suddenly become one of the most dangerous spots in Serbia. A short counsel between Mlle. Christitch and me resulted in the following arrangements.

With her mother, who could hardly be exposed to the hardships of an ox-cart retreat, she would stay at Trestenik for two days to distribute among the needy soldiers and civilians and hospitals the supplies to which she had held so tenaciously. The Government could give her two small ox-carts to go to Alexandrovats, which lay about forty kilometers to the southwest. It was arranged that I should take these carts, and transport the three British nurses, with as much tinned foods and biscuits as we could carry. If at Alexandrovats I found an English or French mission in retreat, I was to hand over the nurses to them, and return to see of what service I might be at Trestenik. If there were no such missions, I should wait three days, unless the danger was pressing, in the hope that Mlle. Christitch and her mother would come on and join us. If they did not come, or if I was forced to go sooner,

I was to accompany the nurses until I found an English mission or until I could see Sir Ralph Paget, who was the representative of the British Serbian Relief and had been detailed to look after the English missions. As I was acquainted with Sir Ralph, and as he was an old friend of Mlle. Christitch, once I could get to him the safety of the English nurses would be assured, Mlle. Christitch felt, and it was the safety of her nurses which was always the first thought with her. I give this arrangement in some detail because of later incidents.

In the dawn of November 4, while it was raining heavily, we said good-by to the Christitches and Miss Magnussen, who, being neutral, would remain with them, and started on our journey.

In company with Mlle. Christitch I had gone to the commandant of the place. I had heard him explain in no uncertain terms the very threatened position of Trestenik. Six weeks later, when in Rome, I had the pleasure of bringing to Colonel Christitch the first authentic news of his wife and daughter. His first question was not of their probable danger under the invader; it was simply:

"Was my daughter brave?"

"Your daughter is a Serb," I replied.

"Thanks," he said, and the expression on his face showed that my answer needed no elucidation.

The three women who were to endure in the succeeding tragic weeks so much physical discomfort and mental strain, were true women of England, although one of them had spent much time in America. The youngest and tiniest of them is a direct descendant of the great creator of "Pilgrim's Progress," a picture of whom she used to wear continually in a locket, and from whose allegory she frequently quoted a paragraph apt for her own wanderings. Then there was the very deft nurse who in London had been the head of the nursing force of a hospital and whose whole life was wrapped up in her blessed profession, as in fact was the case with all three of them. I envied many times their professional attitude toward the innumerable sufferers which we saw later, always knowing what to do and how to do it, while I could only pity. I think no woman ever lived who was pluckier and more uncomplaining than the eldest of the three, a woman well past middle-age with deliberate, gentle manners and the deceptive appearance of being too frail to support even undue exertion in ordinary routine. To think what she went through and how she stood it! Had I known on that dreary morning leaving Trestenik what lay before her I honestly would not have believed that she would ever see England again. When the following days forced upon me the realization of what we were in for, there was always a cold dread within me of what I felt strongly was inevitable for her. My solicitude was unnecessary. At Brindisi, after it was all over, she seemed just the same fragile being who tramped out of Trestenik.

From the very first each of them took the greatest pride in tramping well and "keeping fit." Occasional vain wails for a "wash" were the extent of their complaints. Never a day passed that each of them did not come to me separately and say, "Is n't so-and-so walking splendidly! I was so afraid for her, but is n't she holding up, though!" There was a keen rivalry between them as to their powers of endurance, and none of them would ride—when it was possible—unless I made myself so unpleasant about it that they took pity on me and acquiesced. They presupposed in me a vast knowledge of the country we traversed and of woodcraft in general, to which I could not lay the least claim, but I took care not to disillusion them any more than my manifest ignorance made necessary.

It was not long before we came to know each

other's foibles and how to soothe or ruffle one another. One of us, for instance, was, oh, very ortho-
dox, and two of us were—well, shockingly free in
our view as to the possibility of miracles, let us
say. So on many a night in the savage wilderness
high discussions flew around the camp-fire where we
lay. We laughed at each other, talked at and
about each other, and were, in a word, for many
weeks comrades of the road.

There were no covers on the miserable carts, and
as they were full of supplies the women walked
most of the time. We had been told that it was
one day to Alexandrovats, but hour after hour we
climbed a tangle of hills over mere trails knee-deep
in mud. The oxen were small and, when night
came, were worn out. Having no interpreter, I,
of course, could communicate with my drivers only
by signs, and the old boys were not particularly
bright at understanding things they did not want
to. Tichomir, whom we had taken with us, I
had sent ahead with letters to secure accommodations.

When it grew dark the drivers insisted on stopping, while I insisted on pushing on, thinking it
could not be much farther to the town. Fortunately, the rain had stopped, and the stars shone,

but the road grew worse. It skirted the edge of a precipice. There was no rail, and the earth crumbled away at the slightest pressure. Soon the drivers developed open hostility, holding frequent whispered conferences. The carts stuck in mudholes often, and we had literally to put our shoulders to the wheel and help the weakened oxen. Then they would go only if some one led the front pair. This the drivers refused to do, because it necessitated wading continually in slush up to the knees. So the task devolved upon me.

The women were worn out, of course, and nervous, and distrusted the drivers intensely. For several hours I was able to force the drivers to go on, and about ten o'clock, when we turned a corner, a blaze of light came to us. It was a large army-transport camp, and I thought we had better stay there for the night.

The drivers immediately sat down and refused to move, the oxen following their example. I wished the carts brought out of the road to the camp-ground, and, losing my temper, started to seize the lead-rope of one of the oxen. Five minutes later I recovered my breath. I was lying in a mud-hole about fifteen feet from the ox, and on my right side, along the ribs, my clothing was cut

almost as if with a knife. There was a shallow
gash in the flesh, and one hand was badly cut. I
was a mass of evil-smelling mud. The ox had
failed to get his horn in far enough to do any real
damage. When I got my breath back, discretion
seemed the best cue for me, so I waded through the
mire to one of the blazing camp-fires.

There was a typical group about it. The ox-
drivers of Serbia are as nondescript and picturesque
a crowd as can be found anywhere on earth. I
knew the Serbian word for English woman, and,
pointing to the road, remarked that there were
three English women who must pass the night
somewhere, and I made it evident I thought their
fire was a pretty good place. One young fellow
of about twenty, I should judge, extremely handsome, but in woeful rags and without any shoes,
rose at once despite the fact that he had walked all
day in the rain and was then cooking his meager
supper as he dried himself by the fire. He smiled
as few can smile, and, muttering, "English sisters,"
came with me. It meant that he would get wet
again crossing two bad mud-holes, but he came to
our cart and wanted to carry the nurses over one by
one. We seated ourselves about their fire and offered them a tin of preserved mutton. They had

almost nothing to eat, and this was a rare delicacy for them, but we had to force them to take it. Such are the most ignorant of the Serbians.

Our new protector went back to our carts to give the ox-drivers some well-needed words, and, returning, ransacked the large camp for hay for the women to lie on. He had been walking sixteen hours, he was wet, and he had not had his supper, yet his manner was charming as he offered this hay, much as Lord Chesterfield might have placed a chair for his queen. Strange as we must have seemed to them, dropping out of the darkness like that, they betrayed not the slightest trace of curiosity, observing always an impeccable attitude of careful attention to our every want.

There was one tall, lithe Gipsy among them who appeared to be chief baker. He had long, straight black hair, deep black eyes, and the complexion of a Spaniard, while his teeth were perfect, and always in evidence in the sliest sort of laugh. He had a mellow tenor voice, with which he continually sang songs that were, I am sure, very naughty, he was so obviously a good, gay devil. He was like a Howard Pyle pirate. There was a red turban, such as the people of the *Sanjak* wear, around his head. His shirt was of soft yellow stuff, in tatters, and his trousers were of a rich, reddish-brown homespun. He had no shoes, which did not matter much, because his feet were very shapely.

Before him he spread a heavy gunny sack, very clean, doubled four times, and on this he poured a little mound of wheat-flour. Then from a brown earthen jug he poured some water on the flour and added a little lard and salt. For some time he kneaded the dough on the gunny sack, and at last patted it into a round disk about two inches thick. Raking away the coals from the center of the fire, he uncovered a space of baked earth thoroughly cleansed by the heat and placed his cake there, covering it first with hot ashes and then with live coals. In half an hour he produced a loaf beautifully baked and not at all unpalatable. But one felt all the time that instead of baking bread he should be clambering up the sides of brave ships and kidnapping beautiful maidens.

This was our first night spent under the stars. We all slept comfortably around the fire, and next morning had a wash from an old well near by, our protector bringing us water in a jug. He flatly refused any gift of money, and went away shouting gaily to us, unaware that I had slipped something into his pocket. He was one of the "barbaric

Serbs" whom political propaganda has so long vilified.

While our carts were being brought up, one of the nurses suddenly uttered an exclamation of pleasure and pointed to the western horizon. We were on a high hill, and the mountains shouldered away on every hand like an innumerable crowd of giants. Blue and gold, gray and green, they rolled off from the early sun to the dim west, where, out of crowding mists, a solitary snow-capped peak stood covered with a perfect Alpine glow. Being English women, the nurses had always a keen eye for the scenic side of Serbia, and were delighted with this first snow mountain. But I shall never forget the feeling that the chilly peak brought to me. A distinct vision came to me on that sunny hillside of bleak mountains in a storm through which unnumbered thousands of women, old men, and children struggled, freezing and starving. Mlle. Christitch's earnest words came back, "You will go through Montenegro to the sea with them, if necessary, will you not?" Looking at them now, I wondered if it would not be a death-sentence for these women who were accustomed only to a sheltered London existence. But I cast the vision away as hysterical, which seems very ridiculous to me now, for, if I had spent the whole sunny day dreaming horrors, I still would not have begun to comprehend what soon was to be reality.

Not until three o'clock in the afternoon did we come to Alexandrovats. As we entered the town, a French aëroplane was trying vainly to rise from the open field by the roadside, and a little farther on we saw a heap of splinters, which was all that was left of one that had fallen the day before. When we got into the town we heard rumors that Krushevats had fallen, and I know now that Trestenik was taken by a patrol on the same day. Isolated as it was, Alexandrovats already was moved by a great wave of unrest.

CHAPTER V

A S if to compensate us for the loss of our carts at Alexandrovats, we made a valuable acquisition to our personnel. Driving up to the spotless little cottage that Tichomir had procured for us through the letters he bore, a very short, portly little man, wearing a bright-checked suit and loud golf-cap, rushed out to us, waving a light yellow cane and shouting in English. This gentleman would have excited comment at Coney Island, and Alexandrovats is not Coney Island. It is provincial even for Serbia, yet the man who came to meet us was a cosmopolite. There could be no doubt of it; it fairly oozed from him. The sound of English was more welcome than I can say, for, while letters had made things easy here, I had none for the future, and the constantly louder sound of cannon during the last two days had made me exceedingly skeptical as to the Christitches ever rejoining us.

140

I will not give this gentleman's name, for it might possibly cause him inconvenience, and he certainly did all in his power for us—for himself and us. We shall call him Mr. B——. He is very well known in Belgrade, the head of a large firm there, and the representative of some thirty English companies in the Balkans. No sooner had we arrived than he handed me the keys of Alexandrovats, as it were. Did I have an interpreter? Well, how the thunder did I get so far as this? But it made no difference now; I had met him, and he was absolutely at our service. All the officials of the town were his fast friends, and all the merchants, though he had been there only two weeks. As for languages, he could converse with me in English, French, German, Serbian, Bulgarian, Rumanian, and Italian. His knowledge of the country was at my disposal, and would I see the ladies settled, then come to dine with him?

Even at this early date we were getting tired of tinned mutton and sweet biscuit, so the invitation to dine I accepted with alacrity, despite the fact that he spoke with an unmistakable Teutonic accent. While I have nothing at all against this sort of accent, in a warring country where it is not particularly popular, and when one has others to consider, it is just as well to steer clear even of the appearances of evil.

Mr. B—— was a wonderful interpreter. When I sat down to dine with him, before his German cook, Marie, a poor girl who had been caught in Serbia by the war, had set any dish before us, he apologized for the quality of his meal. He said that as Marie had not known there would be a "ghost" for dinner, she had made no extra preparations. Had he known that a "ghost" was coming, he would have ordered her to prepare one of the six "kitchens" which he had been able to buy that afternoon, for by laborious search he had discovered six fat "hands." Seeing my dismay, he exclaimed testily:

"Kitchens, kitchens, hands. How says it? Feathered files." Then as light broke over me, he ended triumphantly, *"Chez moi, Herr Yones,* I am one good eater!" He was, indeed, the dinner certainly being all that one could desire.

To find in Alexandrovats at that time an excellent meal, faultlessly served in European fashion, was strange, but stranger still was Mr. B——'s apartment. A man who had shown the business astuteness to amass a considerable fortune, as Mr. B—— undoubtedly had, and who has evacuated

Belgrade with nothing but a small hamper of clothes and a very good quantity of books, is unusual. I found on his shelves, in wild Alexandrovats, Heine, Schiller, Goethe, Shakespeare, Thackeray, Dickens, Ibsen, Meredith, Browning, Samuel Butler, Shaw, Voltaire, Bergson, Maeterlinck, Maarten Maartens, the brilliant satire of the last named being sprinkled like paprika over my host's remarkable conversation. He seemed too good to be true, just the man to lead us out of Serbia. And it soon became obvious that he wanted to go. His story was simple.

Twenty years ago he came with his wife from Bohemia to Belgrade. He had no money, but by hard work finally built up the firm of which he was the head. He had a son and a daughter, the son just attaining military age shortly before the war. Twice he had tried to become a Serbian citizen, but Serbia had with Austria a treaty by which a citizen of one could not without the consent of his country become a citizen of the other. This consent was refused because his son would soon be old enough to serve in the army. Just before the war began, the mother, son, and daughter paid a visit to Switzerland, and were caught there by the beginning of hostilities. The offending treaty being abrogated,

of course, as soon as the war started, Mr. B——
again tried for Serbian citizenship; but another law
was in the way. He could not become a Serbian
citizen unless his wife was with him to give consent
and to take the oath of allegiance at the same time.
His wife was in Switzerland on an Austrian passport, and hence could not get into Serbia without
making a journey full of risks and annoyances.
His daughter had died, and the son was an engi-
neer in Geneva. Mr. B—— had been interned
since the beginning of the war, and was more than
anxious to meet his family. He could not leave
Serbia, yet he dared not be captured by his former
countrymen because Austria is not particularly
gentle with her citizens of Slav extraction who for-
sake the country of their birth for the country of
their preference. He saw in us his salvation. All
the Serbian authorities knew him and had confidence in him. I must have an interpreter; he
would be assigned to me, and happily we should
go out together, only he would not leave Marie.
Marie had come to them before the war and could
not get back home. However, a week previously
he had laid in large food supplies, so that they would
not be an added tax on our very insufficient stores.
I quickly decided to take him around to all the

military authorities, and, if they seemed to approve of him, to accept his services.

Mr. B—— proved a great success in Alexandrovats. Everywhere he was apparently respected, liked, almost bowed down to. I began to feel that my position in the place was assured with Mr. B—— as sponsor. For two days we hung about the *narchelnik stanitza* pleading for ox-carts and bread. This officer, chief of the station, is the go-between in Serbia for the civil and the military. To him the ox-drivers go with all their grievances and to get their bread. To him all who have claims on the Government for ox-carts, shelter, and bread must go. All the relief workers come in contact with him. He is a very kind, efficient person, ready to do all in his power for a stranger within his gates. Of course one must have proper credentials, and be able to talk to him in some fashion. On the shoulders of these officers fell a large part of the labor and responsibility during the retreat. When they left at all, they were the last to go. Day by day they listened to civilians and soldiers, sick and wounded, begging for bread and shelter, which they had not to give. They had to look out for the transportation of food into their stations and the proper distribution of it there. When a loaf of bread was selling at five dollars and could not be found at that price, they alone could give the little slip of paper that entitled one to his allowance. The scenes their waiting-rooms presented can be imagined.

Famine was settling on Alexandrovats, and the Germans were close. There were no carts, no bread, and as the Government had long ago commandeered nearly all the oxen of the country, chances of buying any sort of transportation seemed slim, and all the more so as the whole population was beginning to move. Every hour I would bring to the nurses the crumbs of comfort the *narchelnik* let fall, and every hour we were disappointed. At last there came a time when he assured us that we must not wait any longer. We must find by private means any transportation we could and go at once. Now Mr. B—— became a fat little jewel; he scintillated with usefulness.

The chief lawyer of the place, a typical Serb of his class, trained in Germany and at his own university in Belgrade, calm in the face of the general confusion of the community, already forming a league of the leading citizens to take all precautionary measures so that when the enemy came they should find a population that gave no excuse for wholesale executions, was informed of my predicament. His whole fortune had disappeared, he could not but be concerned about his family, if anything happened in the community, he by his prominence would be one of the first to suffer; yet he devoted hours of his time to me. A stout, covered cart was found at a reasonable price, which I immediately paid. To secure horses was more difficult.

We went to another of Mr. B——'s fast friends, the chief baker, whose lowly position had at this moment brought him the popularity of a prince. He was a huge man, with broad, heavy features and small, black eyes that shifted their glance constantly. He had a pair of strong horses that he would sell me for the sake of the nurses. We went to his stable and found a good-looking pair of sorrels for which he wanted a thousand *dinars,* an atrocious price for Serbia, but not in our predicament. The price was paid without much haggling, and as it was then late in the afternoon, we agreed to get an early start next morning, the last day that Alexandrovats would remain uncaptured.

Although our cart was large, it was not large enough to carry food for seven people for an indefinite period, their luggage, and still afford space for the women to ride. Food and blankets might mean life; we must carry all we possibly could of them. So the order went round to cut down personal luggage to the vanishing-point. Hard as this task must have been for them, the nurses mercilessly trimmed down their wardrobes without grumbling. A third of our food-supply—tinned meat, condensed milk, biscuits, tea, and sugar—I felt I must leave at Alexandrovats for the Christitches in case they should come on. I confess it was a hard decision. The lack of this food might very well cost the lives of the nurses for whom I was responsible. We were leaping into the dark. No one knew where or how long we would have to travel. Yet if Mme. and Mlle. Christitch should come that way, depending on us for food, their position would be perilous in the extreme. So a third of everything was left in charge of a man we knew we could trust, with instructions to hold it until the enemy was nearing the town, then to dispose of it as he saw fit.

Early next morning Tichomir drove our cart to the home of Mr. B——, where his things were taken on, and then they came down to us. Mr. B——'s and Marie's belongings filled about two thirds of the cart. There were large wicker hampers, valises, and traveling-bags. I was astounded

The departure became an exodus

that a man and his cook should feel the need of such an amount, and remarked to B—— that he evidently was not in the habit of traveling light. He looked confused, and with an apprehensive glance at Marie said he hoped we could get everything in. That cart looked like the popular conception of Santa Claus's sleigh, but we had the satisfaction of knowing that the load was not heavy, only bulky, and would dwindle day by day.

Alexandrovats was in a furor. Fast retreating troops had struck the town an hour earlier, and were going through at breakneck speed. It seemed as if the sight of these worn soldiers persuaded many more families to go, for the departure now became an exodus. We set out in this mêlée along a road two feet deep with mud. The warm, bright sunshine, glorious autumn woods, and the sight of that top-heavy cart gave our "hearts and souls a stir-up," an exultation that was doomed to a quick death. About two miles out the road tackled a small mountain in a series of switchbacks, not steep, but almost interminable.

We had pushed ahead, leaving the cart and driver to follow, and sat down on a grassy slope to wait for it. No cart came. The fleeing soldiers, thousands of them, passed and were gone. The refugee procession thinned.   An hour went by, and still our ark did not appear.   Then came a dove in the form of Tichomir, but bearing no olive-branch.   With frenzied gesticulations he announced something to Mr. B——, who turned to me groping for words:

"They will not—they will not—will not—*Gott im Himmel*—they will not *do*, those horses!"   His vocabulary did not include the highly significant adjective "balky," but certain experiences with Texas mustangs made me jump to this conclusion.

Leaving the women on the hillside, we returned, and found a very meek pair of beasts as immovable as mountains, which, when the cart was unloaded, still refused to budge.   The only thing to do with that kind of a horse is to get rid of him, but precious time was flying.   Before sunset the enemy might be in Alexandrovats, and of all things I desired to avoid was having the nurses captured in such an isolated position.   Unhitching the pair, we returned to the chief baker, and suddenly entering his shop, we surprised him counting a thousand dinars in ten and one hundred dinar-notes.

In a few well-chosen words I told Mr. B—— to tell him what I thought of his horses and of the sort of man who would play a trick like that.   This did not tend to soften his heart, however, and he flatly refused to return the money. Not to get that money back was unthinkable; without it we would not have enough to buy other means of transportation, and with these horses we could not hope to get anywhere. With touching abandon I threatened and lied. I said I was a government representative, a personal friend of the President. I remarked if the Germans came and found me there with three nurses, Mr. Gerard in Berlin would soon know the reason why. Anything done against me, I demonstrated, would be against my great and dangerous nation, and anything done to hinder the escape of three British citizens would have to be fully accounted for in after years. I represented the deep guilt, the sordid avariciousness of his conduct, and before I finished I had two thirds of the artillery of the world trained with dire threats on that shop; but the chief baker smiled calmly, batting his small pig eyes.

He was sustained by a secret spring of power. My predicament had fast spread through the little place, and the lawyer, the man with whom I had left the provisions, and some leading citizens were holding an indignation meeting about it around the corner. The interest these men took in us, laying aside their own anxieties, is one of the many things I cannot forget about the Serbs. But their hands were tied; they dared not take an open stand against the chief baker. With the approach of the enemy he had become bold, and a truth long suspected was now virtually certain. He was in league with the enemy, and would become burgomaster of the place on occupation. Then he would hold more than the power of life and death over his fellow-townsmen. They stood in deadly fear of him, and so strongly suspected his affiliation with the invader that for fear of reprisals they dared not make way with him. So Mr. B—— and I had to fight our battle alone, and time was passing. Meanwhile the women were watching the sun swing westward on the pleasant hillside.

A small Belgian automatic—from Liège—hung on my belt, less imposing than my mythical cannon, but more tangible. I indicated to Mr. B—— my intention of using this, as a bluff, of course, for law courts and ordered dealings had ceased to be in Alexandrovats. B—— agreed that as a last resort it might be necessary, and all the more so because by efforts of the lawyer four oxen had been found which could be bought for less than the two horses cost. We must have the money. One more frenzied appeal, and the baker softened a little; he would return all of our money except fifty dollars. This he must keep for his trouble. We closed on this finally, and soon had four strong oxen instead of the balky horses.

I shall always wonder where those oxen were procured. What the Government had overlooked, the refugees had taken. One would have been as likely to find South Sea Islanders on Broadway. But I can make a good guess. The man whose house we had occupied for three days and who, although poor, would not accept a cent in payment, had brought them from somewhere. I think they were some he had been saving against an emergency. They might mean much to him and his family later, yet they were sold to me at a price so low that after six weeks' constant travel I sold one pair of them for more than they cost me. Scarcely would he let me thank him.

"Those English sisters," he said simply, "are angels. They came to us in our trouble and risked their lives to save our soldiers. All that any true Serbian has to give is theirs, and," he added earnestly, "when you go back to your own country, you will not say, as the Suabas do, that we are barbarians, will you, American brother?"

The desire to be well thought of, to please, to be a part of Western culture, to do the thoroughly urbane thing, is one of the most striking characteristics of the Serb as he is to-day. One constantly meets examples. It strikes one as being the instinctive reaching out of a people that for centuries drew their very breath only at the pleasure of a terrible oppressor.

In mid-afternoon we were once more on our way, our cart presenting no difficulty at all to the four fine oxen. For three days from that time we were happy, care-free vagabonds. The weather was beautiful, still days bright with sunlight and flaming woods, starry nights through which we slept like logs, lying in the open after the long marches. We saw comparatively few refugees on this road, for we were out of the main line of travel, and would not strike it until we reached the Ibar Valley, one day's journey before Rashka. Some of the most beautiful scenery of Serbia lies in the mountainous stretch between Alexandrovats and Rashka. On many crags stand old fortresses and castles dating from Roman times.

One in particular I remember, Kozengrad, so old that its origin is purely legendary, and on so inaccessible a perch that it is named the "Goat

City," these being the only animals supposed
to have been able to scale its mountain walls.
For a long, hard day we tramped in and out
among the hills, and never got away from it. We
came to detest it as a personal insult. After
that all-day march, it seemed as near as when we
began.

These days were one long picnic for us all except
Marie. Her well-ordered Teutonic mind was
blank with amazement at our mode of life. To
sleep at night in one's clothes, to rise next morning
and begin the march with not an hour to spare for
one to arrange one's hair in a fearful and wonderful fashion, to eat with one's fingers and not have
enough at that—these were the things that out-
raged her housekeeping soul. It was indecent;
she knew it, and would not be comforted. Also
she could not in the least make out what it was all
about, and I was unfortunate enough to be the em-
bodiment of all the trouble to her. Before my
advent there had been no tramping through the
mire, no nasty food. Ferociously she pouted at
me, and viciously answered all her master's efforts
to cheer her up. She took a keen delight in tan-
talizing him by walking, sure-footed enough, on
the very brink of every precipice we passed, and

when to divert her he would cry, *"Marie, Marie, glauben Sie das ist schön?"*

"Ach Himmel! Schön sagen Sie? Haben Sie nicht immer Deutschland gesehen?"

Mr. B—— told me of a little episode which well illustrates Marie's order of intellect. Before they had left Belgrade they were forced to leave their home hurriedly one day to take refuge in a neighboring cellar because big shells had begun to drop on their front lawn. Marie had forgotten something and stole away to get it. She did not return and, after a time, Mr. B——, much worried, went to look for her. He found her setting the house in order, the unavoidable confusion which their hasty departure had caused having left the place littered up. With shells bursting all around the house, Marie refused to leave until she had swept the floors. Only when a fragment of shrapnel came hurtling through the dining-room window, missing her by a fraction, did she consent to go.

But the tug-of-war between her and me came on the third day. The women were getting wearied, and also I was haunted by visions of their plight in case the fine weather should turn into a storm. There was not room in that covered cart for them, and time would not permit us to stop to seek shel-

ter. The thought of them tramping through mud
in a cold, driving rain was too much to be endured.
Some of those great, bulky baskets belonging to
Mr. B—— must come out. We had stopped for
the night at a tiny one-room café, for the sky was
overcast and to sleep in the open seemed hazardous.
After our meal, which was always the same, mutton
and sweet biscuit, with coffee, tea, or cocoa, I put
the situation up to the party. The nurses had already discarded much; I was carrying very little.
Plainly it was up to Mr. B—— and Marie.

Our soldiers brought in the baggage, and we all
began unpacking except Marie. She opened the
hampers, sat down, and gazed. I also gazed. Mr.
B——'s things occupied perhaps a sixth of those
baskets, the rest being Marie's treasured accumula-
tion of more prosperous, happier days. There were
summer hats of straw and lace and pink paper roses,
elaborate white dresses and green dresses and red
dresses—dresses that had been ripped to pieces and
dresses not yet made. There was a huge basket
of mysteries I was not allowed to see, and six or
seven pairs of flimsy summer slippers, some of them
hopelessly worn. It was a regular garret, a rummage-sale. The whole could have been chucked
into the river with less than fifty dollars' loss. It

was a great relief to know that those baskets could be left behind with so little regret.

"Tell her to pick out what she will need for a month, all the warm things, and throw the rest away," I said.

"*Ich will nicht,*" said Marie, with a very frank sort of smile, and continued to sit.

"Tell her she must."

"*Ich will nicht.*"

"Tell her if she does not begin by the time I count twenty, I will do it for her. She cannot carry those things. We will pay her twenty times their value. Tell her we will buy her many new, pretty things, but now the women must have a place in the cart. Tell her this is only fair. She does not want to be selfish, I am sure. Tell her she is a good girl, and we all like her and will get a lot of nice things for her."

"*Ich will nicht,*" with the same smile.

"Tell her we will leave her here in this desolate place with these strange people for the soldiers to get if she does not."

"*Ich will nicht!   Lassen mich.*"

"Tell her we will throw away everything she has, tie her hands and feet, pitch her into the cart and take her by force."

"Gut!   Ich will nicht."

Now, one can outdistance triumphant armies, one can after a fashion break refractory bakers to one's will, one can, if one is forced to, be happy in very extraordinary circumstances, but what can be done against an "Ich will nicht" like that?   Nothing at all, and nothing was done.   The rest of us discarded a little more, the things were repacked, and Marie's rummage-sale moved on to Rashka.

Throughout these days we continually met detachments of soldiers, usually scouting parties of cavalry.   The officers always recognized and greeted Mr. B—— warmly, increasing my feeling of good fortune in having found him.   His constant talk during this time was of Serbia, and his intimate knowledge of the Balkan situation proved very illuminating.   He described the commercial warfare that for years previous to 1914 existed between Serbia and Austria in terms vivid enough to put the thing in the most real light possible.   He had many stories to tell of strange affairs that happened from time to time between Belgrade and Vienna.   Of nothing did he convince me more strongly than that he was heart and soul with Serbia.

Our food was decreasing at an alarming rate despite our attempts to consume it with care.   Also

I began to regret that I had not been provided with papers giving me some official position, in order to get things from the Government. But with the aid of Mr. B—— I expected little difficulty, and at Rashka I felt sure of finding either an English mission or Sir Ralph Paget, whose place it was to look after the British units.

On the morning of the day we came into Rashka we met a group of the St. Claire Stobart Mission of Kragujevats. At the same time we came into contact with the main body of refugees, who were to be our constant companions until we came to the sea. This day a tragic thing occurred. We had passed the English unit before it had broken camp, and so were well ahead of it, but some of the members, pushing forward on foot, overtook us. I was sitting by the roadside chatting with two of them when a soldier rode up and spoke a lot of Serbian to us, from which we could only glean that the two women were wanted behind with their caravan. I continued my way to catch up with our cart, and on all sides I noticed intense excitement in the continuous stream of refugees. As I was unable to understand anything, I was at a loss to explain this. On reaching Mr. B——, I learned that an English girl had been shot on the road behind us, and the news stirred the refugee horde like wind across a grain-field.

While passing along a hillside, some officers had seen horses in a field above them. They needed horses badly, and decided to take these. When they started up the slope, however, they were warned by some peasants on the brow of the hill not to touch the animals. They paid no attention, but continued, and were met with a hail of bullets, which flew wildly over their heads and rained on the road below. As it happened, the English nurses were passing there, and as they ran for the shelter of their carts a girl of nineteen was struck, the bullet passing through both her lungs. At such a time the accident was truly terrible, but as I heard it I could not imagine that it would determine all my future course; yet it did.

Early in the afternoon, as we neared Rashka, lying along the swift and muddy Ibar, a chill wind began to blow and rain came in torrents. It marked the end of our picnic, the beginning of a four weeks' experience as terrible as it was unique.

The town was so crowded to overflowing that I could find no place for the women to wait out of the rain while Mr. B—— and I went to seek accommodations and bread. All four of them crowded into the cart on top of the biscuit-tins and huddled there while we went on our eventful quest.

At Alexandrovats I had got papers for Mr. B——, permitting him to accompany me as far as Rashka, where, I was told, we would find the officer who was in supreme command of interned people. With this permission was a letter explaining my position and requesting that permission be granted to him to proceed with me through Montenegro, or wherever I might find it best to go. From his friend, the lawyer, Mr. B—— had also secured a letter to the military commandant of Rashka, couched in the strongest terms, asking that everything possible be done for us. Armed with these, I of course expected no difficulty, although I possessed nothing but my passport in the way of official papers, nothing to prove that as a head of a unit I was entitled to receive bread and shelter. It is only fair to add that by the time we reached Rashka the situation of Serbia was more desperate than when we were at Alexandrovats, consequently the officials were on even a greater strain.

However this may be, we did not get past the commandant's waiting-room. We were inquiring for him there when he walked in upon us, returning from his lunch. He was not a pleasant creature, rather like a snapping-turtle, and began snarling at the orderlies before he caught sight of me. When at last he did notice me, I saw at once that I was not exactly *persona grata*. Of course I was in tatters—the ox had seen to that—and had not been shaved or washed lately. Also we were both heavily incrusted with mud and soaked to the skin. Appearances count for a very great deal in times of military rule. I took off my cowboy hat and greeted him in French, which he soon made it evident he neither relished nor understood. Then I indicated Mr. B——, who handed the lawyer's letter to him. He scrutinized B—— fixedly for a full minute, made no offer to help, but remarked that we must return in four hours. Then he commanded his orderly to show us out and slammed his door in my face. I was nonplussed. We had thought that the Red Cross and mention of the English women would prove everywhere an open sesame. Plainly those women should not have to paddle about in the rain for four hours, at which time it would be dark.

We decided to try another officer, whose exact title I never learned. Our reception here was the same. At first he disclaimed any responsibility for looking after such as we were, and when he learned that Mr. B—— was interned, he almost kicked us out of his place. Three English women, hungry and cold in the rain, seemed not to influence him in the slightest, but he plainly indicated his suspicions about Mr. B——.

As a last resort we went to the *narchelnik,* although we had no letters to him. The anteroom to his office was crammed, and when after an hour we finally got to him he said he could do nothing for us. He also eyed Mr. B—— suspiciously, and ordered us to go back to the officer from whom we had just come.

As it happened, the Crown Prince, the General Staff, and the Government were then at Rashka, although most of the cabinet ministers had moved to Mitrovitze. Mr. B—— thought of an old friend who he said was rather highly placed in the Department of the Interior. Hither we took our bedraggled way, and there Mr. B——'s presence precipitated events with the rapidity of a violent chemical reaction.

The friend for whom we inquired was gone, but we were shown into an improvised office which presented a scene of the wildest confusion. Imagine what it means to pick up a little thing like the Department of Interior of a nation and carry it about

Serbians about to be shot as spies by the victorious Austrians

Rashka in the valley of the Ibar

on ox-carts.   The archives lay on the floor a foot
deep.   Once orderly letter files were heaped about
in crazy, topsyturvy fashion.   Ink-bottles, empty,
overturned, full, littered the desks, and three or four
subordinate clerks encumbered the rare clear spaces.
The department was in the act of executing its
third move.   We floundered through the paper
snow to the desk where a frail man, dark and very
pop-eyed, and with a tiny goatee, sat drumming
languidly on an American typewriter of ancient
model.

We handed to this gentleman the letter having
to do with the extension of Mr. B——'s permission
to accompany me.   No sooner had he glanced at it,
than he jumped up suddenly and crossed the room
to his colleagues.   From behind B——'s back he
began signaling to me in the most ridiculous manner.   He placed a dirty forefinger on his lips,
wagged his head from side to side, and winked his
pop-eyes very fast.   He reminded one of something
hard and creepy, like a cockroach.   The others con-
versed in low tones a minute, then came over, and
without any prelude went deftly through B——'s
pockets, pulling out all our various letters, which he
was carrying.   "These belong to you," Pop-eyes
exclaimed to me in French.   "Guard them as you

would your life!" Seizing B—— by the shoulders,
they marched him out of the room none too gently.

Next they set to cross-examining me as to my
whole acquaintance with B——. It was growing
dark and cold, and the rain still poured. I could
not get my mind off the nurses, miserably huddled
in the cart; but neither the strength of my voice nor
my French was equal to the task of interrupting
the stream of interrogations fired at me. Hopelessly was I submerged, until who should walk in
but a young American Serb whom I had known
previously. In a way he was known to the clerks,
and, as I found out later, he entertained rather
definitely correct ideas about them. He came to
my rescue, and with him as interpreter I made more
progress.

They wished to know just what dealings I had
had with Mr. B——, and said I should never be
allowed to see him again. It happened that Mr.
B——, because he had nothing but Serbian paper
money, had paid for the cart and oxen, and I had
promised to repay him at the current rate of ex-
change in gold, for fortunately all my money was
in gold. This transaction had never been completed, and I now said I must see him for a moment
only, as I had a little matter of slight importance

to settle. Wild excitement followed this simple
statement, and I was asked for every detail of the
affair. I then remarked that I owed him a little
money for the cart and oxen. They brought him
in, and I was astounded at the change in him. He
was trembling, and appeared on the verge of a nervous breakdown. As a matter of fact, he was in very
real danger.

I took out my purse and began counting the
napoleons. When the clerks saw the gold, which
of course at this time was much sought after by
every one, they appeared surprised and jubilant.
One of them went out, and returned before I had
finished. He had a lot of Serbian notes in his
hand, which he gave to B——, pocketing the gold
himself. "He is a suspect," he lucidly explained
to me.

After this transaction, I was able to convince
them that three English nurses had really been out
in the rain for hours, and that shelter must be found
at once. They held a consultation among themselves, which the American Serb later said he over-
heard. Then one of them came with me, saying
that he would find us a place to stay and that Mr.
B—— might spend the night with us there. I did
not quite understand this sudden leniency toward

B——, but was glad of it, because an interpreter was our greatest need, and I wanted to keep him as long as possible. The young clerk showed us every courtesy, first offering to give up his own quarters to us; but just as it grew dark, a large empty room was found where there was a stove.

No sooner were we settled here than the clerk left us and the American Serb appeared. Mr. B—— was in a high state of excitement, but Marie knew nothing of his agitation. The Serb called me aside, and asked if I felt kindly to Mr. B——, or if I did not care what became of him. I replied that he had been kind and invaluable to us, and that I was distressed at his position. The Serb then said that he had good reason to believe that the clerks, relieved of the presence of their superiors, were planning to rob Mr. B——, knowing him by reputation to be a wealthy man. I was at a loss to know what to do when I heard this. It was obviously in their power to do anything they wished at such a time, yet because of the nurses I could not afford to be implicated in anything savoring of spies.

I called Mr. B—— and told the Serb to tell him what he knew. Mr. B—— heard with no apparent surprise, but resigned himself at once. "They cer-

tainly can do anything with me. As a suspect, they
will make me deposit all my money with them, and
then they will go away, and I will have no redress
because everything has gone to pieces. They can
do with me what they like, and they will. You can
do nothing for me personally, but you must take
Marie. I give her into your hands; you must take
her along as one of your nurses. You can keep this
for me," he added, handing me a package which he
drew from his coat. He had known me less than a
week, and the only tab he had on me was a New
York address which I had written down for him because I did not even have a card. He could give
me no address for himself, but wrote down that of
an uncle in Bohemia. The package contained
twelve thousand five hundred dollars.

Mr. B—— then turned away and passed down
the dark street without saying a word. I confess
that, sorry as I felt for him, the overpowering sense
of having Marie on my hands took a larger place in
my thought. I turned and went in where the
nurses were setting out mutton and sweet biscuit.
Those biscuit had grown sweeter and sweeter at
every meal until now they were pure saccharine.
Stepping out a little later I saw a figure lurking
close by, and felt convinced that our place was being

watched. Soon the Serb came to me again, saying that Mr. B—— had sent him to get Marie and some of their luggage. I told him of the guard, and they took precautions to get away unobserved.

The department clerks were under the impression that B—— was still with me. Later the Serb came back alone and spent the night with us. He said Mr. B—— had met an old friend and was in hiding. Contrary to expectation, we were undisturbed during the night.

In the morning there was no sign of our guard, and no one came to get B——, as I had thought. I went down to the town, and was standing idly on a corner when a soldier passed by me and shoved a piece of paper into my hand. It was a diagram of the square where I was standing and of a street which led off to the west. It was fairly accurate, and a door some four blocks from where I stood was marked with a cross. After a short time, I found it—a low house surrounded by high walls, the only entrance to which was by a heavy wooden gate that let one into a small garden, with the house on the left. In the garden, on a camp-stool, animatedly chatting with a group of French aviators, I found Mr. B——. He glowed with joy at this new cosmopolitan company which he had found; also he had just received good news. He had found an old friend in the street the night before who had hidden him at his home, and early in the morning he had despatched a soldier to find me, not daring to show himself or even to write anything. Just before I found him, the news had come that all the rest of the Government had been ordered to evacuate in the middle of the night. Long before dawn Pop-eyes and his retinue had taken the rough road to Mitrovitze. Joyfully I returned all his cash and all claims to his cook. I could no longer have him. I do not know what became of him, but I hope he escaped capture.

CHAPTER VI

ALONG THE VALLEY OF THE IBAR

AFTER losing my interpreter, and with him the food which he had brought, I was faced with the necessity of doing something quickly. Food could not now be bought at any price. At least it was impossible for one not speaking the language to find it. First I went back alone to the *narchelnik*. The crowd was larger, more pathetic, than on the preceding day. It was scarcely nine o'clock, yet hundreds of wounded soldiers had already dragged themselves there to beg for bread.

As I fought my way in, pushing and crowding, a beast among beasts, I came face to face with a handsome young peasant woman coming out, led by two soldiers fully armed. She was crying bitterly in a hopeless sort of way, great sobs shaking her whole body. In broken French a wounded man gave me her story. She was a young widow with several children, her husband having been killed during the first invasion. Some starving soldiers

176

had passed her hut, and seeing that she had some corn-flour started to take it. With her children behind her, she had ordered them to leave. They came on, however, so seizing a rifle she had killed one of them, a petty officer. The military authorities had just had her under examination.

When I came into an inner room, immediately adjoining the *narchelnik's* office, the crush was not so bad. Only my frenzied "Americanske mission" had obtained my entrance there. A few very badly wounded soldiers lounged about, and a small group of tired-looking officers stood conversing in one corner. At the opposite side of the room, sitting on the floor, with head and arms resting on a bench, was a ragged old man, a cheecha of the last line. He was at least sixty-five years old, and rested there motionless, without a sound, his body seeming inexpressibly tired. No one paid the slightest heed to him. As I was looking at him four orderlies came in and picked him up. Only then did I realize that the old man was dead. As they turned him over, a terrible wound in his right breast came to view. It was plain, how, weak from hunger and loss of blood, he had dragged himself over the dreary mountains into the town and, with the last spark of energy left in him, had sought the source of all help, the *narchelnik,* only to die there in the lonely night.

My interview with the *narchelnik* brought me nothing; neither interpreter, bread nor papers of any description. When I came out, it was with a deep feeling of discouragement. The tragedy of this retreat was becoming more and more manifest; the starving, the wounded, the dying, and dead increasing hourly.

Only one thing was left. I must find the English mission and turn over my nurses to them at once. I knew they were in the place, but I did not know where, and I could not ask. Walking across the principal square, trying to decide where to go, I met Colonel Phillips and the Italian military attaché, Major de Sera, talking to one of the English nurses. The colonel was especially glad to find me, as Major de Sera, whom I had not met previously, had just received a cable from his Government to inquire for news of Mme. and Mlle. Christitch, the Serbian military attaché at Rome, Captain Christitch, being a son of madame. I was able to give them what amounted to definite news of their capture, but nothing more.

Colonel Phillips became at once interested in the plight of the three British nurses whom I had, and while I was explaining the situation to him Admiral

Troubridge came up. I remarked that whereas we had got along very well so far, our food was going fast, and, as they knew, I had no facilities for getting anything either from the Government or by private means. A chance remark of mine to the effect that I had not started out prepared for such emergencies brought this question from the Admiral: "What did you come out here for, anyway? Joy rides?"

I replied that I was ready, as an American, to place myself entirely at the disposal of the British Government in aiding the retreat of the English nurses, but, as even he must see, the women were suffering from a state of affairs that it was impossible for me to control. He seemed to understand the logic of this, and offered to walk across the town with me in order to introduce me to the head of the mission, which, he said, was being better looked after than any other because it was under the guidance of Dr. M. Čurčin of the University of Belgrade, who had been appointed by the Government to look after affairs connected with the English units.

We found the head of the mission, Dr. Elizabeth May of Manchester, and the Admiral explained the situation. Dr. May said she must speak to Dr. Čurčin. When she returned, she replied that Dr.

Čurčin was unwilling to take on any one else, as a number of additions to the party had been made since the beginning of the retreat, and the food question was growing more difficult. However, they were leaving immediately, and I might travel with their *kommorra,* which consisted of about thirty carts, thus avoiding isolation in case of capture. She said that she could not assume any responsibility for the nurses as to food or shelter, but would "hand them over" to Sir Ralph Paget at Mitrovitze, whose duty it was to look after them, she said.

I was surprised at this, but at least it was something to go along with them, and we would have enough food to bring us to Mitrovitze, where things would be settled. I said we would be prepared to go at once. She told me to be punctual, as they could not wait; but on returning to my cart, I found that Tichomir had had to go out into the country for hay for the oxen, and would not be back for several hours. So we had to remain behind, and did not take the road until early next morning. We were again isolated, with the enemy close behind us, without Mr. B——'s helpful tongue and with alarmingly short rations. Also the fear began to haunt me that winter would begin. I hated to think what this would mean to the women when we had no shelter.

During the afternoon of the forced delay I scoured Rashka for food, which I did not find. The refugee locusts had picked it clean. While on this search I was standing in front of a low, red building that served as army headquarters. A row of automobiles was drawn up before it and at the door of one of the limousines stood a very important-looking man in a heavy fur coat. He was altogether a dignified looking person, the sort that made me feel my rags the more. Thus I was very much surprised when a natty young officer of perhaps twenty-five, spotless, shining like a tin soldier from his patent-leather gaiters to his gold pince-nez, strode down the steps and, coming up behind him of the fur coat, thumped him resoundingly on the back, crying in Serbian "Good day." It looked like lese-majesty to me; but I had the thing twisted: the thumper, and not the thumped, was Alexander Karageorgovich, Crown Prince of Serbia. He seemed like a young American lawyer, clean-cut, with suppressed energy in every movement as he walked down the street, followed at some ten paces by a single Serbian major. His inheritance was dwindling to the vanishing point, scarcely one third of the fine army of which he was commander-in-chief remained, and in all probability he was about as hungry as the rest of us, but one would have thought from his face that he was going to dress parade.

The Serb has an astonishing ability to suppress all traces of feeling when he so wishes. I have never yet seen one admit that misfortune had got the better of him. The officers we had met at Stalach talked with humor and brilliancy, when everything in the world they cared for had gone to destruction. With seeming light-heartedness, the crown prince took his afternoon walk while his kingdom crumbled. I remember later meeting in Montenegro an officer I had known in happier days. He had passed through butchery as bad as anything on any war front, he had seen his regiment almost wiped out, his country devastated, his private fortune and his home destroyed, his family in peril, and had himself frozen and starved for six weeks, he who until 1912 had never known a day's hardship. After greeting me warmly and happily, his first act was to give a very funny pantomime of how necessity had taught him to conceal the very significant fact that he had to scratch. Lack of feeling? A few minutes later I

caught him off his guard, and a clearer expression
of abject misery I hope I may never see.

The valley of the Ibar is one of the wildest and
most beautiful in the world, but in that three days'
march we came to regard it as monotonous beyond
endurance.   Twenty or thirty miles of it out of
Rashka surpasses the far-famed Gorges des Loups.
The road that twists along the tortuous, shelving
cliffs that form its banks is as marvelous as the
Route des Alps and as beautiful as any Corniche
road must be.   Also it is just about as bad as a
road could be and still remain a road.   Rashka lies
in a narrow plain at a widened part of the valley.
The road leads out along this plain for a little way,
then follows the rapidly rising banks, first on their
crest, and later, when they tower to extraordinary
heights, is cut from the living rock midway up their
sides.   With the rising of the banks the valley nar-
rows to a gorge, so that it is like a great funnel, in
the wide-spread mouth of which lies Rashka.   Converging at this place, the refugee throngs from most
of northern Serbia flowed through this gigantic
funnel.   The surface of the way was trampled out
of all semblance to a road.   The unbuttressed outer
edge crumbled away under the tearing pressure of
heavy army-lorries and the innumerable ox-carts

that passed over it. The narrow foot-paths along the sides and on the slopes above became serpentine rills of slush incessantly beaten by crowds of men, women, and children marching from horrors behind to horrors ahead. For the most part these throngs were forced to go in single file over the narrow trails, which strung their numbers out into an interminable silhouette against the hills that seemed to be tirelessly moving in some great, blind pageant of suffering.

We became a part of the moving hosts, and soon were winding along the high cliffs half way between the beautiful river, five hundred feet below, and the jagged pinnacles above. A November sun flooded all the valley with bright sunshine, picking out the figures of refugees and carts far ahead and behind. When I found a suitable place, I scaled a rocky point at a curve in the valley, which rose more than a thousand feet above the river, and from it, where there was scarcely room to keep a footing, got a photograph of three or four miles of the refugee train as it wound along.

In the afternoon a motor ambulance passed us, in which were some nurses of the Scotch mission. Motoring on that crumbling road was not an unalloyed pleasure, and we were not surprised to find,

Crown Prince Alexander of Serbia

After the blizzard in the Ibar valley

farther on, this same ambulance at the foot of a steep slope, smashed to pieces. Loaded full of British women, it had tumbled down the hill when the road caved from under it. One of the nurses was killed instantly, and others were severely bruised.

Late in the afternoon we heard an army-lorry snorting behind us. It was taking the inside of the road, and the road here consisted mainly of inside. Carts were pushed to the crumbling brink, and, just ahead of us, one which had not quite cleared the path of the heavy car was bowled over the side with its team of horses. The people in it flew out like peas from a pod, but miraculously escaped serious injury. The horses fell on the top of the cart, which had lodged against some small trees about half way down to the river. They were on their backs, entangled in the wheels, and were kicking each other viciously. With his usual presence of mind, Tichomir seized our only ax, and, leaping down, set to hacking away indiscriminately at trees, wheels, cart, and horses. Soon the whole thing rolled on down into the river, and our ax with it.

We continued the journey, tracking until almost nightfall, because there was literally no room to sit down along the road. At last we descended to the level river bank and sought a resting place. There was a chill wind, and the only wood for fires was the great sycamores growing along the river. A large straw stack looked inviting to us, but on its further side we found numerous families already ensconced, who shooed us away vehemently. Next I tried to get into a small military camp where big fires were burning, but with no success. Our pride now being injured, we decided to "go it alone."

A fire was the first of all necessities, and I sent Tichomir to beg, borrow, or steal an ax. He did none of them. There were dozens of camps about with axes, but none could be borrowed, he said. Meantime I had been raking twigs together and breaking off small green branches with my hands. It was not easy, but necessary, and I ordered him to help. He was tired and out of humor and refused. With what joy would I have pitched him into the river, but I needed him too much. He plainly indicated that he considered the whole affair useless. What we could gather with our hands would be gone within an hour, and then we would be colder than ever; we might as well freeze at once. With sarcastic waggings and wavings, I conveyed to him what I thought about his losing our ax. *"Nay dobra, nay dobra"* ("no good, no good"). I danced up and down and shouted at him over and over, while the nurses huddled together about the tiny blaze we had kindled and ate their mutton and sweet biscuits.

Tichomir's imperial eyes flashed and, with only a calm shrug or two, he said quite unmistakably, if I thought it possible to get wood, why didn't I go and do it? So off I went, thinking to find a drift down the river. I passed a camp where I saw great piles of neatly split logs, all ready to keep a fire going the whole night. It was evidently the camp of some high civil dignitary. Through the walls of a neat, little tent warm light glowed, and I could hear the murmur of conversation within. By the side of the tent a man was busily engaged in cooking supper. Three delightfully savage ragamuffins were at work making things as comfortable as possible. At a glance one could see they were rascals. I passed close to one of them, and rattled some money in my pocket. He looked up as if it were a sound he had not heard lately. *"Piet din-ars"* ("Five dinars"), I whispered, pointing to the pile of wood, and then to a spot of deep shadow some fifty yards distant. With a pained expression he made signs toward the tent, conveying the illustrious ownership of that wood, and making plain the fact that he was an honest man. *"Decit dinars"* ("Ten dinars"), I bid up, and in twenty minutes we were roasting our toes at a fine fire with enough split logs in sight to keep it going until morning. Tichomir was perplexed. However bad humored I might have been, he had hitherto regarded his American *braat* as strictly honest.

Along this march we began to see increasing instances of starvation. In places where the road was particularly bad Austrian prisoners were always found tending it. Seeing the cross on my arm, these men would come to me begging medicines, for many of them were suffering from malarial fever. "Can't you give us bread? Can't you give us quinine?" they begged. To be unable to supply these simple wants was very sad. There were few soldiers guarding these prisoners; indeed, frequently they were virtually alone, but starving as they were, they remained peaceable and calm. They obeyed orders willingly and, it seemed to me, regretted the suffering among the Serbs as much as their own hardships. Their guards suffered just as their prisoners did. When there was any bread, it was share and share alike.

Coming across a particularly wretched group of these prisoners in one of the most desolate parts of our way, I saw a tall Austrian weakly leaning against a rock and weeping in an insane manner. He sobbed and blubbered, and bit his lips until the blood ran. He was mad from hunger, dying by inches, and not alone, but while thousands of people passed him, and three hundred of his comrades there, faced the same fate. A gray-haired man came by, apparently a Serb who had seen better days, but who was now walking the muddy road with a pack on his back. Seeing the prisoner, he stopped and asked a guard what was the matter. "No bread," was the brief answer. The Serb reached into his pocket and took out a large hunk of white bread, the first I had seen in a long time, for bread of that sort was not to be had at any price. The starving man seized it, turned it over and over in his hands, and then devoured it in an incredibly short time. For a brief moment a sort of ecstasy came into his eyes, and then he grew violently ill. He vomited up the precious food and fell to sobbing once more.

Frequently, after bread and flour gave out, the prisoners would procure an ear or two of Indian corn. They never knew where they would get any more, and as this was all that lay between them and starvation, they hoarded the grains as a miser would so many diamonds. By repeated counting they knew the number of rows and grains on a cob, and would allow just so many rows for a meal. They either parched the grain in hot ashes or boiled it in old tin cans, and sometimes, when they found a dead animal, they made soup.

Searching about for wood when we made camp that night, I came across a slightly wounded soldier lying inert among the bushes. It was chilly, the ground was wet, and he was in rags; but when I stumbled over him he did not move. I turned him over and looked at his face. He was a mere boy, not more than twenty. He was dazed, and when he did become aware that some one was near him, he mumbled over and over in Serbian: "Is there any bread? Is there any bread?" I dragged him to our fire, got some mutton and biscuit, and placed them in his hands.

For fully five minutes he looked at the food, turning it about, bewildered. Then he dropped it on the ground, and took out of his pocket a cob from which he had gnawed nearly all the corn. Counting a dozen grains, he bit them off, carefully replaced the cob, and lay down in the mud. It was with the greatest difficulty that we awakened him out of his lethargy to the extent that he realized we had real food for him. Next morning we had to leave him by our smoldering fire with the scanty food I felt justified in taking from the stores. Continually during these dreary weeks we had thus to make compromises with our better feelings. To leave a man like that in the wilderness was simply murder, but there were the women of our party to be thought of. And why choose him for life when hundreds and thousands of his fellows were in a like predicament? The only respite from such trying decisions came when they had grown so common that no one felt them any more.

In watching Serbia die, we came to attain what Nietzsche terms "metaphysical comfort," and the heroism of the Serbs supplied the exaltation of a Greek tragedy, showing as nothing else could the strange, paradoxical pathos and yet utter insignificance of individual lives. When heroes die by tens of thousands, each is none the less a hero, but how inconsequential each!

To get into Mitrovitze is like chasing a mirage. About eleven in the morning we came to it. It was perhaps three miles away, but the swift, treacherous current of the Ibar lay between, and there was no bridge. So for four hours we followed the river as it wound about the city in a series of broad curves, until on the opposite side from which we approached we found a long bridge spanning it. On the hilltop, just before we descended to this bridge, we passed a brand-new cemetery by the roadside. It had the unmistakable, extemporaneous air which the swift ravage of typhus last year gave to many Serbian burying grounds. There were perhaps fifty graves, none of them more than a week old. Typhus was beginning in Mitrovitze, and two victims were being buried as we passed.

On crossing the bridge I found it impossible to get our cart into the town itself because of the refugees, and left it outside among the innumerable *kommorras* then encamped there. With Tichomir as the best excuse for an interpreter I could get, I went into the town to find Sir Ralph Paget, who I knew was there, as well as many English nurses. It was about three-thirty in the afternoon, and I was anxious that the very tired women should have some shelter that night, because for three nights they had had none. I thought to hand them over, with the remainder, thank Heaven! of the mutton and biscuits, to Sir Ralph, and then decide what I should do. Alone I could travel fast, and the retreat, despite its terror, was intensely interesting. I should have to trust to luck about finding food.

My alternative was to stay in Mitrovitze until the Germans came, and then return home through Austria and Switzerland.

By this time my personal appearance was truly awful, and the gendarme at the other end of the bridge kept me almost half an hour before Tichomir could persuade him to let me go on. He would never have dreamed of stopping me if I had worn a smart uniform. What inquiries we could make among the anxious crowd brought us no information. No one seemed ever to have heard of Sir Ralph Paget, but somebody said they thought there was an English mission in the *casern* by the hospital. As corroborating this, I suddenly sighted an English nurse standing on a corner watching the crowd. She informed me how to reach the *casern,* and told me a special train at that moment was leaving Mitrovitze with a hundred and twenty nurses who intended to reach England as soon as possible. Their train journey would be only three hours, when they would again have to take ox-carts and start for the mountains. But there were many more nurses left in Mitrovitze, for, even as late as this, some still hoped to be able to remain and work. These would stay as long as possible. To have arrived a few hours earlier would have enabled my three nurses to join this hundred and twenty. To come in one end of the town as they were going out the other, did not tend to put one in an enviable humor.

After a few minutes I found Dr. May at the *casern.* She could give me only general directions where to find Sir Ralph, but offered me a room for the nurses, having secured more shelter than her party needed. Grateful for this aid, I set off to find Sir Ralph, and met his secretary, Mr. Leslie, in the street. I put the situation of the three nurses before him in detail, with the assurance that, as previously, I was ready to do all in my power to aid the British women in any manner. I asked him to bring the matter to Sir Ralph's attention as soon as possible, for it was then late, and I could not go in person, but had to return to my party outside the town to bring them to the quarters Dr. May had kindly loaned me. Mr. Leslie said he would tell Sir Ralph at once, so that I felt the nurses' safety was assured, at least to the extent of the other British women in the place. While we were talking, Captain Petronijevich came up, and the comic side of my predicament seemed to strike him forcibly. We laughed together, and I went away feeling greatly relieved.

All of our party were dead tired and could not be

thankful enough for a roof that night, as it rained heavily. Despite a warning I had received that the people in the house could not be trusted, I slept soundly on the floor in the hall of a Turkish house where we were. Relieved of the necessity of getting under way next morning, we all slept late, and it was nearly nine o'clock when I went out from the secluded court where our house stood, through two outer courts, to the street.

One of the liveliest scrimmages I have ever seen was in session. There was a terrific jam, automobiles, ox-carts, and carriages grinding mercilessly into one another, and the town could not be seen for the people. Acquaintances were shouting excitedly to one another across the street, and children were howling. The gate through which I came opened on a large square where nearly all the streets of the town emptied, and from which the road to Prishtina ran. The trouble was that everybody was trying to take this road at the same time, and no one was succeeding very well.

In the center of the square I suddenly spied English khaki, and recognized Admiral Troubridge and Colonel Phillips. They were seated in an ancient *fiacre*, and wasting a good deal of energy trying to impress on a nondescript coachman the necessity of speedily getting free from the tangle. The Admiral caught sight of me, and beckoned me to him.

"Where are the three nurses? You will have to get out before noon," he said all in a breath.

"I have reported them to Sir Ralph; he has made arrangements for them, I presume. What is the matter, anyway?"

"The Serbs seem to have had an awful knock. Word came after midnight to evacuate this town at once. The road to Prizrend may already be cut; if so, think of Ipek. Remember what I say: think of Ipek as a refuge. And if you want to see Sir Ralph, you had better hurry to his house; but he has already gone, I think. Good-by, good luck, and remember Ipek," he shouted at me as the *fiacre* plunged through an opening in the crowd.

I hurried down the street, dimly recollecting some directions, crossed a bridge, and, turning to the left along the river bank, saw Sir Ralph just getting into his touring-car, which was piled high with luggage of various descriptions. He saw me coming, and ceased arranging his baggage.

"Good morning, Mr. Jones. I began to think I should go away without seeing you. Mr. Leslie told me about the three nurses. I am extremely

sorry that I can do nothing to help you. I hope
you understand how it is."

"But, Sir Ralph, you know the circumstances
under which I have these English nurses? Having
no official standing and no interpreter, I am unable
to get anything for them. Also, I feel that the responsibility is growing too great."

"I am very sorry, but I can do nothing. The
General Staff has been ordered to go, and I must
go with them. After they go I am powerless. I
should advise you to go on to Prizrend, where there
are sure to be parties forming to go over the mountains. Really I am most awfully sorry."

"Had I not better turn them over to Dr. May?
My oxen are getting weak, and our food is almost
gone. I am sure that unaided I can never get the
nurses to Prizrend."

With the sort of accent that American actors
strive a lifetime to attain, looking back at me as the
chauffeur started the car, "Yes," he said, "that is
best, if you can *persuade* Dr. May to take them."

"Good morning, Sir Ralph."

"Good morning, Mr. Jones." I turned on my
heel and walked away. At least I had expected
a brief note recommending that Dr. May look out
for these English women, who were in a very dan-

gerous situation. I had gone only a little way when I heard running steps behind me, and Mr. Leslie rushed up shoving three books into my hand. One of them was in a postal wrapper, the other two were uncovered.

"Sir Ralph wishes to know if you will be kind enough to deliver this book to its owner, if you happen to find her, and the other two he thought you might like to read in your spare moments."

Saying this, he fled to catch the moving motor.

I stood gazing stupidly down at the books in my hand, and finally became aware of two words staring blackly at me from a yellow cover. "Quo Vadis?" they impishly screamed at me, "Where are you going?" "Quo vadis, quo vadis?" And I could not answer at all. Subtle humor to meet in an Englishman!

Having told my nurses the night before that everything was sure to be all right now, I had no heart to go back to them with these fresh complications. Instead, I wandered up the street a short way to think, though the crowds that swept me along left little time for mental gymnastics.

It is a Turkish custom for women to mix bread at home; then they take it in large shallow pans to the public bake-shops, where it is baked for a small con-

sideration. The good Turkish housewives were
now engaged in this daily pilgrimage along the
streets of Mitrovitze.   As every one was ravenously
hungry, they were the cynosure of all eyes as they
marched gracefully along, the wide, round pans ex-
pertly balanced on their heads.   Going forward in
a "brown study," I quite unpremeditatedly collided
with the fattest and ugliest of these bread women
and both of us were showered with the sticky, yellow maize batter.   It ran down the good woman's
face like broken eggs, and down my back in nasty
rivulets.   Immediately there was a throng, with
shouts and excitement, while the old woman seized
the copper pan and started for me.   A wall of grinning soldiers cut off all retreat; so ignominiously I
bought forgiveness and liberty with ten francs.

This collision brought me to my senses, as it were,
and I decided to try another appeal on Dr. May.
It was about ten o'clock when I arrived at the
casern and found my way to the huge room the
party of forty had occupied.   They did not seem
alarmed by the general exodus, and were only then
eating breakfast.

I found Dr. May seated before a bowl of porridge, which she generously wanted to share with
me, but I had no appetite.   She, of course, wished

to know what Sir Ralph had done with the nurses. I told her about the brief interview, repeated my predicament, and asked if she did not see her way clear to taking on the three nurses. She replied that she sympathized with me deeply, but that Dr. Čurčin had refused to take on any more, and she did not think she could do it. I then remarked that I had done all in my power for the three English women, and if their own countrywomen would not make the very small sacrifice that receiving them into their own unit would require, now that my power had ended, I did not know what would become of them. Again she expressed her sympathy for their position and regretted exceedingly not to be able to take them. However, she made the same offer as at Rashka, namely, that our cart might come along with theirs, and whereas food and shelter could not be provided, in case of capture the women would have the advantage of being with them. This was the final arrangement, and Dr. Čurčin agreed that when it was possible to get bread from the Government he would ask for an allowance for us. In the middle of that same afternoon, the sixteenth of November, we all left Mitrovitze together, taking the road over the Plain of Kossovo.

A silhouette against the hills moving as in a pageant

CHAPTER VII

ON THE "FIELD OF BLACKBIRDS"

TO American readers the name Kossovo doubtless calls forth little recognition. But to every Serbian, Kossovo brings up an image of past glory when the present dream of every Serbian heart was a reality. A powerful Slav nation existed until more than five hundred years ago, when the Turks won a crushing victory on the Plain of Kossovo, and the ancient kingdom, whose power stretched from Mitrovitze to Prizrend, became a memory.

The great battle that took place here resulted in such slaughter that for generations it became the synonym for all that was terrible. Because of the great flocks of vultures that were said to have gathered over the plain after the battle, it has always been known as the "Field of Blackbirds."

To me the name of Kossovo calls up one of the most terrible spectacles I shall ever see. The plain on the day after we left Mitrovitze epitomized all that is sordid, overwhelming, heartrending, and intermingled in that strange maze, which is ever the wonder of onlookers at the tragic puzzle of war, all that is noble, beautiful, sublime. Until that day I did not know the burden of the tiny little word "war," but never again shall we who traversed the "Field of Blackbirds" think of war without living again the snow-filled horrors of our march.

From Mitrovitze to Prishtina is scarcely more than twenty-five kilometers. I am sure that never before in human history has more suffering, heroism, and patriotism been crowded into so small a space. As usual, we were with the army, or, what the day before had been an army. I think from the Plain of Kossovo what had been the most stoical fighting body in a war of valiant armies became for the time being no more an army, no more the expression of all the hope and valor of a nation, but a ghost, a thing without direction, a freezing, starving, hunted remnant that at Belgrade, Semendria, Bagardan, Chachak, Babuna Pass, Zajechar, and many other places had cast its desperate die and lost, and needed only the winter that leaped in an hour upon it on the "Field of Blackbirds" to finish its humiliation. For it was on the dreary stretches of Kossovo that the cold first came upon us. In an hour a delightful Indian-summer climate changed to a temperature so savage that of all the dangers it was the greatest.

Forty English women made the march that day. They made it without food and without drink; most of them made it on foot and in clothing intended only for Balkan summer. I think it can be said that the party of English women stood it better than the Serbian refugees and fully as well as the Serbian army. Of course girls who entered the march mere girls came out in the evening old in experience. They saw the things that generations of their sisters at home live and die without the slightest knowledge of—the madness of starvation, the passion to live at all cost, the swift decay of all civilized characteristics in freezing, starving men. They understand now better than any biologist, any economist, could have taught them the struggle for existence and the survival of the fittest. At the end they smiled, made tea, slept forty in a Turkish harem, and next day marched their thirty kilometers. They are the heroines of the Serbian tragedy, and they realized it not at all.

When we left Mitrovitze at two-thirty in the afternoon, we were in the center of that ever-surging refugee-wave along the crest of which we sometimes moved, but behind which never. Just out of Mitrovitze the road climbs in steep ascents over a small range of hills, then dips to the level of the plain. There are no trees on Kossovo, a detail; but have you ever seen an army in zero weather go into camp without wood? The plain continues almost to Prishtina, where the road begins to climb once more in snake-like zigzags, every curve of it a bog, until from the top of a range Prishtina is visible, lying in a snug cove among the mountains.

We had scarcely descended to the plain outside of Mitrovitze when the early dusk came on, and we turned aside to camp in a corn-field, having come about six kilometers in two hours and a half. There was a warm breeze from the south, and the clear sky looked like midsummer.

Our little party camped near by, but separately from the main *kommorra*. As we were once more partaking of mutton and sweet biscuit, about a brightly blazing camp-fire, Dr. May came over to see us. She said she had a "bargain to drive" with me, and I said, "All right." She told us the nurse who had been shot on the road to Rashka had had to be left at Mitrovitze with two women doctors and a nurse. Mitrovitze was expected to fall any day, but she desired to send back the one motor-ambulance they possessed to see if the sister could be moved. The young British chauffeur she hesitated to send back to almost sure capture, but I was neutral. If I would take the ambulance when it caught up with us next day and return with it to Mitrovitze, there to place myself at the absolute disposal of the doctors, either to bring the wounded girl on or to stay with them and be captured or go anywhere they might send me, she agreed to take the three nurses as her own and see them through with the rest of her party. I replied that I was ready to do this, and she took on the nurses at once.

The ambulance did not reach us until Prishtina, however, so I made all of the march next day and returned from Prishtina to Mitrovitze, but more of that later. At last I had secured the safest possible provision for the nurses. From this "bargain" on, I cannot say too much for the kindness and consideration shown me in every way by the English women. Later when I fell ill during a bitter cold spell, I feel that I owed my life to the attention which some of them found time to give me despite their own hardship and sufferings. Nor can I exaggerate the thoughtfulness and unselfishness of both Dr. May and Dr. Čurčin in looking after the comfort and security of the mission in every possible particular.

On the stretch of road we had traversed that afternoon I counted fifteen army-motor lorries hopelessly bogged in the mud. The mire was well above the hubs of our ox-carts, and it was all the powerful beasts could do to pull the carts along. Before, as far as one could see, was a squirming, noisy, impatient stream of carts, automobiles, and carriages, while behind us from the thousands of camps spread about Mitrovitze an unbroken torrent of vehicles flowed out on the road. I estimated that without an instant's pause day and night, at the rate oxen could go, it would require at least three days for the ox-carts about Mitrovitze so much as to get on the road. Indeed, many hundreds were taken there by the Germans five days later.

There were crowds of Austrian prisoners at work along this part of the road, their best efforts only being sufficient to prevent the way from becoming absolutely impassable. Here I saw my first and only German prisoner. For some reason he was not working with the others, but stood on the roadside looking down on them. The Austrian prisoners were in tatters. For weeks they had not had sufficient to eat. The German presented a striking contrast. Superbly equipped, helmet shining, his wonderful gray-green uniform successfully withstanding the hardest usage, a comfortable great coat over his shoulders, well shod, and exhibiting every indication of being well fed, I concluded he had not been captured very long. He was loquacious enough, and while we listened to the German guns then booming not very far from Mitrovitze he naïvely asked: "But why is every one going in a hurry? What does it mean?" If it was irony, it was well veiled, and I turned the subject to Frankfort, his home, and found him an enthusiastic reader of Goethe. He was a fine soldier, but I do not forget what the cheechas of Chachak did to his kind.

Plowing along with our *kommorra*, I had seen many carts overturned while trying to go around the motors that were *en panne*. Especially do I remember one handsome carriage, drawn by a fine pair of blacks and containing a man, his wife, and several children, to say nothing of what was in all probability their entire household possessions. In attempting to pass a motor, this carriage tumbled over a ten-foot bank into a miniature swamp. Owing to the softness of the ground, the family escaped serious injury, and immediately continued their journey on foot, leaving all in the bog, not even waiting to finish the horses, which were lying in distorted positions entangled in the harness and wheels. Thousands of soldiers were marching by us all this time, and when we camped it was in the midst of them.

Soon after Dr. May's visit, we went to bed in the open, there being, indeed, no other place to go. At twelve o'clock we were awakened by rain-drops in our faces, and until daylight the rain continued in torrents.

We got under way about five o'clock the next morning, while it was yet pitch dark, in the hope of doing several kilometers before the creeping glacier of vehicles should begin again. This was hopeless, however, for every one else had the same inspiration, and already the road was full. I use "road" from habit; on this day it was a turbid stream, sometimes ankle-deep, sometimes up to the drivers' waists where wet-weather torrents had broken their banks and overflowed it.

Through this highway, long before it was light, thousands upon thousands of ox-carts, carriages, and automobiles were plowing their way. For the most part the road was so narrow that there was no chance of passing those in front, the ground on each hand being impassable mire. After an hour

Long trains of oxen were pulling the big guns from the camps along
the wayside

In many places on Kossovo swift torrents swept across the road

or so, when all the gaps were filled, this meant that if far ahead in the environs of Prishtina an ox slipped his yoke or a cart-wheel broke or a horse balked or an automobile stuck or a driver wished to light a cigarette or any other imaginable contingency came to pass, a few minutes later carts just leaving Mitrovitze would be held up until the other carts twenty kilometers ahead should move. This was the condition on all the mountain roads of Serbia. It added at least fifty per cent. to the time required to finish one's journey.

Every one was drenched. Few people had had any sort of shelter during the night, and the rain had been such as to come through the tiny tents some of the more fortunate soldiers possessed. The women of the English mission took the road soaked to the skin. Either in their miserably covered carts, uncomfortably perched on top of the meager luggage that they had been able to save or walking along beside the drivers when it was possible, I saw them pass from the flooded corn-field where they had slept, or, rather, spent the night, on to the road.

The army, too, was beginning to awaken. Long trains of oxen—the army, of course, had all the best oxen, huge powerful animals, far better than horses for the Serbian roads—were pulling the big guns

from the camps along the wayside. From twelve
to twenty teams were required for each gun, and
even then they had to strain every muscle in the
frequent mud-holes. They would go forward a
few meters, all pulling together in a long line, then,
as the heavy guns sank deeper, some of the wilder
ones would begin to swing from side to side, oscil-
lating like a pendulum, each swing wider, until all
the teams were in hopeless disorder, while yokes
broke, and drivers cursed. At last they would
come to a standstill, all the waiting thousands behind perforce following their example, bringing
comparative silence, in the midst of which the German and Serbian cannon could be heard incessantly,
like rumbling thunder. Then the caravan would
move on again, only to stop once more. This was
repeated all day long, each day for weeks and
weeks.

During one of these lulls we heard a great commotion behind us. There was a loud trampling
of men's and horses' feet, and a lot of shouting,
which steadily grew louder, and finally sounded
abreast of us. Out in the marshy fields along the
road I saw a thousand or fifteen hundred Serbian
youths, ranging in age from twelve to eighteen.
They were the material out of which next year and

the succeeding years Serbia was to replenish her army. Not yet ripe for service, the Government had ordered them out at the evacuation of every place, and had brought them along with the army in order to save them from being taken by the enemy into Austria, Germany, and Bulgaria as prisoners of war. For it is these boys the invaders are especially anxious to get. They are the force of to-morrow, and to-morrow, it has been my observation, the Teutonic allies now dread above all else in the world.

One of the Austrian official *communiqués* recently read, "And here we also took about one hundred and fifty youths almost ready for military service." It is the only official mention I have ever seen of such captures, although in the fighting of last year they were common. It is a bare statement of one of the most terrible aspects of the Serbian retreat.

The boys I saw in the flooded fields were not strangers to me, but now for the first time I saw them bearing arms. When the trouble first began I had seen these and other thousands all along the railway-line from Belgrade. Many for the first time in their lives were away from their own villages, and most of them had never before been

separated from their families. There was no one
to look after them. They did not even have the
advantage of a soldier in getting food and shelter.
If there was bread left over at the military stations,
they got it; if not, they did not. Never were they
sheltered, but slept where they happened to stand
when night came on. Few of them had sufficient
clothing; only those whose mothers had been able
to supply them with the warm, durable, homespun
garments which the peasants make were adequately
protected. I used to see the smaller of them sitting on top the railway-cars crying together by the
dozens. They were hungry, of course; but it was
not hunger or thirst or cold; it was pure, old-fash-
ioned, boarding-school homesickness that had them,
with the slight difference that they longed for homes
which no more existed. "The capture" of such
as these to be honored with an official commu-
niqué!

When the retreat took them from the railway,
they marched over the country in droves. There
were no officers to oversee them. They were like
antelope, roaming over the wild hills along the Ibar.
They ate anything they could find, rotten apples,
bad vegetables, the precious bits of food found in
abandoned tins, and yet most of them had arrived

safe and sound at Mitrovitze, where the Government had large magazines of munitions.

Now, when the order came at midnight, like a clap of thunder, to evacuate Mitrovitze immediately, they were rounded up by some officers on horseback, and to each was given a rifle, a canteen, and absolutely all the ammunition he could stagger under. They were delighted, tickled to death to have real guns and to be real soldiers, and as the officers were insufficient, they were soon riddling the atmosphere with high-power bullets in every direction, creating a real danger. If a crow flew over a mile high, half the company banged at him on the instant. A black squirrel in a wayside tree called forth a fusillade that should have carried a trench in Flanders.

They were not particular about the aim. There were plenty of cartridges and, after all, it was the first good time they had had in many a week and perhaps the last.

Joyously they had left Mitrovitze with us the afternoon before and, like us, they had camped in the open, but here the analogy must rest. We had tried to sleep, at any rate, whereas they had made night hideous with violent attacks on bats, rats, rabbits, and even the moon before the clouds came to her rescue. But they had been soaked and had had nothing for breakfast and were getting tired of their own exquisite sport. So they were loath to march with that enthusiasm and at the rate the officers on horseback desired. This accounted for the commotion.

It was very simple. A few would lag, then more and more, and soon the entire thousand would simply be paddling about in the fields like so many ducks. Then the officers, infuriated, would ride full tilt into them, heavy riding-whips in their hands, and spurs in their horses' sides. I saw many of the boys ridden down, tumbled in the mire, and stepped on by the horses. Blood streamed from the faces of scores of others whom the whips had found. The rest at once regained their enthusiasm, and rushed forward with cries of fear. I saw this performance recur several times before the herd passed out of sight around a curve.

Months later I was to learn by sight and report the staggering denouement of this childhood drama. An account in the "New York Evening Sun" sums it up with a clarity and fidelity to detail that is terribly adequate:

When the frontier between Serbia and Albania was reached a gendarme told the boys to march straight ahead

and pointing to the west, he added, that there would find
the sea and ships, and then left them.

Without a leader or guide the boys crossed the frontier
and marched through Albania in search of the sea and
the ships which they hoped to find in a couple of days at
the utmost. They were overtaken and passed by columns
of old soldiers, armed, equipped, and officered, who gave
them all the bread they had and encouraged them to follow.

No one has described how long it took these boys to
reach the sea, and how much they suffered from hunger,
exposure, and fatigue. They ate roots and the bark of
trees and yet they marched on toward the sea. At night
they huddled together for warmth and slept on the snow,
but many never awoke in the morning and every day the
number decreased until when the column reached Avlona
only fifteen thousand were left out of the thirty thousand
that crossed the frontier.

It is useless to attempt a description of what they suffered, as the story of that march toward the sea and the
ships is told and understood in a few words. Fifteen
thousand died on the way and those who saw the sea and
the ships "had nothing human left of them but their
eyes." And such eyes!

The Italians at Avlona had no hospital accommodation
for fifteen thousand. They could not possibly allow
these Serbian boys covered with vermin and decimated by
contagious diseases to enter the town. They had them
encamped in the open country close to a river and gave
them all the food they could spare, army biscuits and bully
beef. The waters of the river had unfortunately been con-
taminated as corpses in an advanced state of decomposi-

tion had been thrown in, but the Serbian boy soldiers
drank all the same.

By the time that the ship to convey them to Corfu arrived the fifteen thousand had been reduced to nine thousand. About two thousand more boys died during the
twenty-four hours' journey between Avlona and Vido, and
thus only seven thousand reached the encampment in the
grove of orange and olive trees by the sea on the island
of Vido.

The French and Serbian doctors attached to the encampment said that if it were possible to have a bed for
each boy, an unlimited supply of milk, and a large staff
of nurses, perhaps out of the seven thousand boys landed
at Vido two thirds could be saved. There are no beds,
no milk, no nurses at Vido, however; and despite the hard
work of the doctors and their efforts to improvise a suitable diet, during the last month more than one hundred
boys have died every day.

As it is not possible to bury them on the island, a ship,
the *St. Francis d'Assisi*, steams into the small port of Vido
every morning and takes the hundred or more bodies out
to sea for burial. The allied war vessels at Corfu lower
their flags at half-mast, their crews are mustered on the
deck with caps off, and their pickets present arms as the
St. Francis d'Assisi steams by with her cargo of dead
for burial in that sea toward which the boys were ordered
to march.

And the survivors lying on the straw waiting for their
turn to die, "with nothing human left of them but their
eyes," must wonder as they look at the sea and the ship
with the bodies of their dead comrades on board whether
this is the sea and the ship that the only leader they had,

Kossovo stretched away in the dreariest expanse imaginable

Now and then the storm lifted its snow veil
Crossing the "Field of Blackbirds" in the blizzard

the Serbian gendarme that saw them safely to the frontier, alluded to when he raised his arm and pointed to the west and told them to march in that direction.

To go through long weeks of horror and pain to achieve victory at the end is not easy—we call it by superlative names. To go through what the young boys of Serbia tasted first in full tragedy on Kossovo and in succeeding weeks drank to the dregs of lonely painful death, is a thing that I, for one, cannot grasp. But any American worthy of the name who has seen such aspects of life as it has come to be in the world would gladly make any effort in order to show the honest disciples of unpreparedness in this country even a little of the real terror of invasion by a ruthless enemy—and enemies have a habit of being ruthless. The Alps of Albania and the islands of Greece bear on their gleaming passes and their rocky shores *the lifeless bodies of twenty-three thousand boys*, but the Alps of Switzerland still are undotted with the dead of Switzerland, and the plains of Holland, separated from a conqueror-created hell only by electrified barriers and well-trained troops, are not yet soaked with the blood of Holland's boys.

Of course we felt sorry, but something else claimed the attention of all. The rain had stopped.

Every one began to hope for a bright day, but the clouds still hung low, heavy, and purplish gray and as we watched the stream of refugees go by a breath of distinctly cold wind struck us.

These refugees were inextricably mixed with the army. A rickety little cart drawn by scrawny oxen, and containing a whole family's treasured possessions, would follow a great gun pulled by its fifteen splendid spans. A handsome limousine laboriously accommodated its pace to a captured Austrian soup kitchen.

Theoretically the army always had the right of way; but when there is only one way, and it is in no manner possible to clear that, theory is relegated to its proper place. Few people had sufficient transportation to carry even the barest necessities, so they waded along in the river of dirty water. Dozens of peasant women I saw leading small children by each hand and carrying Indian fashion on their backs an infant not yet able to take one step. Old men, bent almost double, splashed about with huge packs on their shoulders, and many young girls, equally loaded, pushed forward with the wonderful free step the peasant women of Serbia have, while children of all ages filled in the interstices of the crowd, getting under the oxen and horses, hanging on the automobiles, some whimpering, some laughing, some yelling. Every one was wet, every one was a mass of mud, every one was hungry, but summer was still with us, and no one was freezing. Affairs were rapidly approaching the limit of human endurance for many in that snake-like, writhing procession, but as yet none had succumbed. Then it began to snow.

It was about eight o'clock in the morning when the blizzard began, first some snow flurries, then a bitter cold wind of great velocity and snow as thick as fog. The cart in front, the cart behind, the pedestrian stream on each side, and one's-self became immediately the center of the universe. How these fared, what they suffered, one knew. Beyond or behind that the veil was impenetrable. We were no more a part of a miserable mob. We were alone now, simply a few wretched creatures with the cart before and the cart behind, struggling against a knife-like wind along a way where the mud and water were fast turning to ice.

In less than an hour our soaked clothes were frozen stiff. From the long hair of the oxen slim, keen icicles hung in hundreds, giving them a glittering, strange appearance, and many of them despite the hard work were trembling terribly with the cold.   For a short time the freezing wind accelerated the pace of the refugees on foot.   The old men shouted to the women, and the women dragged along their children.   But soon this energy was spent.   The hopelessness of their situation was too obvious even for Serbian optimism to ignore.

Why were they hurrying?   There still remained a good hundred and fifty miles before the sea, and most of this lay over the wildest Balkan mountains, infested with bandits, over trails where horses could hardly go, and which frequently reached an altitude of seven or eight thousand feet.   Along that way were no houses for days, and not one scrap of food. Also, whereas this gale had blown from us the sound of the German guns behind, it brought—the first time we had heard it—the sound of the Bulgarian guns ahead.   For as the Germans were sweeping down from Rashka, the Bulgarians were striving to cut off the line of retreat between Prishtina and Prizrend.   The last line of hills had been taken. No more than six kilometers of level ground and the Serbian trenches lay between them and the road. For four weeks retreating from one enemy, at last we had reached the wide-spread arms of the other and, by all Serbians, the more dreaded invader.

The plight of these refugees seemed so hopeless,

it brought us the ever-recurring question, Why did all these people leave their homes? Surely nothing the invader could or would do could justify them in a thing like this. But all the peasants had heard stories of the fate of Belgium, and many had seen what the Bulgarians were capable of doing. So here they were. It seemed foolish to me, but for them it was obedience to an instinct.

While the wind at no time diminished, now and then the storm lifted its snow veil as if to see how much was already accomplished in the extermination of these feeble human beings. At such times we came once more into the life of the throng, and it was possible to form some idea of what this whim of nature meant. Less than two hours after the beginning of the snow the mortality among oxen and horses was frightful. Already weakened by long marches and insufficient food, the animals now began to drop all along the line. When one ox of a team gave out, the other and the cart were usually abandoned, too, there being no extra beasts. An ox would falter, moan, and fall; a few drivers would gather, drag the ox and its mate to the side of the road, then seizing the cart, they would tumble it over the embankment, most frequently contents and all; and then the caravan moved on. Automo-

biles also were being abandoned, the occupants con-
tinuing their journey on foot.

I find in my notes of this date the following .im-
pressions:

"On every side the plain stretched away in the
dreariest expanse imaginable. At great intervals
a tiny group of miserable huts built of woven withes
and mud, typical of the *Sanjak,* was visible through
the storm.   Other than these there was nothing, not
a trace to indicate that human beings had ever before traversed Kossovo.   Tall, sear grass and very
scrubby bush covered the ground as far as the eye
could reach, until they in turn were covered with
the snow, leaving only a dead-white landscape devoid of variety or form, through the center of which
the thousands of people and animals crept, every
one of us suffering, the majority hopeless.   Scores
of dead animals were strewn along the road, and
many others not yet frozen or completely starved
lay and moaned, kicking feebly at the passers-by.
As the day wore on, I saw many soldiers and prisoners, driven almost insane, tear the raw flesh from
horses and oxen, and eat it, if not with enjoyment,
at least with satisfaction.

"In many places swift torrents up to the oxen's
bellies swept across the road.   In these carts were

lost, and two huge motor lorries that I saw. It was impossible to salvage anything. The swift current caught the weakened oxen, and before even the driver could jump from the cart all was swept off the roadway to deep pools below. Sometimes the occupants were rescued, sometimes they were not. One of the wagons of our kommorra, filled with invaluable food, was swept away, lost beyond recovery.

"This was heartrending, but as nothing compared with the sufferings of the peasant refugees who splashed along on foot. By making wide detours, they were able to cross these streams, but each time they emerged soaked to the skin, only to have their garments frozen hard again.

"We now began to overtake many of the peasant families who earlier in the day had gone ahead of us, walking being about twice as fast as ox-cart speed. They were losing strength fast. The children, hundreds of them, were all crying. Mothers with infants on their backs staggered, fell, rose, and fell again.

"Into our little snow-walled circle of vision crept a woman of at least sixty, or, rather, we overtook her as she moved painfully along. Methodically like a jumping-jack, she pulled one weary foot and then the other out of the freezing slush. She had no shoes or *opanki*. She was utterly alone, and seemed to have not the slightest interest or connection with any that were passing. Every effort she made was weaker than the preceding one. Death by the side of the fleeing thousands stared her in the face. A soldier came up, a man of the second line, I judged, neither young nor old. Hunger and fatigue showed on his unkempt face. The woman bumped against him, and the slight impact sent her over. He stooped and picked her up, seeing how weak she was. Impulsively he threw down his gun and heavy cartridge-belt, and half carrying the old woman started forward. With every ounce of strength she had she jerked away from him, snatched up the gun and ammunition, and, holding them up to him, motioned where the cannon could be heard, and she cursed those horrible Serbian oaths at him, saying many things that I could not understand. Again he tried to help her, but she flung the gun at him, and began creeping forward again. She must have known that before the next kilometer-stone she would be lying helpless in the snow. So did we witness a thing that medieval poets loved to sing about. It had happened almost before we knew. Like a flash of lightning, her act showed the stuff of that woman and of the people from which she came; but it was n't poetic. It was primitive, crude, and cruel, and it was n't the sort of thing I want ever to see or hear about again.

"For some time I had noticed an old peasant couple who moved along just at our speed, staying within view. They were very aged even for Serbs, and carried no provisions of any sort that I could see. The old woman was following the old man. I saw them visibly grow weaker and weaker until their progress became a series of stumbling falls. We came to a place where low clumps of bushes grew by the roadside. The snow had drifted around and behind them so as to form a sort of cave, a niche between them. This was sheltered from the gale to some extent. By unspoken consent they made for it, and sank down side by side to rest. Their expression spoke nothing but thankfulness for this haven. Of course they never got up from it. This was quite the happiest thing I saw all that day, for such episodes were repeated with innumerable tragic variations scores of times. The terrible arithmetic of the storm multiplied them until by the end of the day we had ceased to think or feel.

"At last a change came over the army. I think

it was the young boys to whom arms had been given at Mitrovitze who began it. After a few hours of marching that day every ounce one had to carry counted greatly. Rifles, camp things, and over-flowing cartridge-belts are heavy. At first I noticed now and then a belt or canteen or rifle by the roadside. Soon it seemed as if the snow had turned to firearms. The surface of the road was thickly strewn with them; from every stream bayonets protruded, and the ditches along the road were clogged with them. The boys were throwing away their guns and, like a fever, it spread to many soldiers until the cast-away munitions almost impeded our progress.

"Although scarcely four o'clock, it began to grow dusk. The aspect of the plain seemed exactly the same as hours before; we did not appear to have moved an inch. Only the road had begun to climb a little and had grown even muddier. The snow ceased, but the wind increased and became much colder. No one seemed to know how far we were from Prishtina, but all knew that the oxen were worn out and could not go much farther. However, to camp out there without huge fires all night meant death, and there was nothing whatever with which to make fires.

"We climbed a hillside slowly. It was darker there than it would be on the crest, for the sun set before and not behind us. A little before four we reached the top. At most we could not travel more than thirty minutes longer, but we did not need to. Below us lay Prishtina.

"This ancient Turkish town was very beautiful in the dusk. It stands at the head of a broad valley, and on three sides is surrounded by hills which now were gleaming peaks. Lower down, the mountains shaded from light blue to deep purple, while a mist, rising from the river, spread a thin gray over the place itself. Hundreds of minarets, covered with ice and snow, pierced up like silver arrows to a sky now clear and full of stars. The snow was certainly over, but it was incredibly cold on the hill-crest, where the wind had full sway. Some bells in a mosque were ringing, and the sound came to us clear, thin, brittle, icy cold. But no place will ever seem so welcome again. It was blazing with lights, not a house, not a window unlighted, because, as we soon learned, not a foot of space in the whole place was unoccupied. On the right, down the broad stretch of a valley, for at least five miles, was a remarkable sight. We had moved in the middle of the refugee wave. The crest had reached Prishtina the day before, had surged through its narrow, crooked, filthy streets, and debouched over the plain beyond in thousands and thousands of camps. Now this huge camp-ground was lighted from one end to the other by camp-fires for, blessing of blessings, along the river was firewood. There must have been five thousand carts in that valley. This meant ten thousand oxen and five thousand drivers, and every driver had his fire. The thing stretched away along the curving river like the luminous tail of a comet from the blazing head at Prishtina. The contrast from the plain we had come over brought exclamations of pleasure from every one, and for a minute we paused there, watching the plodding refugees as they came to the top and gazed down into this heaven of warmth and light.

"A woman dragging three children came wearily up. There was a baby on her back, but for a wonder it was not crying. She stopped, sat down on a bank, and had one of the children unfasten the cloths that held the baby in position. Then she reached back, caught it, brought it around to her lap. She shook it, but it was frozen to death. There were no tears on her face. She simply gazed from it to the children beside her, who were almost exhausted. She seemed foolish, sitting there holding it. She was bewildered. She did not know what to do with it. Some men passed, took in the situation, and promptly buried it in two feet of mud and snow. The whole affair had lasted perhaps ten minutes.

"We moved on down the hill into the town, no longer a town. It was an inferno. The tens of thousands rushing before the Bulgarians and the tens of thousands ahead of the Germans met and mingled at Prishtina before pushing on their augmented current to Prizrend. The streets of Prishtina are narrow, so two carts can pass with difficulty. They wind and double upon themselves in the most incongruous maze, and they are filthier than any pigsty. The mob filled them as water fills the spillway of a dam. There were Turks, Albanians, Montenegrins, Serbs, English, French, Russians, and thousands of Austrian prisoners. They crowded on one another, yelled, fought, cursed, stampeded toward the rare places where any sort of food was for sale. Sneaking close to the walls, taking advantage of any holes as shelter from this human tornado, were numerous wounded soldiers, too lame or too weak to share in the wild mêlée. Here and there in some dim alley or in the gutter dead men lay unnoticed. And everywhere, on the sidewalks, in the streets, blocking the way, were dead animals, dozens and dozens of them. There was here not even the semblance of law that had obtained at Mitrovitze. The Government was crumbling, a nation was dying, and all such superfluities as courts of justice and police were a thing of the past. In lieu of street-lamps, however, flaring pine-torches had been stuck at dark corners, and the weird light they afforded put the last unearthly touch to the scene.

"Fighting one's way down these lanes of hell, stumbling over carcasses, wading knee-deep in slush and refuse, looking into myriads of wild, suffering eyes set in faces that showed weeks of starvation and hardship, the world of peace and plentiful food seems never to have existed. Yet less than two weeks before this town was a sleeping little Turkish city where food and shelter were to be had for a song, and where life took the slow, well-worn channels that it had followed for a hundred years. If ever there was a hell on earth, Prishtina, which from the hilltop yesterday afternoon looked like heaven, is that hell.

"In an hour and a half I came about six blocks to a street where shelter had been found for the forty English women in a harem where absolutely none of this turmoil penetrated. Never before have I realized what is the peace of the harem."

In regard to this remark in my notes, I would say that at Prishtina, at Prizrend, Jakova, and Ipek, when the retreat had reached its last and most terrible stage, before it was shattered to bits on the Albanian and Montenegrin mountains, the harems invariably proved to be havens of refuge. However wild the struggle in the streets without, however horrible the situation of the unnumbered thousands that descended in a day on these towns, however imminent the danger of invasion, life behind the latticework and bars moved uninterruptedly, steadily, peacefully, tenderly amid incense and cushions. The Turk did not suffer for food because, at the first hint of danger, each had laid in a supply for months. In this region they alone had any money; they are the buyers and sellers, the business lords of the country, and they had nothing to fear from the invasion, for were they not of the Teutonic allies? Their kindness to the English, French, and Russian nurses everywhere throughout the retreat is one of the fine things to be found in that awful time, and many English women I know have gone home with a confirmed conviction that "the terrible Turk and his harem" are a very decent sort after all.

My notes continue:

"Last night I found no shelter here [Prishtina] and was forced to follow my ox-cart outside the town, where thousands of others were incamped. All night long the freezing crowd wandered in the streets. Most of them had no blankets. They could not lie down on the snow and live. From fire to fire they wandered, and always in search of food. My blankets were soaked from the rain of the night before, but I wrapped them about me and lay in the bottom of my cart, an affair made of latticework through which the wind whistled. Soon the covers were as stiff as boards, and sleep was impossible. Through the night I listened to the oxen all around moaning in the plaintive way they have when in pain, for there is no hay about Prishtina, and they are starving.

"The sun came up this morning in a perfectly clear sky except for a slight mist over the mountains that turned it for a while into a blood-red ball. It touched the peaks to pearl and the hundred minarets of Prishtina to shafts of rose. Also, as far as the eye could see, it caused instant activity in that mighty camp. Men roused themselves and began

Last night I found no shelter, but followed the ox-carts to a camp outside the town

by thousands to cut wood along the river. Fires were replenished, meager breakfasts cooked, oxen still more meagerly fed. Along the slope behind me I saw a small squad of soldiers approaching. There was an army chaplain among them, and some men in civilian clothes. They trudged up the hill towards the rising sun. I looked on a moment, and then followed. Soon they halted. When I came up I saw five empty graves. In each a wooden stake was firmly driven, and the five men in civilian clothes were led to them, forced to step into the graves and kneel down with their backs to the stakes, where they were tied. Three of them were middle-aged and sullen. Two were young, scarcely twenty, I judge. They obeyed the quiet orders mechanically, like automata. One of the younger ones turned and gazed out over the camp just breaking into life, then he looked at the shining peaks and the minarets. From the town came the sound of morning bells. For a moment his face worked with emotion, but neither he nor his companions spoke. An officer stepped forward, and before each read a long official paper. He spoke slowly, distinctly, in the somewhat harsh accents of the Serbian language. After this the priest came forward and read a service. The men remained silent. When the priest finished, they were blind-folded and ten soldiers shot them at a distance of thirty feet. They pitched forward out of sight, and were buried at once. They were Bulgarian spies. Along the road below, the *kommorras* were getting under way, more than I had as yet seen, more than at Mitrovitze. As I returned down the hill and neared the highway they were moving away end-lessly, ceaselessly, to renew the endless, hopeless march. Ten kilometers down the road the cannon began to boom, and the tramping of the oxen on the snow and the creaking and rumbling of the thousands of carts were like the beating of torren-tial rains or the surge of the sea at Biarritz."

CHAPTER VIII

BEHIND THE LIVING WAVE

THE day following the great blizzard was warm and full of sunshine, so that most of the snow was turned to muddy slush, making, if possible, the highways more difficult. But cold winds soon began again, and while there was no more snow, the way of the refugees from Prishtina was anything but easy, the Bulgarian lines, only five kilometers distant, adding nothing to its attractiveness.

But I did not move at once with the hordes along this part of the way. Instead, I waited for Dr. May's ambulance to arrive from Mitrovitze, in order to make the trip back to that place, according to our arrangement. The main part of the English unit went on at once, but one Englishman remained behind with his cart to take on the man who was bringing the ambulance. He was to have overtaken us the day before, but did not, and so we were momentarily expecting him. However, not until late afternoon did he arrive; so that I had a whole day of idleness in Prishtina, and did not start back to Mitrovitze until next morning.

Although unnumbered thousands were leaving all the time, more poured into Prishtina to take their places, and all that day the congestion remained constant.   As soon as the English party had gone, I wandered out into this maelstrom purely as a sight-seer.   It felt queer, after so many weeks of retreating, during which always "the great affair was to move," to have nothing to do but loaf and watch others flee.   In the bright sunshine the streets were not weird, as they had appeared the evening before, though quite as revolting and terrible.

I went first out on a long search for small change. Every one had been hoarding their silver money for weeks, and things had come to such a pass now that one could not buy even the scant things that were for sale unless he had the exact change or was willing to give the seller the difference.   After a dozen or more futile attempts I found a druggist who was willing to give me silver francs for gold, but franc for franc, although gold was now at a great premium.

Shortly after this fortunate find I wandered to the principal square of the place, on one side of which stood an immense stone building which was temporarily occupied by the General Staff. Strings of new American touring-cars were drawn up in front of it. They were piled high with baggage, and the chauffeurs were standing alertly around, as if expecting urgent orders. No one knew when instant evacuation might be necessary.

On another side of the square was the office of the *narchelnik stanitza*, whom the Englishman, Mr. Stone, and I now sought out on some trivial business. At his outer door we met Mrs. St. Claire Stobart, who, unknown to Dr. May's section of her unit, had come into Prishtina that morning with the second army.

When hostilities were renewed last autumn, Mrs. Stobart left her main unit at Kragujevats, and with several ambulances, hospital tents, doctors, nurses, and orderlies formed what was unofficially known in Serbia as the "flying corps." They followed the army in all its moves from northern Serbia to Ipek. This necessitated forced march, sometimes of thirty-six hours' duration. It frequently meant three or four moves in twenty-four hours, and much more traveling at night than in daylight. It required taking automobiles where automobiles had never been before, and where it will be long before they are again. It entailed an endless routine of putting up and hauling down tents, of scanty meals and broken rest, of being cold and soaked and tired to death. The chauffeurs were men, but much of the most arduous labor was done, and done superbly well, by young girls.

For instance, the authoritative person who was responsible for the proper putting up and taking down of the numerous tents was a London girl of scarcely twenty. How would you like to see to the striking of four or five large tents in the dead of a freezing night, while the wind was blowing great guns, and the orderlies, whose language you could not speak, were so numb they would not work? How would you like to be held responsible for the placing of everything in the proper order, only to be forced to pitch the lot again after a sleepless ride of hours in a springless cart, or perhaps spent in pushing an ambulance through mud-holes, when all the army had gone past and nothing remained between you and the enemy, but a few kilometers of road? How would you like to subsist on black bread and thin soup and get so little of it that when meal-time came you felt like a wolf in famine. Three months after I saw the flying corps at Prishtina I met this young lady again. It was Sunday evening, and we were dining in the pretentious restaurant of a pretentious New York hotel. The room was filled with beautiful women in beautiful clothes, who laughed and sparkled, sipped their wine, and toyed with their food; but none of them laughed or sparkled or sipped or toyed with greater vivacity and light-hearted charm than this luxurious girl whose pastimes it had been to watch German "busy-Berthas" drop seventeen-inch shells about her hospital in Antwerp, or to pitch frozen tents on bleak Serbian hills for shot-riddled men to die in. Since seeing the English women in Serbia and elsewhere, a wonder which never troubled me previously has been daily growing in my mind. Why does n't England turn over this war to her women?

This by way of digression. Mrs. Stobart had business at general headquarters, and we accompanied her there, I being secretly gratified. I had been wishing for some pretext to take me into that building, teeming with its harassed and desperate officers, but in war-time, and such war, one does not scout about without some good excuse. Quite intentionally I got lost for a little while, and went about peering into doors to see what the general staff of an army such as the Serbian one was at that

moment looked like. The main thing I remember
is that in many of those rooms where the staff officers worked were piles of hay in the corners where
they slept, littered boxes standing about off which
they dined, and portemanteaux out of which they
lived. Ordinarily the Serbian officer is the smart-
est and most faultlessly got up of any of the armies.
There were haggard-looking men at the rough
tables covered with maps and documents. Halting
cheechas went to and fro as messengers, and here
and there in dark places orderlies cleaned much-
bespattered gaiters or burnished dull swords and
rusty pistols. Of course nowhere that I stuck my
head was I wanted but at the simple remark,
"Engleske mission," all my imbecility seemed covered by a cloak, or at least explained to them; so
much so that I decided to use it instead of "Americanske" in future, and continued to wander a bit.
They were faced with awful things, this General
Staff who dined from tin-cans and slept on hay, but
in some manner they seemed to be getting their
work done.

It was now about eleven o'clock, and as Mr.
Stone and I had breakfasted early on a handful of
corn-bread and some cognac, we followed Mrs. Stobart with what may be described as the keenest

pleasure back of the general staff building, where the flying corps were serenely encamped in a side street. We had dined the previous evening, after that blizzard march, on a bit of cheese, some tinned meat, and hard tack, and before that we had dispensed with lunch, and still before that had breakfasted on tea and biscuits, and before that a backward vista of tinned mutton and sweet biscuit too long and monotonous to be recounted in one modest volume. Hence when we saw the Austrian *goulash Kanone* that the flying corps had acquired steaming in the midst of the automobiles, we looked upon the world and saw that it was good. We had coffee and cheese and cocoa and rice and nearly white bread and a hearty welcome from the corps. Greatly did I fortify myself, for I saw no chance of anything more until I should arrive at Mitrovitze next day.

In mid-afternoon the long-expected ambulance arrived, much the worse for the wear of the road. By this time the traffic had completely destroyed all effects of any road-building that had ever been done on the Plain of Kossovo. The rest of the day I spent fitting on new tires, plenty of which the flying corps let me have, and overhauling the car in general.

An English clergyman, Mr. Rogers, had come over on the ambulance from Mitrovitze, but was determined to go back with me, there to remain with the women doctors and nurses who were staying behind with the wounded sister.   In all likelihood this meant his internment until the end of the war, whereas there was a good chance for the women who stayed being allowed to return home.   Also, there appeared to be no great necessity of his remaining; but he knew and I knew that it would make the women feel a little more protected.   It seemed to me an act thoroughly in character with the best sort of Englishman, and the kind I had always expected from them, though after what I had seen of British men in Serbia, it came as a distinct surprise to me.   I was indeed glad to have him as a companion for the return trip to Mitrovitze the next day.

That night I discovered a hay-loft belonging to a jolly old Turk who would not let me set foot in his harem, but assured me of an unlimited welcome to his hay.   The mercury dropped to the neighborhood of zero as night came on, and it was a great comfort to be able to burrow into the very center of a great stack of warm hay, a fine improvement on my cart of the previous night.

About five next morning I rolled out of my nest, and spent an hour in violent contortions incident to cranking the frozen motor before daylight. Mr. Rogers had some dry bread, which we ate, and then we started on our return journey.

On the top of a hill outside the town we came to four large guns standing beside the road, and beyond, in a muddy grain-field, we saw a little group of tents.

"It must be some of Admiral Troubridge's men," said Rogers. "I should like to stop and speak to them a minute."

"All right," I replied. "I 'll sit in the car."

In a few minutes he came back and asked me if I would like a cup of hot coffee, real coffee. Would I! · We wallowed through the field to the tents, where we found a cheecha broiling meat over a camp-fire, and between times watching a large kettle of porridge and the coffee-pot. We entered the largest of the tents, which we found warm and dry, hay a foot deep on the ground, and braziers of coals making everything comfortable. I think there were eighteen or twenty men lying about, and a more cheerful, hospitable crowd could not be found anywhere. We had excellent jams, coffee, tea, rice, and beef for breakfast, and they made Rogers bring away some potatoes and beans to help out his provisions at Mitrovitze. These things had mostly been sent out from home before the trouble began.

More than half of the men looked scarcely older than boys. I remember one "mother's boy" who did not look eighteen, with his innocent blue eyes, curly hair, and cheeks as fresh as a baby's. But they had all seen hard enough service, having been unrelieved at Belgrade since the preceding March. They gleefully related to me how they had got into Serbia.

They left England on a battle-ship which took them to Malta. There they disembarked, and their uniforms were taken from them, but each was given a suit of citizen's clothes. They assured me that these were the worst clothes that anybody ever had to wear for the sake of his country. Rigged out in this ludicrous raiment,—the Government had seen no necessity of taking their measures,—they boarded a passenger-boat, and came to Saloniki as "commercial travelers." They were allowed little time to ply their trade, however, for a train was waiting to whisk them across the Serbian border, where they resumed their real character.

These marines represented all that England did toward the actual defense of Serbia until the last attack. There were eight guns stationed in and around Belgrade, and a forty-five-foot steam-launch that had been ingeniously fitted with torpedo-tubes. In the first encounter that this heavy craft had with the enemy, it attacked two Austrian monitors, sinking one and forcing the other to return to Semlin, where afterward it succeeded in keeping such dangerous boats bottled up. The work of their guns, they said, had been greatly hampered by the activity of Austro-German aëroplanes. These immediately spied out any position they would take, and directed the enemy's fire accordingly. In Belgrade and throughout the retreat the French aviators appeared either unable or unwilling to give any protection against scouting and bomb-throwing. The opinions which those marines expressed would, to say the least, have shocked the boulevards.

In expressing freely adverse opinions about their allies, the marines were no exception to other British soldiers with whom I came in contact. My experience among British military men has not been wide, but within its narrow scope I never heard one of them say a good word for anybody except the Germans. It seems to be an axiom among them, a tradition from which there is no appeal, this in-

significance of all but the British and of the enemy
that has taught them many things. I heard very
little mention of German atrocities in Serbia, but
generous praise from British men and officers of
German efficiency and bravery. These marines
despised the Serbian soldiers, spat on the Italians,
tolerated the French. I am not sure they knew
Russia was fighting.

"What do you think?" one of the older of them
said to me. "These Serb boys don't get anything
for serving! Now, is n't that calculated to make a
man fight with a good heart, not getting a penny,
and knowing that his wife or mother won't get anything! Are n't they a fine lot, now?"

This man was a fine fellow, and, I am sure, as
unselfish and brave a soldier as England has, although he would be horrified if you told him so.
His own solid, well-ordered, comfortable system
represented to him all that could possibly be good
in the world. Of the indefinable, even mystic, motive force which drove hundreds of thousands of
ignorant Serbian peasants, in a fight that from the
first was hopeless, to face separation from everything which human beings prize, and to endure tor-
tures the like of which armies have seldom known
in order that those who did not die might return to

renew the holy war, of a very practical patriotism
for a very beautiful and ideal cause, he knew nothing. If you had asked him why he was fighting,
he would have told you because it was his business,
and to his business, whatever it may be, he has a devotion that makes him one of the most formidable
of enemies. Government says fight, and ages of
experience have taught him that Government
usually has something worth while up its sleeve
when it says fight; so, volunteer or regular, he fights
with bravery and abandon. It seems to me that
the average British soldier follows his Government
with an implicit faith surpassed only by the Germans.

The difference in this war lies in the wide gulf
that separates the somewhat less dangerous desires
of the one Government from the altogether dangerous and abominable ambitions of the other.
The soldiers of both nations follow without very
much thought as to the real objects at stake. But
most French know pretty well why they are fighting, and you can be assured the average Serb knows
why. Whether you believe in the Serb's ambitions
or not, you instantly see that he believes in them,
worships them, dies for them with a gladness that
takes little account of self or family. It would be

utterly impossible for a Serbian statesman to hold his nation at bay while he wrote half a dozen notes on such a thing as the *Lusitania,* no matter how big the offender. If it meant sure defeat, they would still jump in and fight for their liberty until utterly exhausted. They can not help it; they are built that way. They may or may not be too extreme in this. It is well for Americans, who can sit calmly and weigh the advantages and disadvantages of fighting no matter what is involved, to *realize* that such peoples do exist.

Of course, in trying to make even the slightest analysis of the feelings of various armies, one is treading a path hopelessly confused by numerous exceptions; but, after all, there is a common type which can be more or less sharply defined. I simply wish to state the impression, perhaps entirely erroneous, which the British soldiers I saw, and the Serbian soldiers I lived with, made on me.

As Mr. Rogers and I breakfasted, they told us of their work at Belgrade and their retreat. Near Nish they had lost two of their guns. These had become bogged on a mountain-side, and the enemy was so close behind that there was no time to dig them out, but only to blow them up and hurry away. There were four guns with them at Prishtina, but ammunition was running low. "Only fifty rounds left," one told us, "but fifteen of them are 1915 lyddite, and, I tell you, sir, when you name it, take off your hat, for you're in the presence of your Maker!"

The next morning—for I returned that way next day—I stopped to leave some medicine which Mr. Rogers had sent them, and had breakfast with them once more. This was the last I saw of them until three weeks later, when we again met on the bleak, wind-swept pier at Plavnitze, where we waited to take the tiny boat across the lake to Scutari.

No one would have recognized them. For two weeks they had been crossing the mountains. Their own stores having been exhausted, they had had to live as the Serbian soldiers had been living for at least ten weeks. It was an interesting comparison in endurance. Under regular conditions all of these men would have been pitched into an ambulance and taken to a base hospital. One week more, and most of them would surely have died. Their spirit was splendid. One staggered up to me,—he of the lyddite worship,—and when I inquired how he felt, said he was all right, and even had something to be thankful for. His gun was the only one that had not been destroyed. They had dug a hole and buried it intact! His devotion to that gun was as sincere a thing as I ever saw. Hardly had he finished speaking when he fainted before my eyes from exhaustion and starvation. Several of his comrades also had to be carried on to the boat.

When finally we returned to our car and took the road again, we encountered a difficulty which was entirely unforeseen. Bottomless mud-holes, deep ruts, impossible hill-climbs I expected as a matter of course, but I had not exactly realized what it meant to go against the tide of refugees even yet pouring toward Prishtina, to be the only persons in the country going toward the invader. The ambulance explained us to some in the incredulous mass we passed, but many there were who, seeing we were foreigners, and concluding we had lost our way, made frenzied gestures indicating the folly of our course. Some of them would not be deterred from their well-meant warnings, but, placing themselves in our path, forced us to stop and listen to their harangues, which we could not understand. As we drew away from Prishtina, however, the refugees thinned, and before we came to Mitrovitze we had seen the last of these hordes.

Around Mitrovitze itself there were great camps

of army-transports, which were delaying to the last minute and never got away.   When we came into the town we found its aspect much changed.   All traces of the mad riot in which I had seen the Admiral and the Colonel were gone.   The dirty, primitive streets were empty and silent; where had been terror and panic, was only ominous solitude. Nearly every house was tightly shut, boards having been nailed over the windows of many of them. Only soldiers were to be seen, and now and then a leisurely Turk waddling by.   Around the *casern* a large number of soldiers were bringing field-guns into position, and also about the hospital, not far away, air-craft-defense guns were being set up. Feebly armed, Mitrovitze awaited her inevitable fate.

My mission was in vain.   The unfortunate nurse could not be moved again in any circumstances. She had already been completely exhausted by thirty-six hours of continuous journey in a springless cart over roads so rough that the automobile was thought worse than the primitive cart. Imagine making a trip like this when one had been shot through both lungs and the temperature is about zero.   Think of being put down in an overcrowded military hospital, with cannon guarding it from bombs and with the enemy expected any hour. Picture having to lie there day after day listening to the guns without and the moaning of the wounded within, deprived of proper food. Can you conceive of a mere girl living through such an experience? Yet I understand that she has recovered. Needless to say, she is a British woman.

It was decided that I should return to Dr. May, whom I would find at Prizrend, with the ambulance, taking letters, and, if possible, come back to Mitrovitze with whatever provisions could be spared by the unit. The food situation at Mitrovitze was serious. This plan meant a race against time. The Germans were right on the town, and would certainly come in after two or three days. I would have to return before they took the place or I could not get in. Although my bargain with Dr. May in return for the care of the three British nurses placed me unconditionally at the orders of her doctors at Mitrovitze, they kindly put the matter up to me as to whether I cared to return to Mitrovitze. No one could have been anything but glad to be of the slightest service to these women who were cheerfully remaining behind with their wounded companion. However, the question was arbitrarily settled for me within forty-eight hours.

A well-known army surgeon, an Austro-Serb, who had been attending the wounded girl was to accompany me to Prizrend.   In all probability, capture for him meant summary execution, and while he was loath to go, the others insisted that it was a useless sacrifice for him to remain.   There were other physicians who could care for the patient.   This doctor was a man of broad education, unusual culture, and polished manner.   He spoke five or six languages, and, besides being a physician of high rank, was a delightful conversationalist on almost any subject.   He was a man who had a comprehensive, intelligent, sympathetic view of international questions, a fine product of the best in civilization.   He was the sort of man the United States seems rarely to get as an ambassador anywhere.   All that kept him from being marched out into a corn-field and shot like a dog was a few kilometers of road.   He had left the land of his birth, and had gone to the land of his choice to join himself to the people whose nature corresponded to his own; for this he would be shot.   His case is a glimpse at the under side of Balkan politics.   The method which without doubt would be applied to him if he were caught has been applied unnumbered times perhaps by all the Balkan countries, but certainly on a greater and more heartless scale by Austria. It is logical and simple. It is the only way to hold together polyglot empires made up of unwilling remnants that have been torn from peoples burning for that illusive thing called nationality.

The correct definition and establishment of this nationality seems to me to be the greatest question in the world to-day. It can never be based on racial differences, because the blood strains are hopelessly mixed; nor on language boundaries, because people who could not possibly live together frequently speak the same tongue; nor on religious differences, because peoples of the same faith vary widely in location, temperament, and progress; nor on topography, because such "natural barriers" mean less and less as communication is perfected; nor on the previous ownership of territory, for whereas one nation may be the possessor to-day, another was the day before: on the preference of the people concerned, and on that alone, will any sort of satisfactory scheme ever be built up, directed, of course, and modified somewhat by essential economic considerations. When this principle is followed, Austria will find herself no longer forced to hang whole villages, and shoot and burn

and terrorize as in Bosnia since 1878 she has had
to do, because Bosnia will no more be Austrian.
However, several million pages may still be written about this matter without exhausting its difficulties, and mine is not the story of things as they
might be, but of things as they were in Serbia during the ten weeks it took to make her once more a
part of the polyglot system.

This interesting doctor, whose name I do not feel
free to mention, and I started from Mitrovitze in
the freezing dawn of the day following the afternoon on which I had arrived. ·We faced a chilling
wind as we descended to the bleak and now empty
Plain of Kossovo. It had been only three days
since I had taken the same road, but how different
now! Ragged patches of snow still spotted the
earth, souvenirs of the blizzard, but where was the
creaking procession that had suffered so that day?
The question came to mind, and with it a picture
of them as they must be, still floundering somewhere farther along the road. Their trail had been
left there on the desolate plateau, written in a
waste of debris and objects too repulsive for
description. What had been a country, was now
a desert, strewn with unburied people and animals, in which there was no food, no drink, no eco-

nomic life, no trace of happiness. The whole world suggested a feeling of suspense, a waiting for something unknown, such as one feels in a theater when the warning bell has rung.

The road had dried somewhat, so we went along with less difficulty. We came within view of Prishtina about ten o'clock, but it was one before we had traversed the town. This delay was due to the fact that the huge *kommorras* about the place were all breaking up, and the narrow streets were literally deluged with ox-carts. New York traffic policemen could not have handled that mass, and there was no guiding hand. The result was a jam so inextricable that for two days many carts in the town did not move at all. People camped under their chariots, and the oxen lay down by their yokes. At last we found a way that skirted the town and which, because it was nothing but a marsh, was less crowded than the central streets. The liquid mud came up into my motor when we ran along the shallowest part, a narrow strip in the center of the roadway; on each hand was mire that would have swallowed the machine whole, as some ox-carts that had strayed there only too plainly told us. Luck and that marvelous little engine were with us, and just at lunch-time we came in

A group of transport drivers

What had been a country was now a desert

sight of the Stobart "flying corps," camped on the farther side of the town. I was surprised to see them still in Prishtina, but also delighted, for it meant some sort of lunch.

We were welcomed, fed, and again took the road, but with an addition to the party. In case the Germans took Mitrovitze before I returned from Prizrend, I, of course, would not come back. In this contingency Mrs. Stobart wished the ambulance with her corps, though I was at a loss to see why, for it was then most obvious that everything had gone to smash, and nothing was left but for the units to get out as best they could. However, she asked to send a Serbian chauffeur, Peter, along with us to bring back the car in case I should not need it.

Peter was a typical Serbian chauffeur; when I have said that I have said the worst thing I can. About fifteen kilometers out was the most threatened spot in the whole route. For a short time the Bulgarians had succeeded in taking the road here, but had been driven back again, and the line was then three or four kilometers east of the road, the ground between being almost level farmlands. Here the Serbians had temporarily intrenched themselves, and were endeavoring to hold the enemy back from the road as long as possible. Farther on, the road drew away from the battle-line, and in the rear, Prishtina was not as yet threatened. It was simply this small salient which was in immediate danger, and, as it happened, here the road was not at all bad. It was level and smooth, and wide enough to enable us to run past the trains of military transports, hospitals, and artillery that were hastening to get past this danger-point. For some inscrutable reason a deep hole had been dug on our side of the road, a pit perhaps five feet deep, four feet long, and three wide, running lengthwise with the road. We were going fast, the hole was plainly to be seen, and there was ample room to right and left of it, but Peter, with splendid nonchalance, preferred to take it straight ahead, on the jump. The front wheels hit the farther edge, bringing us to quite the quickest stop, with the exception of one that was to follow a few hours later, which I have ever made.

When we picked ourselves off the floor of the car, we found our Ford with its nose in the ground and its heels in the air, like a terrier digging for a chipmunk, a position never dignified for an automobile and particularly out of place, it seemed to me, just four kilometers behind a very fickle battle-line. Peter crawled out first, remarking casually in very bad German, his only language besides Serbian, that he did not know what in heaven was the matter with the steering-gear. Whatever may have been its previous state and condition, that important feature of an automobile's anatomy was certainly "on the blink" now. Yet nothing other than the triangle was injured in the slightest. I really never wrote an advertisement in my life, and shall not begin now, but when a car can stand up against Peter's idea of sport with nothing except the triangle injured (which was not made at Detroit, but in a Serbian shop), it deserves honorable mention in the despatches, and a new triangle.

The moment I looked at those tortured, twisted rods, I knew that we would never be able to straighten them so that they could be induced to fit again. But the optimistic Peter did not share my views, and was confident we could straighten them in a jiffy. It was then about three o'clock, the sun was nearing the horizon in a perfectly clear sky, and the temperature was not far above zero. In passing, it may be said that every account I have ever seen of the Balkans in winter lays frequent and eloquent stress on the peculiarly penetrating cold. One writer who had endured the unbelievable temperatures of Siberia, said that he had never felt anything like this damp, searching, congealing chill, which nothing seems thick or warm enough to shut out. They do not exaggerate; the Balkan cold cannot be overstated. I tried my best in stern Anglo-Saxon to do it while I wrenched and hammered and squeezed with gloveless hands the frozen steel, but it was hopeless. Nothing I could think of to say even approached an adequate expression of that cold. A good part of my conversation on the weather was really meant for Peter, but he was none the wiser. Yet even at this stage I had not lost my temper. I was sorry afterward that I had not; it left me with so much reserve force a little later when I really did blow up.

I was holding the misused triangle as firmly as it is possible for numb blue hands to do while Peter attempted inexpertly to smooth out the numerous spots where the rods had buckled. My appearance would have done credit to a Gipsy. I was ragged, covered with mud, and my coat, which a tall Englishman had given me at Prishtina to replace the one torn by the ox, was yards too long for me. It flapped sadly about my knees in the biting wind. As I bent over the iron rod, my face was hidden by a tattered felt hat. So intent was I on the work that I did not see a major ride up and dismount.

He was a smart officer, whose glory, however, had
been somewhat tarnished by sleeping in haystacks
and pigstys.   This also had not improved his temper.   From the demeanor of his attendants it was
plain that he was a dreaded man.   What he saw
was an ambulance in trouble, with the doctor in
spotless uniform standing beside it and a fairly
decent-looking Serbian soldier hammering on some
steel rods which were being infirmly held by a nondescript beggar evidently requisitioned for the job.
It was not any of his business, but, oh, cursed spite!
he was the sort born to set all things right.

I first became aware of stentorian tones shouting
what I recognized as the vilest Serbian epithets.
The voice threatened instant annihilation, and
looking up in astonishment, I saw his gestures
threatened likewise.   I was not holding the rod to
suit him.   My feet were ice, my ears were ice, my
nose was ice, my hands aching, skinned, covered with
frozen blood, all because of an idiotic chauffeur who
had run us into a hole and insisted on trying a job I
knew to be hopeless, and now—this specimen!
You know the sensation—all your injured feelings,
acquired and inherited, coming suddenly to a head
in the sublime detestation of one person.   With exquisite relief I turned on him a torrent of abuse, an

orgy of anger, saying everything that as a little boy I could remember I had been taught not to say. Still, what I said to him did not equal what he had said to me; nothing can equal Serbian oaths in vileness. But the next minute I was thoroughly ashamed of myself. The troop had stood petrified when I had shouted at him. They could not believe their ears, but when he heard my English and saw my face, he slumped completely. I never saw a deeper humiliation. Of all things, the Serbs avoid most even the appearance of impoliteness to foreigners, especially neutrals engaged in relief-work. The major's mistake, not my retaliation, crushed him. Sputtering some sort of broken apology, he meekly mounted his horse and rode away, leaving me quite as conscience-stricken as he.

After wasting three precious hours, Peter came to my way of thinking and agreed to follow out an arrangement which I had suggested some time before, and which was made more reasonable when a military hospital came by and took the doctor with most of his luggage along with them. Peter was to walk back to Prishtina, secure a new triangle from the flying corps' supplies, and return early next morning. We would then fix the car, pick up the doctor at the next town, where he said the hospital would camp, and go on our way. I was to stay with the disabled ambulance in the meantime.

Soon I was left alone, with half a pound of black bread for dinner and only one blanket for covering. The bare fields round about afforded no material for a fire. My three heavy blankets had been stolen from the car on the previous day, leaving me in a bad situation. Woolen blankets were getting to be worth a great deal, for it was impossible to buy them. Fortunately, the English unit had evacuated with a plentiful supply, from which I was later refurnished. It was ridiculous that a person's life should depend upon two or three blankets, and yet this was virtually the case at that time.

This night, after closing as tightly as I could all the curtains of the ambulance, I lay down in the place designed for stretchers, with my piece of bread and my blanket. It was not warm there, but after my night in the cart at Prishtina, it did not seem so bad. Of course it would have been much better to have spent the night tramping about to keep up circulation, but fatigue made this almost impossible. So I lay and shivered, watching the blue moonlight through the rents in the curtains.

The noisy traffic on the road had ceased. The tired men and oxen had long since turned from the melancholy road to desolate camps, those behind thinking that on the morrow they would pass the danger-point, those ahead feeling a sense of comparative security because it was passed. But I thought I heard more distinctly than formerly the rapid-fire guns and rifles crackling across the fields. It seemed to me the firing was freshening, but I was too tired to think about it very much and dozed for a time. I was awakened by the sound of an automobile rushing by at full speed, with the cutout wide open. Then began a stream of cars tearing past, which, crawling from my shelter, I recognized as the motors of the General Staff. Prishtina was being evacuated at midnight and seemingly in something of a hurry. Furthermore, beyond the cornfields things were unmistakably getting more lively.

I was not left long in doubt as to what was happening. A large touring-car slowed up as it approached me, and from the running-board a figure sprang which I recognized as Peter carrying the coveted triangle. The automobile had not stopped completely, but shot away again without losing a minute. In German, Peter announced that Prishtina was being evacuated, that the Serbs expected to retreat across the road, and that we had three hours in which to repair the car and get away.

"We must work very quickly, very quickly," he remarked, and in true Serb fashion therewith put down his burden, seated himself on the running-board, leisurely pulled out a package of tobacco, then cigarette-papers, carefully made a beautiful cigarette, hunted listlessly through each of his many pockets, and at last asked me for a match. When I handed it to him from under the car where I had scuttled at his first words, he lighted the cigarette, and began smoking, rapturously drawing in the fumes as if he were passing a dull hour gazing out of a club window. Nor did my heated remarks move him to hasten. Lying there in the freezing mire, hammering my fingers in the darkness, I hated him almost as I had hated the major. The fighting came closer. We could now spot in a general way the position of the machine-guns as they sputtered, and the rifle-fire became a host of separate sounds, like raindrops falling, rather than the conglomerate cracking we had heard before. A triangle is a troublesome thing for two inexpert men to put in at any time; now it seemed as if it would never be made to fit. We had no light, and under the chassis it was almost pitch-dark despite the placid arctic moon that sailed overhead. I did not know I had so many fingers to smash, I did not know lying in freezing mud could be so uncomfortable, I did not know that there ever lived so big a fool as Peter seemed to be. While the sounds of battle drifted over the moonlit, frosted fields, I lay under the car and battered away, thinking of the hot summer days in Long Island City, where I had seen the operation I was trying to perform done in the twinkling of an eye. How simple! how easy! and now how—hellish!

Two hours and a half went by, in which we got the rounded knob at the apex of the triangle almost fitted into its socket; but it would not slip in, despite innumerable manipulations with levers, jacks, and hammers, and turning of wheels and straining the front axle. Then four soldiers came by whom Peter persuaded to help us, and with the combined strength of these the job finally was done. We had fifteen minutes left of the prescribed time. Slightly wounded soldiers were straggling back from the trenches. We had only to put back several important screws, that was all; but Peter discovered he had lost two of them. We had no extra ones, and the chance of finding them in that trampled mud by moonlight was *nil*. For the first time Peter swore; and it was not at high heaven or me or the Bulgarians or even himself; it was at the two screws for letting him lose them.   I could not help but laugh, and we stuck in some wire, hoping it would hold.

The four soldiers who had helped us Peter now insisted would be much offended if we did not give them a lift.   I objected that it would overload our tires, which I knew were weak, but he finally gained his point.   I also hated to ride away from them when they had aided us.   At last, just on the three-hour limit, we started.   Within half a mile' one of the tires blew out.   I then ordered the soldiers to get out and Peter to drive on with the flat tire. This he did, for the battle was rolling on behind us and the camps along the road were breaking up in the wildest confusion, the tired oxen being forced once more to take the road.   The countryside now became lighted with dozens of fires, where the re-treating soldiers burned haystacks, granaries, and supplies which they could not take.   Now and then a peasant cottage would break into flames, and the farm stock ran about.

In an hour we came to the town the doctor had spoken of.   Our inquiries failed to bring any in-formation as to the whereabouts of him or the hospi-tal.   I told Peter we would spend an hour searching for him, and that, while he did this, I would put on a new tire. The arrangement appealed to him, but at the end of the hour the only information we had was from the commandant, who said the doctor could not be found, and that he would doubtless go on with the hospital to Prizrend. So we started on without him. Our lamps were out of commission, but for two hours the moon afforded quite enough light, even though we had to run along the left, boggy fringe of the road because of the ox-cart trains. The ox-drivers were worse humored that night than I had ever seen them. To our constant horn and cry of *"Desno! desno!"* ("To the right"), they paid no attention whatever, purposely sticking in the middle of the road, leaving not enough room to pass on either side, and forcing us to accommodate our pace to theirs. We were continually running on first speed on account of this and the heavy roads, and water boiled out of our radiator in a very short time. Then I would descend, break the two-inch ice on the stream-filled ditches along the way and fill up with the freezing water, which instantly gave the tortured motor relief for the moment.

Once when the drivers were particularly irritating about not giving the road, Peter descended, like

the wrath of heaven, and beat one of them soundly
with a stick, screaming hair-raising threats meanwhile.   After this we fared somewhat better, for
the news passed along that line far faster than we
could travel.   Once we were stopped by an old soldier who could hardly drag himself along.   He was
wounded in the leg and was faint from loss of
blood.   He asked a ride, and we put him in the
ambulance, where now and then he moaned a little.
Peter had brought me some bread, which I had not
eaten, and it occurred to me this old fellow might
be hungry.   I do not believe he had had anything
to eat for days.   He seemed considerably "bucked
up" afterward, and when we had to stop because of
darkness, during the brief period between moonset
and daylight, he left us, hobbling away we knew not
where.

At dawn I took the wheel, and almost at once we
came up with what I always refer to as the "long
kommorra."   It was where the road leaves the
plain and begins in gradual, tortuous ascents to
wriggle up a narrow gorge.   Of necessity the way
is narrow, too, cut out of the cañon's side, with an
unspeakable surface.   There is no balustrade on
the outer edge; only the crumbling brink, unsafe
for any heavy weight.   This stretch is between

twenty and thirty kilometers long, and without a single gap the whole was clogged with trains of carts. A more harrowing fifteen or twenty miles I hope never to drive. Even when the carts crowded against the inside bank, there was no room safely to avoid the dangerous edge. But seldom could my hoarse shouts of *"Desno! desno!"* repeated unceasingly, persuade the drivers to go so close in, and so the car had to run on the narrowest margin—a margin that in some instances I could distinctly feel give beneath me. Peter slept through it all, loudly snoring in the back of the ambulance.

At last it ended in a steep ascent on which I passed the head of the procession, and climbed on a road that had now become very good to the top of the range. I had not realized we had climbed so high. In the morning sunlight I looked over a tremendous expanse of hill ranges and thickly wooded valleys, now brown and gold and blue with the tints of late autumn. Down the side of the mountain on which I was the road ran in endless leaps and turns on a regular, but steep, grade, narrow, but with a perfect surface, as smooth as glass. I could see it gleam for miles and miles ahead until it was lost in the valley, only to rise again on the

farther side, and lead over the next crest.   Not that
I stopped to take in this picture.   It flashed on me
in the brief time in which I glimpsed it as, with
power shut off, I glided on top of the divide.   I had
shut off my power so as to begin the downward run
as slowly as possible, for long before I had received
the ambulance all the brakes had been worn out.
Also, the reverse was gone, and the first speed so
worn that I dared not use it as a brake.   Up to
that time this lack had inconvenienced me little, but
as I looked at the long coast ahead, I knew that I
should have to do better driving than I had ever
done before if I got to the bottom.   Of course I
had virtually had no sleep for two days and nothing
to eat except a little bread for twenty-four hours
and was fagged with the train of misfortunes that
had followed us, and especially with the drive just
ended.   I was really in a sort of coma, which kept
me from realizing what driving that stretch without
any brakes meant.   Peter was still snoring.

In two minutes we were going like an express-
train, in three twice as fast, for we had hit the steep-
est grade, and at its bottom was a short turn to the
right, almost a switchback.   It was there that
Peter got the joke on me.   I did not drive that
curve; it drove itself.   What I did was reflex.   All

that I know is that, when headed like a cannon-ball for the five-hundred-foot precipice, I waited until the road turned and then swung the wheel for all I was worth. I am confident that all four wheels left the earth; but we had made the curve, only to see another, sharp to the left, right ahead. Before I even realized there was another turn, we had gone straight ahead into a deep, muddy ditch, and the front wheels and radiator face were buried in a soft clay bank. It was a quicker stop than Peter had given us, and a more violent one. It threw Peter over my shoulder upon the radiator, and woke him up. I was whirled into the middle of the road. Neither was hurt, and we set to work inspecting the wreck. But there was no wreck. As I said before, I do not write advertisements, but when a car can stand up against Peter's and my ideas of sport, it does deserve honorable mention in the despatches. Nothing was injured except the triangle; that was buckled as before. Now by the deep contempt with which Peter looked at me, I realized how much he must have despised himself for running into that hole.

I looked over the car, and saw that the rod was bent in only one place, and could be straightened with patience. I was sure it would take a long

Where the Bulgarians threatened the road

time, however, and I was afraid that Dr. May would leave Prizrend next morning. So when I was told it was only a five-hour walk to Prizrend, I took a small bag on my back, gave Peter two napoleons to salve his feelings and hire helpers, and pushed on alone.

It had been the unit's intention to go to Monastir by way of Albania from Prizrend. Once at Monastir, they could take the railway to Saloniki. This trip would require six or seven days on horseback. The road had long been cut by the Bulgarians, but of course I did not know this. There were two alternative routes. Either they could go by horse-trails through Albania to Scutari, or they could go north by cart to Ipek, and from there cut across Montenegro by horse-trail to Androvitze, where a wagon-road led to Scutari via Podgoritze and Scutari Lake. When I set out to walk to Prizrend, I knew none of this. I only knew that they intended going to Monastir, and that, if they left Prizrend before I arrived, I could not overtake them; and although the road back to Mitrovitze had been cut so that I could not hope to return there, I still wished to deliver the letters to Dr. May. I was right in my supposition that they would be leaving next morning, for we did actually all leave together then, though it was by the route to Ipek.

I had been told that it was five hours to Prizrend. I began walking at eight o'clock, and at one I was told it was three hours to Prizrend. By this time I was completely fagged, mainly on account of sleep and hunger. At two I descended the last range of hills and began crossing a plain, dimly on the farther limit of which I saw for the first time the savage heights of the Albanian Alps. I could not see any sign of Prizrend, and could walk only about half as fast as formerly. I was thirsty, and left the road a minute to get a drink at a clear mountain stream. While standing on the bank, I heard a motor and, looking up, saw Peter flying by in the ambulance. If only I had been on the road! I resumed my march with many refugees, who were growing much more in evidence. Luck at last favored me, for I soon spied the ambulance standing in the road, and, hurrying, I came up just as Peter, with two soldier comrades, was ready to set off. In the distance Prizrend showed indistinctly, crammed right against the mountains.

In fifteen minutes we could see the surly old fortress on the hill above Prizrend, and soon neared the outskirts of the town. As I looked out, I had a curious sensation of being among familiar surroundings. It puzzled me a minute, and then I knew it was the refugees. We were in the thick of them again. By the tens of thousands they swarmed around Prizrend, ants in an ant-hill, bees in a hive, flies about a carcass. We were submerged in them, buffeted, hindered, stopped, amalgamated with them. Swirling with them into the narrow maw of Prizrend, we became a part of them again. The old life had begun once more — the life it seemed to me I had led a thousand years instead of a few short weeks, the astounding, restless, tragic life of the living wave.

CHAPTER IX

ABOUT four o'clock in the afternoon I arrived at Prizrend, and at four next morning I left it. It was not a long stay, but quite long enough to leave an indelible picture with me. The life of the retreat was always crammed full of incident, rich in striking or colorful detail, a pageant that day and night rolled over Serbia costing thousands and thousands of lives and a nation's existence. To have marched with it was to see the most savage face of life and to become the familiar of death. To look back on it is to feel its dream-like quality seemingly extending over years and years. To write about it is to contend with a bewildering maze of narrative threads, the brightest of which it is not easy to choose; but Prizrend, in the sunset half-hour that I saw it and in the misty dawn as I left it, certainly deserves to be picked out of the tangle.

I came there trailing the refugee masses, just ahead of the battle-storm, dangerously late. All three Serbian armies were converging on the Albanian and Montenegrin frontier between Prizrend and Ipek, some of them planning to take the route across Albania to Scutari, the rest to go through Montenegro by way of Ipek, Androvitze, and Podgoritze to Scutari. The road to Monastir, as we learned at once, had been cut; the General Staff had already announced the evacuation of Prizrend, and were preparing to go to Scutari by the Albanian route.

In time of peace Prizrend numbers about fifteen or twenty thousand inhabitants. It lies on the edge of a broad valley so close to the mountains that a good half of it clambers up a steep slope for hundreds of feet, and ends in the huge gray fortress which gives an appearance strangely reminiscent of Naples around San Martino. At the foot of this slope, through the center of the town, runs a swift mountain river, the quays on each side being lined with the spacious harems of the wealthier Turks. Farther up-stream these quays become grassy banks, and instead of old houses, are deep groves of sycamores. Where the main street strikes the river is an ancient stone bridge that consists of one incredibly long arch springing from massive piles of masonry on each side.

When we came to the bridge, Peter and I were at a loss to know where to turn, when we spied one of the English nurses in the crowd. She had seen us, and was soon guiding us by a precarious road along the river-bank to a filthy alley a little way up which was the house which the ever-watchful Dr. Čurčin had succeeded in getting for the mission. I was met with the news that the unit was leaving for Ipek the following morning. Dr. May was happy to get what slight good news I could bring of the wounded girl—they had expected her to die—and as all question of sending back the ambulance was settled, kindly invited me to travel along as one of the unit. This I was happy to do, and am frank to say that at this late date I do not know what I should have done otherwise; for although I had gold, food was not for sale. I made the journey as far as Rome with the unit, and can never forget the kindness shown me without exception by all the nurses and doctors.

Soon after I arrived I met Admiral Troubridge again. He seemed worried; as near it, that is to say, as I ever saw him. Major Elliott had been sent with fifty marines to go out by way of Monastir, and soon after he left the Admiral had got information that the road had been cut by the Bul-

garian forces.   Since then he had had no word from
his men; so whether they were captured or not he
did not know.   As a matter of fact, they succeeded
in getting out shortly before the enemy came.   To
add to the uncomfortable situation, Colonel Phillips had fallen ill, and was in no condition to make
the trip across Albania to Scutari.   What caused
the Admiral most anxiety, however, was the condition of the prisoners at Prizrend.   He said that the
English women must be got out of the town as soon
as possible, next day at the latest.   The Serbs had
about fifty thousand prisoners in the old fortress,
with insufficient guards, and more were coming in
all the time.   There was no food for them, and they
were going mad with starvation.   What he feared
was that they would overpower their guards and
deluge the town, looting, murdering, and burning.
As he talked, I got a vivid picture of what fifty
thousand haggard, ragged, freezing, starving men
would do if turned loose in that place.   I believe
with him that this could easily have happened, for
there were very many more prisoners than soldiers
in the place, and with the wild confusion that prevailed they would meet with little organized resistance.   Affairs certainly bore no pleasant aspect.
The phenomenally good behavior of the prisoners

of war will always remain something of a mystery to me.

Beside the tremendous number of prisoners, there were more refugees gathered at Prizrend than at any other place during the retreat. At last the stream, which had arisen in the north along the Save and the Danube and in the east along the Bulgarian frontier, and which had inundated the entire nation for two months, was dammed. The dam stretched away to north and south in a wild, beautiful tangle of shining peaks. When the refugees looked at the mountains ahead and heard the guns behind, they realized finally that Serbia was lost, abandoned to three strong invaders, betrayed by three strong allies. This was the general sentiment. I heard it continually from civilians, soldiers, officers, and government officials. "Why did not Russia come? Where are the French? Has England forgotten us?" These questions were so common as to become a sort of national threnody.

When I came, there were at least eighty thousand refugees here, with perhaps ten thousand more to come ahead of the moving armies. These hordes, combined with the fifty thousand prisoners, overwhelmed the little city. There was no food to be had for the masses. The Government was faced with three starving armies beside the one hundred and thirty thousand civilians and prisoners. In all that crowd I am sure not one had enough to eat, and thousands were facing actual starvation—thousands of women and children without any food, without any shelter at the close of November, and in the town congestion so great that contagious diseases were only a question of days.

I find myself wondering what Prizrend is like to-day. The refugees had to remain there. To cross the mountains was an impossibility for families of women and children without food. After two months of untold hardship, at last they had to sit here and starve until the enemy came, only hoping that he might bring food. If he was unable to do so, Prizrend is indescribable now. It is about fifty kilometers from the railway, and in winter the road is terrible. Only by ox-cart can food be brought in, and the armies operating in Albania must be provisioned. It was not a bright outlook for the refugees.

The streets of Prizrend are precipitous and tortuous, and down their whole length, from houses on each side, old grape-vines hang in graceful festoons, which in summer must cast the town in delicious shade. Now of course there was no foliage,

only the serpentine stems under the forlorn net-
work of which unnumbered thousands of starving,
homeless peasants fought their way about, filling
the streets with an unending stream day and night
that crushed against the houses and swirled in restless pools around each dirty square.   The red and
white fezzes and gorgeous bloomers of the Turks;
the Albanians, with their white skull-caps and great
flaming sashes; the tall Montenegrins, with their
gay jackets and tiny round hats; the people of the
Sanjak, with glaring, pirate-like turbans; the Serbian peasant women, with their vari-colored, brilliant stockings, multiform *opanki*, exquisitely embroidered short skirts and jackets, and bright
head-dresses; the Serbian men in their brown and
black homespun trousers, tight as to leg, volumi-
nous as to seat; French majors and colonels and
captains in dress uniform; English and Serbian
officers tarnished and business-like; gendarmes in
bright blue, with gold lace and braid; the royal
guard, with red breeches and sky-blue tunics; the
bluish gray of the Austrian prisoners; the grayish
green of the Bulgarians, the greenish yellow of the
Serbian soldiers—all flowed in barbaric masses of
color through the streets of Prizrend, like Prishtina,
but on a larger and more varied scale.   Such street-

scenes were one of the most remarkable aspects of
an invasion unique in many ways. In no other
circumstances could one ever see such a conglomera-
tion of races in a setting that is still medieval.

Up these streets in the dusk, playing havoc with
the crowds, luxurious French limousines, shining
American touring-cars, huge snorting motor-lorries
nosed their way. The life of a whole nation had
suddenly burst upon Prizrend, and everything was
confused, turned topsy-turvy, business destroyed,
and shops closed because, if opened, they were
wrecked by the crush of too eager customers. Only
the life of the harems moved on. The world might
go to smash, but the Turk had his larders full, his
money in gold, his own philosophy, and alone he
walked the streets unperturbed.

As night drew on, I stood in a little niche of the
old bridge's balustrade. Lights were sprinkling
the heights around the dark fortress, and the
river's surface below was spread with ruddy and
golden reflections from the latticed windows along
the quays. There was the usual heterogeneous
clamor of great crowds. Soldiers came toward the
bridge shouting in Serbian and pushing a way
through the throng. I was pushed hard against the
wall as they opened a way before them. They were

followed by some dim figures.   A hush came over us.   As the party came within the circle of light opposite me, I recognized for an instant the thin, keen features of King Peter.   It was a curious setting for a king, and brought to mind a fleeting memory of the German emperor reviewing his incomparable army on the plain near Mainz in 1913, a wonderful illustration, I thought, of cause and effect.   The crowd began to heave and squirm again, restless as before.

I had never happened to see the King before, but of course had heard and read the many wild conflicting tales about his checkered life—whispers of a young man's Bohemian existence in Paris around the Café du Helder before he dreamed of being a king; stories of a care-free life at Geneva not unmixed with plots; descriptions of him as an almost penurious, threadbare man in Petrograd, choosing the less-frequented streets to bring his children to and from their royal school, where royal favor permitted them to go.   These I remembered now, and wondered if he, too, were not lost in memories of beloved Paris, or feeling again the sweet breeze that on summer evenings sweeps in from Lake Leman, or walking with the young princes along the quiet streets of Petrograd.   Certainly his ex-

pression was one of brooding, and well it might be,
for this was his last day on the soil of his kingdom.
The following morning he plunged into Albania,
and before reaching Scutari had to be carried on the
backs of his soldiers.

Not one tenth of the refugees could get shelter
in the town. Broad camps stretched about the
place, filling the numerous Turkish cemeteries. A
Turkish cemetery is the most desolate thing in the
world. They plant their dead—and how innumerable their dead seem!—on any barren space that lies
near at hand, for they always live in the midst of
their departed. They stick up rough-hewn slabs
of stone, which seem never to fall completely, but
only to sag from the perpendicular, adding much to
the chaotic *ensemble*. Then they seem promptly
to forget the graves forever. In space of time
these sink, leaving depressions which, when the
wind is right, are partly sheltered by the gravestones. Filled with hay, they are not bad couches
—for a refugee. Now all about Prizrend in the
November dusk camp-fires burned brightly amid
the tipsy gravestones, and hundreds of inert forms
were stretched beside them on the grave. A weird
sight, those living cities of the dead, but only in
retrospection strange. For there is a point which

people sometimes reach when nothing is strange but peace and happiness, and nothing natural but the instinct to exist.   Prizrend's self-invited guests had reached it.

CHAPTER X

IN that future for which all Europe hopes, when stability and peace shall have come to the Balkans, Serbia will doubtless become a tourist's playground such as is the Midi or Switzerland. Then the road from Prizrend to Ipek will be as famous as the Corniche Road or the Brünig Pass. It winds along broad, fertile valleys, skirting the northern Albanian Alps. There are old and very beautiful arched stone bridges, carrying it across cañons of savage magnificence. The finest of these is the thin half-circle of masonry that marks the border between Montenegro and Serbia. At Jakova it breaks into narrow Eastern streets full of the yet unspoiled glamour of the Orient, and winds about the crumbling Turkish fortifications that loom upon the grassy plain like the battlements of Aigues-Mortes. Then it dips into the foot-hills, and leads after a time to the mouth of a deep and narrow valley two kilometers up which, surrounded by crag-tipped heights and dark forests of pines, is a large monastery with a fourteenth-century church, the interior of which is still covered with unrestored frescos of the period. Its final stage is straight over another plain to Ipek, lying at the foot of roadless mountains. The peaks that overshadow it are majestic as few mountains are, but to us who as refugees came that way, they spelled only hardship, and the road itself was very bad.

If we had known at Mitrovitze that the way to Monastir was cut, we should not have gone to Prizrend at all, but should have gone directly from Mitrovitze to Ipek, a distance of only twenty-five kilometers. As it was, the march to Prizrend had required four days, and now, reversing our direction, the march from there to Ipek would require two more, although on ordinary roads, in an automobile, it could be done in two hours. Thus five days' unnecessary march were made in describing the two legs of a triangle, the base of which lay on the line between Mitrovitze and Ipek. Having come to Prizrend, however, we chose the Ipek route to Scutari rather than the one across Albania, because the latter had been rendered exceedingly unsafe by the wild native tribesmen, who were rising everywhere and attacking all parties not strong enough to offer formidable resistance. Had the

King Peter of Serbia

Prizrend from the river bank

refugees at Prizrend wished to do so, they could
have made the additional two days' march to Ipek,
but comparatively few of them did.   Having been
driven to a realization of the hopelessness of their
situation, they decided that it was just as well to
starve at Prizrend as farther along.

The total absence of news or reliable information
of any sort, which had brought us so far out of our
way, was one of the striking things of the retreat.
Even the army was for the most part ignorant of
what was taking place at other points, so great was
the problem of communication in the general confusion.   There was a field wireless or two which did
good work interrupting German messages, and
couriers were riding this way and that, but the
rumors which came to the masses were of the wildest character and always of rosy burden—a half
million Russians through Rumania, a quarter million troops of the Allies from Saloniki, and the railway freed again.   We heard that Germany was
withdrawing her troops to protect her borders from
the French, who had driven them beyond the
Rhine.   No one believed these stories; all repeated
them with additions.

Always one moved blindly with the throng, itself
a blind leader, knowing nothing for certain except

the never-ceasing guns behind. The fortunate
people who came out early met little of this chaos,
and, arriving at Prizrend, made the journey to
Monastir before the cold set in, if not in comfort,
at least with a fair degree of safety. The members
of the American Sanitary Commission were able
to do this, as well as a good many Russian and
French nurses. Most of the English sisters arrived too late, and made the trip to Scutari either
through Albania or Montenegro. Those who came
out late saw the real retreat. The far more fortunate earlier ones heard only the distant rum-
blings.

Early in a foggy dawn we passed through the
streets of Prizrend, still crowded with the abnormal
life that all night had not ceased to stir, and got out
upon the road among those dreary graveyards, now
turned into huge bivouacs. Just outside the town
two automobiles passed us filled with queer, furry
creatures who were hardly recognizable as men.
Hung all over the cars were rucksacks, bales, and
bags, all tightly stuffed and quite obviously intended to be transported on pack-horses. Each
figure carried a rifle, which made him look like a
trained bear in a circus. Cheery French chatter
came to our ears as they passed, and, inquiring, we

learned that they were a party of aviators and mechanics starting on the Albanian road to Scutari. They would be able to go only a few kilometers in the cars, which they would then burn and take to pack-horses. The entire party would number about fifty, all well armed. I found myself wishing to be with them.

The march to Jakova was one of the longest we ever made in a single day. Part of the caravan, indeed, did not go all of the way, but camped by the roadside and came on the next morning. It was a beautiful day, full of sunshine, and cold enough to make walking a pleasure. Strange as it may seem, tramping was really becoming pleasant to many of the nurses. They were now experts at it. They had learned the steady gait that does not tire, and they found the deep sleep that is bought only by long hours of hard exercise. The sparkling air and savage mountains delighted them, and the knowledge that they were playing a part in the wildest drama even these old, romantic lands had ever known added much to their pleasure. So the hunger and cold and exhaustion, even the multiple tragedies around them were, to a degree, compensated for. "I should love to tramp forever and ever," they would say after a cold night in the open, when the warming dawn brought a nameless delight just because it was dawn and warm. We know they are heroines, but they would say they were merely happy tramps. Not only was the march to Jakova one of the finest because of the mountains that always watched over us, but its pleasure was undisturbed by many refugees. Few were traveling the road with us.

A good many soldiers were on the road, however, and our ambulance had an exciting episode with one of them. At Prizrend the car had been turned over to Mr. Boone, a fine English boy of scarcely eighteen who had come out with the Stobart unit and who, although ill most of the time, showed an unfailing cheerfulness and good humor that threw him into glaring contrast with most of his country-men whom it was my fate to meet in Serbia. If I had never seen any Englishmen except those who dumped themselves, or were dumped, on that un-happy land, I would conclude without difficulty that the percentage of the species we know as *men* among them is so small as to be negligible. For-tunately, it was possible to realize early that Serbia had been made the military and diplomatic scrap-heap of England and France, and that the specimens to be found there were no more to be taken as representatives of those two great nations than the contents of an ash-can can be held to be the true symbol of the mansion from which it comes. Wholesale criticisms are seldom in good taste and rarely true. If here and in other portions of this book the opinions expressed seem too sweeping, the only apology is that they never pretend to a wider experience than was actually the case, and are not founded on any personal opinion of what may or may not be wise or stupid, but are rather the outcome of an indignation aroused on occasions too numerous to enumerate. I speak of the unrestrained and oft-repeated expressions of mean, lying, and contemptible sentiments from men sent out to help Serbia. The wide-flung declaration of facts, obviously false, the cynical, egotistical criticisms of the nation which was dying through the fault of these critics' own nations; the ill-timed, vulgar, and abominable mouthings of persons whose business it was to fight and keep their mouths shut, but who showed no perceptible liking for doing either; and finally the cold heartlessness of an English journalist whose only apparent conception of a country's crucifixion seemed to be that it was

a God-sent opportunity for him to spread picturesque slanders, make it impossible for me to keep
such paragraphs as this out of my story.

In perhaps the widest circulated of our weeklies
an article appeared entitled "The Difficult Truth
about Serbia." It is a fine reading. About no
country, in my knowledge, is it more difficult to get
the truth. The truth about Serbia is, indeed, difficult to learn, but a pleasure in these days to tell.
It is a truth at which, in a stay of less than a month,
even the perspicacity of the woman journalist who
wrote the article could not hope to arrive. Filth
is no criterion by which to judge nations who have
faced what the Balkan nations have. It is like
criticizing Milton for the lack of a manicurist. To
say that of late years Serbia has had time to recover from the effects of centuries of degradation is,
through ignorance or design, to ignore many things.
With the easy grace characteristic of a certain type
of feminine mind the author of that article leaps
over the economic isolation of Serbia, the deadly
trade wars with Austria, soars over the most significant factors in the growth of nations, knocking
down not a single fact. You cannot learn a nation
in a week. You cannot measure the potentialities
of a people by their lack of smart *fiacres* or the

abundance of vermin in their inns any more than you can fairly revile them because, with world dramas on every side, as yet the cinematograph has failed to bring them the "Perils of Pauline." After a stay of a fortnight you cannot convincingly impugn the honor, kindness, pride, and hospitality of a people in whom for a generation English, American, French, and German travel-writers have praised these qualities almost without exception. When you attempt to do such things you become to the informed reader stupid or laughable, but to the unsuspecting millions pernicious.

The right to this opinion I do not base upon as intimate a knowledge as I could desire, but it is given on at least two months' extensive travel over the country and close association with all classes, on four additional months of "root-hog-or-die" existence with the soldiers of the line, with their officers, with their martyred wives and children, and finally on the illuminating sight of Serbia in the moment of her death, that moment which on the road to Ipek we were fast approaching. The Serb is not an angel, frequently he is not clean, but, thank Heaven! he is a *man*.

All of which is by way of digression. Boone was bounding along in the ambulance alone except for two wounded soldiers that he had picked up, and who, with the supplies he had to carry, were all the car would hold.   Some slight trouble forced him to stop, and before he could start again a Serbian petty officer, who had called to him in French a short time before, ordering him to stop, came up. He wasted no words, but harshly ordered Boone to give him a place in the car.   Boone refused to do this, showing him the wounded soldiers.   When he saw the soldiers, the young brute became furious, and ordered Boone to throw them out and to take him.   Boone again refused to obey the order. Then the officer drew his automatic and pressed it against Boone's temple, repeating the demand. Boone still refused to throw out the wounded men, but they had seen the situation, and of their own accord got out.   The officer then forced the English boy to get in and drive him on, holding the pistol to his head all the time.   Finally a tire blew out, much to Boone's relief, and as repairing it required some time the officer went away swearing.   Such incidents as this were inevitable at such a time. Examples of brutality are not lacking in any army anywhere.   When I read wild tales of Serbian soldiers having mutinied, murdered their officers, and looted the houses of their countrymen, I cannot but think they have their foundation in more or less isolated crimes. The splendid dignity, the great restraint, and the almost perfect behavior of the soldiers and civilians after their Government had crumbled caused frequent comment among the foreigners making the retreat. Had the gentleman who described Krushevats as dead drunk seen this episode, the world might have been treated to an account of how the Serbian officers in a delirium of fear turned on the Red Cross workers, and we at home would have believed it!

At about three in the afternoon those of us in the front party crossed over the bridge which marks the boundary between Serbia and Montenegro. It was dusk when we came to Jakova, and almost an hour later before we found a resting-place in a Turkish school-room. Jakova furnished a good illustration of the isolation that still exists in this region. Thirty kilometers away was the inferno of Prizrend. At Jakova, the day we arrived, one would not have known that there was such a thing as war. Silver money could be easily obtained, and food was for sale. Next morning I bought quantities of cigarettes, and because we had had no sugar for some time, a store of raisins and sticky "Turkish Delight." But with us came the first sign of the

deluge, and on the second day after we arrived
enough refugees and soldiers had come to give the
inhabitants a sense of uneasiness, so that when I
went out to shop on this day, I found conditions
much changed.   In vain I hunted for more "Turkish Delight" and cigarettes. They and nearly
every other article had disappeared.   I did not believe the stock had been sold out so quickly, and was
puzzled.

Finally in the window of a little shop I saw an
empty box that had without doubt contained the
coveted sweet.   I went in and directed the ancient
Turk's attention to it, mentioning divers moneys.
He shook his head stolidly.   I repeated the operation, although I was confident he had understood
the first time, but with no more success.   Then I
had an inspiration.   At college I had learned a
disgusting trick, which consisted of smacking the
lips and rubbing the stomach in unison, a perform-
ance that made up in buffoonery what it lacked in
elegance.   I now had recourse to this, nodding
meanwhile at the empty box.   At first the good
Moslem brother looked startled, as if I should not
be loose; then over the wrinkled, inscrutable pie-
plate that he called his face a grin flickered, and
diving into a back room, he brought half a dozen

boxes and sold them to me, thus proving that not everything learned at college is useless. The shop-keepers had begun to hoard, taking all tempting articles out of the sight of the soldiers, who might not prove overscrupulous about a little raid.

I continued my search for cigarettes. There were any number of tobacco shops where on the previous day these could be had, but now nothing but smoking tobacco of a very inferior grade was for sale. I could think of no vaudeville stunt calculated to soften the dealers' hearts. Disconsolately I looked into a tobacco-shop window when a Turkish gamin of ten came by, puffing a cigarette as large as his two fingers. He stopped and looked at me as I looked at the empty window. I patted him on the head, told him in English he should not use tobacco, pointed to his cigarette, and held up five *dinars*. He promptly led me around a corner, winked, and disappeared. Soon he was back with two hundred excellent cigarettes. I pocketed them, and held up five more dinars. Again I received two hundred, and he pocketed the ten dinars. My conscience now suggests that in the evening when papa Turk came home to his harem, he may have worn out an embroidered velvet slipper caressing the anatomy of my sly friend, but I wager he saw nothing of the ten dinars. *Dans la guerre comme dans la guerre!*

At Jakova I sold one pair of the oxen I had bought about six weeks before at Alexandrovats. They had come all that distance through terrible hardships and were much weakened; but I received thirty dinars more than I had paid for them, and I sold them to a Turk! All things considered, it was the greatest financial stroke I ever performed. One day's journey away was Ipek, where all the oxen would have to be abandoned. There a few days later I gave the other and larger pair to Ticho-mir, who sold them for eighty dinars. Our noble chariot was burned to warm his lazy limbs.

We left Jakova in the beginning of our second snow-storm; but it was not so cold as on the Plain of Kossovo, and there was no wind. Also the way was not so encumbered with refugees, though full of the army. The fall was exceedingly heavy, and delayed us some, so that it was nearly dark when we turned up the cañon to seek refuge in the monastery where Dr. Čurčin had made arrangements for the unit to stay, the journey on to Ipek requiring only about three hours. For thirty minutes we fol-lowed a makeshift road between ever-heightening mountains. The creaking and rumbling of our

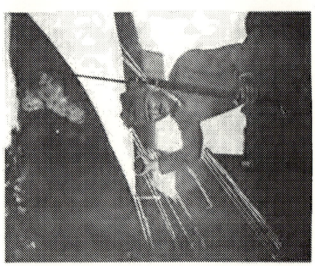

Soldiers of Serbia

In 1912 they gave up comfortable homes in America to fight for the freedom of the southern Slav

carts was the only sound in the snow-laden forest. Far ahead we saw the great building, with hundreds of ruddy windows sending rays of light down the valley. It looked cheerful enough, and even had something of a festive air, which made me suddenly remember that it was Thanksgiving day. Being the only American in the party, I had quite forgotten this occasion. When we floundered up to it, we found the great quadrangular building as white as an Eskimo hut, and entering by a high arched portal we plowed about the extensive courtyard, deep in great snow-drifts. On the eastern side of the court stood the ancient church, streaming light from the windows illuminating in patches its rich façade of colored marbles, while the numerous gargoyles in the shadows above had become terrible pale shapes that grinned and writhed, strained and snarled, in the gathering night.

No doubt they have seen many strange sights, these odd, old creatures, which were white with the whiteness of new marble when the Serbia of ancient days was ground to death under the Turkish heel, from which the rest of Europe had only with great difficulty been delivered by a valiant Pole under the very walls of Vienna. They had looked on while for five centuries a race, persecuted with every conceivable form of atrocity and oppression, had kept alive the dream of the Southern Slav, and in times so recent that to them it must have seemed but yesterday they saw that dream come to flower in a little nation which, whatever its faults, is certainly as brave and as unfortunate as any nation ever was.   Four years ago they saw it redeem a large stretch of territory from its ancient enemy, and then, bullied by a treacherous ally, turn and inflict a stinging defeat upon her.   They saw this new-born nation live through those breathless days of 1914, when the whole world watched her.   They saw her confronted with demands more humiliating than any free nation had ever been called upon to accept, and they saw her make broader concessions than any free nation had ever done before, but to no purpose.   Then they saw her invaded by an army three times the strength of her own, they saw her desperate and suddenly, before the world realized, gloriously victorious under General Mishich's brilliant leadership, but wounded and exhausted, so that disease and famine spread over her for six months, creating a situation terrible enough to call the whole friendly and neutral world to her aid.   That Thanksgiving night they were witnessing the passing of a shattered, starving army, the plight of a hopeless, starving people, and now without doubt Bulgarian officers pass to and fro beneath them.

It seems impossible for one who saw it to speak or write coldly about this period of the retreat.   It was the death moment.   After it the flight over the mountains seemed merely the instinctive departure of men who for the most part did not care whether they lived or died.   Two or three days later all three armies would be in Ipek, except several thousand who already had gone into Albania from Prizrend.   The road having been cut, part of the second army was coming across country, without any roads at all, over frozen plains and snow-covered hills, fording icy streams every few miles, dragging their cannon and ammunition with them.   The three field commanders would soon hold their council in Ipek.   King Peter, the crown prince, General Putnik, and the general staff were already on their way to Scutari.   The Allies had failed her; Serbia was lost.

Throughout the long night carts struggled up to the monastery, and men bearing stretchers filed in. They carried Serbian officers, many wounded, some dead from cold and the cruel exhaustion of the carts.   All night long the queer monastery boys, in their tight, bright-red trousers and abbreviated blue jackets, ran up and down the long corridors with flaring lights, while the brown, silent monks stole to and fro. There were cries and groans and curses, and every hour chimes in the old tower. It was bitter cold. A more grotesque night I never expect to spend.

No, one cannot write calmly of Ipek then. No matter where one's sympathies may lie in this war that has divided the world, if one knows patriotism and has any admiration for pure grit, that last camp of the Serbian army, already on foreign soil, could call forth nothing but the deepest feeling.

We came to Ipek after two days' delay at the monastery, which allowed the weaker of the party to regain a little of their strength. It was a great question at this time whether we should ever get to Ipek, or, at any rate, out of it, before the Germans came. Mitrovitze had been in their hands for several days, and Mitrovitze was distant only twenty-five kilometers. A part of this way the invaders had already come, and we did not know whether they would be opposed by the Serbs or not. But it is not easy to arrange quickly at such a time for a party of forty women and the necessary attendants, guides, guards, and food to cross the mountains of

Montenegro.   Dr. Čurčin and some Serbs had gone ahead to make such arrangements as were possible.

On the second day we started for the town.   As soon as we reached the cañon's mouth and turned into the main road, the coldest wind I had ever felt struck us full in the face as it swept off the bleak, Alpine peaks behind Ipek and raced unbroken across the icy plain.   In crossing this plain we undoubtedly suffered more bitterly from the cold than anywhere else on the whole retreat.   Nor was it cheerful to think that, if we were freezing on this plain, what would happen when we took the two-foot trail across the summits of those mountains, now so blinding in the bright sunshine that we could scarcely look at them.   I could see great clouds of driven snow swirling around those lofty ice-fields, just as on any clear day they may be seen blurring the summit of Mont Blanc and showing the violence of the gales.   Perhaps it was foolish, certainly it was no compliment to the oncoming Teutons, that in a choice between them and the cruel desolation of those vast, trackless wastes the women of England unanimously chose the latter.   But I do not think it was really fear of the invader at all.   In the first place, as far as we could learn, there had been no reason to fear the Teutonic invaders in Serbia.   I

say as far as we could learn, for we were ahead of
the army, and hence would naturally not come in
contact with atrocities, if any had been committed.
But according to Admiral Troubridge, Colonel
Phillips, and Serbians with whom I talked, they
had no reason to believe that the Germans were not
following a humane policy in Serbia.   We heard
that on entering Belgrade—what was left of Belgrade—they sealed the houses which had been left
intact, and disturbed nothing except to take all the
brass, copper, and bronze which they found.   Since
coming out of Serbia I have heard many seemingly
authentic stories of barbarities committed there by
the Teutons and by the Bulgarians, but from personal experience I know only what I have stated.

I think it was the strong aversion the nurses felt
at the possibility of having to nurse back to fitness
for the trenches the men whom their fathers and
brothers were fighting that was the deciding factor
in their decision to go over the mountains.   To see
any live thing suffering made these women almost
wild unless they could do something to relieve it;
and then it seemed to me that they were rather
jubilant, their professional feeling drowning everything else.   A prisoner never failed to draw sympathy from them, but when it came to being pris-

oners themselves and nursing men who would be
sent back to fight—well, the unknown, icy trails
were preferable, even though they were ragged and
starved, footsore and weary.

The wind that nearly took us off our feet and
whistled through our clothing, chilling us to the
bone, also removed the light layer of feathery snow
that lay under foot, and uncovered a solid expanse
of slippery ice on which every moment animals and
people lost their balance and fell heavily. It was
like a skating-lesson. At times it was impossible
to move at all against the wind with such insecure
footing, and many ox-carts stood immovable in the
road, with both oxen vainly trying to rise.

In the sheltered cañon we had met wild, little
Gipsy boys who did a brisk trade in wormy apples
about the size of lemons, wormy chestnuts, and
hard, green, little pears. Lead a precarious existence out of tin cans for weeks, and see if you would
not welcome such fruit as this. We did abundantly. But those pears were dum-dum bullets.
They raised all their mischief inside, and, combined
with many a chill among us, was many a stomach-
ache of the real, near-fatal, small-boy variety. At
last with eyes that smarted and wept under freezing slaps of the wind, we saw Ipek splotching the

826 WITH SERBIA INTO EXILE

arid, white waste at the base of the mountains, a straggling, irregular, crimson-and-yellow blot on the snow. It looked as if a Titan had dropped a titanic tomato of titanic over-ripeness. I do not love Ipek, but I shall be dust and ashes before I forget it.

Of course we did not have so many refugees to make life terrible, but here it was the army that took the star rôle in our masque of horror. There were just enough civilians to make the town really congested. Around it on the ice and snow the army camped, or, rather, lay down in the frosty open, nursed its wounded, and took stock of its dead. When I saw the Serbian soldiers at Ipek I said to myself that I had seen the hardiest men on earth reduced to the furthest limit of their endurance. Again, like the quick-trip journalists, I was very ignorant and foolish. Had a pressing contract to write up the court etiquette of Timbuctoo in 1776 called me hurriedly away at the moment, in all good faith I would have cabled any newspaper that had been unfortunate enough to retain me that the Serbian army had reached the end of its rope, was merely scratching around in the snows of Ipek for a place in which to die, and would never get ten miles over the mountains toward Scutari. I might

The army that cannot die
Starving soldiers pouring into Ipek

have padded this information with more or less veracious details of hungry soldiers eating live oxen on the half-shell, and fastidious officers living on consommé made from expensive Russian boots, and in all probability I would have established myself as an authority on Serbia.

As a matter of fact, two war correspondents, one English and one American, did find time and inspiration to make part of the retreat. They took the route through Albania to Scutari and thence to Rome. They were the first two; I happened to be the third curiosity to arrive in the Eternal City from the great retreat. As such, Ambassador Page questioned me extensively, with his habitual Southern courtesy. Among other things, he asked how many Serbian soldiers came through. When I replied, not less than one hundred thousand, he laughed politely, but very heartily. It was impossible; it could not be; besides, the two eminent correspondents differed radically from me. One said about thirty, and the other about forty thousand, had escaped. Mr. Page was inclined to split the difference at thirty-five thousand. Last week His Highness Alexander, Prince Regent, announced that one hundred and fifty thousand Serbs were now completely reorganized, reëquipped, and suffi-

ciently rested to fight again on any battle-field.
Sixteen thousand of these came out by way of Saloniki, the rest through Albania and Montenegro.
So much for the quick-fire reporters. Despite
their manifest shortcomings, what would we do
without them?

The army that huddled around the cheerless
town of Ipek really did not seem to have enough
reserve strength to make any further exertion. I
knew, as I looked at the drab, bedraggled groups
clustering about fires that their transport-wagons
fed, that these men were doomed to death or capture at Ipek. Three weeks later, watching the
same men crawl into Scutari, I knew that I had
been mistaken previously, but that, unless Scutari
was safe for months and ample food and clothing
came, they would die or surrender there. Further
mountain retreating for that mechanical mass,
scarcely instinct with life, was impossible. Again
I would have cabled lies to my paper. I was ignorant again. They did not get rest at Scutari nor at
San Giovanni di Medua, but they made the indescribable march to Durazzo on rations that were
criminally short, hundreds and hundreds perishing
by the roadside, and then they fell into boats, and
only on the islands of the Adriatic and in southern

Italy did they find food and rest. Now, after scarcely two months, comes the amazing announcement that they are ready and eager for the battle again! Such were the men I saw evacuating the hospitals, such were the men I saw crowding the long refugee-trains in indescribable discomfort, such were the men I saw, wounded and bleeding, tramping the muddy roads through the wilderness; such were they whom I saw freezing and starving around Ipek, who died by the hundreds there and by the thousands in the mountains; such were they who, when they could have surrendered with betterment to themselves, and dishonor for their country, did not, but made a retreat as brave and as glorious as any victory of this or any other war—a retreat that dims the flight from Moscow in suffering. Such is the Serbian army, the army that cannot die.

The economic life of Ipek was interesting. Splendid oxen could be bought here for ten or fifteen dollars a pair, their former price being about one hundred and twenty-five dollars. The food situation was acute, but not so bad as at Prizrend. However, the supply, such as it was, was purely temporary, and before I left had been completely exhausted. The price of boots was a phenomenon.

Since the first day of the retreat footgear had sold at constantly increasing prices, until the amount paid for a pair of boots was fabulous, amounting to sixty or seventy dollars. In the streets of Ipek there were quantities of excellent Russian boots for sale at four or five dollars, the normal price of these in Serbia being about twenty dollars. Government magazines had been thrown open to the soldiers, and many of those who happened to be more or less decently shod preferred to sell. So the bottom dropped out of the boot market. Bread, however, was at the same famine prices that had prevailed before. I saw a pound loaf sell for eight dollars.

The council between the three generals was on. All communication with the General Staff was cut off. It devolved upon the field-commanders to decide upon the final abandonment of Serbia. Their conference lasted two days, and, according to all reports, was stormy. General Mishich was for an offensive even at that date. With those emaciated regiments out there in the frozen fields, killing their transport-beasts for food, burning their transport-wagons for fuel, and having enough of neither, with most of his ammunition gone, together with a great part of the very insufficient artillery which the army had possessed, he still felt that there was a chance,

and that is all that is necessary for the Serbian soldier. They are not fools, they do not die need-
lessly, as the Montenegrins are popularly reported
to do, but if there is a chance life counts nothing to
them. During the months that I lived with them,
slept with them on the ground, ate their bread, saw
their battle-lines, I learned this beyond all else.
Soldier for soldier, I believe them to be the best
fighters in the world. Most soldiers are brave
men; the Serb is also a marvelous stoic, a rare op-
timist, and built of steel. But the odds there were
too great. The other two generals favored the
course which was carried out with a very remarkable degree of success—a general retreat through the
mountains with as many of the smaller guns and as
much ammunition as possible. So the evacuation
of Ipek was announced.

The next morning loud explosions were heard at
one end of the town. The purchase of horses was
keeping us in Ipek, and I found myself with nothing to do, so, with my camera, I wandered toward
the explosions. At the edge of the town, where the
highway that was a skating-rink led out, a lot of
field-guns were finishing their short, but checkered,
career. They were just about obsolete and worn
out, anyway. Fate had not been very kind to them,

and few vacations had been theirs since, new and efficient, they had been turned on the Turks in 1912 with a result too well-known to recall. In 1913 they had been reversed, and had spoken successfully the Serbs' opinion of the Bulgarians. In 1914 they blew Austria's cumbersome legions to shreds, and stuck up a "Keep off" sign over Serbia that Austria did not feel justified in disregarding until Germany and Bulgaria could aid her. After that they had been dragged and carried the length of Old Serbia until fate had concentrated them in groups of two or three along the Ipek road.

The men who were smashing their breeches or blowing up their carriages looked as if they hated themselves. The army lined the road to watch. The only sounds were the ringing sledges and the detonations of the explosions. As I photographed some of those yet untouched, it came to me rather forcibly that this was the first time I had ever seen Serbian soldiers work without laughter and song.

A gunner whose gun I had photographed came up to me and in broken German asked if I would send him a photograph. I took out my note-book and pencil and told him to write his address. He hesitated. He had forgotten something; he had no address any more. He had nothing but that gun,

which he had worked since 1912. In a few minutes
he would not have that. We could hear plainly the
enemy fighting with the rear-guard out toward
Mitrovitze. The man began to curse, and war was
the object of his curses. Again I was forcibly impressed; it was the first time I had ever heard a
Serb curse war, though all had lamented it. Also
for the first time I was seeing a Serbian man weep.
I could hardly believe it. Standing there with his
back to the mountains and his face turned toward
the enemy, shaking with the cold, the man, for a
Serb, went to pieces: four tears rolled down his
cheeks. Turning to me, he said, "America *dobra,
dobra, dobra, dobra*" ("America good, good, good,
good"). Then they came and knocked his gun to
pieces. Most forcibly of all there came to me the
conception of a new sort of value in artillery—a
value that is not strictly military, nor particularly
effected by the model or life of a gun.

In Ipek there were many automobiles—motor-
lorries, limousines, and touring-cars. They were
drawn up around the public squares in imposing
rows. Apparently from habit the chauffeurs pot-
tered about them, polishing the plate-glass and
nickel and cleaning the engines. But when evacuation was announced they drove a little way out of

the town. Some of them had brought hand-grenades, and leaving the engines running, they lifted up the hoods, struck the percussion-caps of the bombs, which they dropped beside the cylinders, and then ran. A Serbian grenade explodes in from seven to ten seconds after the cap is struck, so that one could not get very far before the racing motor was blown to scrap-iron. Fire usually consumed the body. Other chauffeurs saturated their cars with petrol and set them on fire. In the case of limousines this was spectacular. With all the upholstery soaked well with benzine, and everything closed tight except a small crack in one window through which the match was thrown, the luxurious cars became roaring furnaces for a minute, and then literally exploded into glorious bonfires. But these methods were as nothing compared with what one chauffeur conceived and, by setting the fashion, brought several others to adopt. The man who thought about it ought not to be a chauffeur at all; he ought to be at the head of a cinematograph company.

The mountain horse-trail does not begin in Ipek itself, but is approached by three or four kilometers of regular road, which at a rightangular turn shrinks into the two-foot trail. At this point it is cut in the side of a sheer cliff three or four hundred feet above a little stream. There is no balustrade; the earth simply ends, and space begins. Having arrived at this point, to step out of the car, let in the clutch, and push down the accelerator was less dangerous than the grenade, easier, quicker and far more exciting than the fire. It was a great game. There was a long gray Cadillac that took the brink like a trained hunter, leaping far out over the edge. As its power was suddenly released from the friction of the road, the car roared and trembled like a live animal during the infinitesimal instant that it hung upright, held by its own momentum. Then the motor dragged its nose downward as true as an arrow until it struck the steep slope, down which it did quick somersaults, the tires bursting with bangs that could be heard above the crash. Before it had rolled into the stream it became a ball of fire. A ponderous Benz limousine followed, and tucked its nose into the slope without a spectacular leap. It was like a fat old lady falling down-stairs. Its tires blew out, and its body came loose from the chassis, both running a race to the river. An expensive-looking Fiat behaved much in the manner of the Cadillac, and was followed by a large French motor-lorry, which plowed a terri-

ble path down the cliff, pretty well giving knock
for knock, and finally grinding to splinters the
wreckage on which it hit at the bottom. Others
followed, each taking the leap in an individual manner. Sometimes they flew almost to bits. The
tires invariably blew out with loud reports. Since
it had to be done, one did wish for every small boy
in America to watch it. I think the chauffeurs
who burned or blew up their cars were sorry.

It is doubtless permissible to add that one very
famous and very cheap American car made the
leap. It had up good speed and its well-known
characteristic of lightness sent it far beyond the
brink, where it floated four hundred feet above the
river. It acted quite as if it wanted to fly, and with
a little encouragement and experience might have
sailed on over the mountain-tops, headed for Detroit. But once started on its downward course,
it gyrated with incredible swiftness, quite as fast
as its wheels had ever turned, and, bouncing on the
river-bank, flew beyond the other cars, swam the
stream, and came to an eternal resting-place on the
farther side. It was just the sort of a stunt one
would expect from a nervy little thing like that!

Buying horses at Ipek was a difficult gamble.
By the time we arrived, the horse-market had been

thoroughly picked over, and everything that could be mistaken for a real horse had already been taken through the mountains. After three days' strenuous search, one horse for every two members of the unit was procured. They were miserable, weak animals, with large sores on their backs and discouragement enshrouding them like a cloak. It took a lot of will power to put the rough, wooden pack-saddles on those raw backs and to load them down with what to a regular pony would have been feather-weights.

You may be wondering what there was to carry. The largest item in our outfit was our bedding. Every person had not fewer than three heavy, woolen army blankets, and most of the women had twice as many; but six were frequently insufficient. Then there was the irreducible minimum of luggage which the nurses had to carry. This was usually rolled up in the blankets, and a piece of rubber sheeting tied over the outside as a protection from the rain and snow. Fortunately, the unit had evacuated Kragujevats with large quantities of rubber sheeting. Had it not been so, they would oftener than not have slept in soaked blankets. We gathered together three days' rations, consisting of two loaves of bread, tea, coffee, and a little bit

of sugar, a can of Oxo, and two small tins of condensed milk, for each person. Every one was supposed to see to the carrying of his own provisions.
In addition, there was a community cheese, a
glorious cheese, three pounds of oleomargarine, a
few tins of bully-beef, and a little extra milk. The
remainder of the stores, which had been carefully
hoarded because none knew what lay ahead, we
could not take with us, and gave away. We had
been told it was three days to Androvitze, and we
believed it. At Androvitze a wagon-road led to
Scutari. There were rumors of Montenegrin
autos awaiting us there. Thus our provisions
would be sufficient, we thought. It was little
enough for a party of fifty to start off with on a
journey through the most barren part of barren
Montenegro. We thought to find provisions of
some sort at Androvitze. For fifteen days, however, we had to live on the country, never having the
slightest idea where our next meal was coming
from, but frequently knowing that it would not
come at all.

Light as our possessions were, when we came to
pack the horses, they seemed endless. The giant
Montenegrin whom we had retained as a guide,
Nikola Pavlovitch, was the only pack-horse expert

A Serbian gun just before it was blown up at Ipek

among our men, and he could not pack twenty horses. Packing a horse properly is far more difficult than higher mathematics. To begin with, it requires a born diplomat to persuade the owner of the pack to throw away half of his belongings before the packing is begun, and half of the residue after the first tumble. In the second place, one must be an animal-trainer to conquer those mountain ponies; third, only a juggler with a wire-walking instinct of balance and with a stock of patience such as would make Job look like an irascible editor, is adequate for this work. There is no such thing as perfection in the art. A perfect pack is a purely hypothetical joy. It is an intangible, spiritual ideal to the outer court of whose sanctuary Nikola approached, while the rest of us floundered in pagan darkness. I say "us," because I determined to pack Rosinante myself. Rosinante was a horse I had bought; more about her later. After two hours I turned out a job that stopped Nikola, passing by, and made him exclaim in horror. He acted as if I had blasphemed the cult of horse-packing by what, to me, looked like a masterpiece of cunning and ingenuity. Nikola was wise. He did not argue; he said nothing. He simply seized the bridal and led Rosinante at a fast walk for ten yards. Then Rosinante found herself in what she must have felt to be an exceedingly undignified and embarrassing position. She was low and short; the pack, as I had created it, was high and bulky. When it neatly slipped under her belly she was pivoted on it, her toes—she had toes I know, or later she could not have done all she did—barely touching the ground. Nikola started to untie my pack, but grew faint before the maze of knots, and slashed the ropes. In ten minutes he had my stuff and some more besides on Rosinante, and his pack was perhaps a third as large as mine. Nikola was severely classic in his pack building. I fear mine leaned—leaned is the right word—toward the most flamboyant of Gothic creations.

I am going to detail the costume which I finally assumed at Ipek. Not because it was typical, but because it was not. Despite the fact that some of the nurses, after considering the peaks before them and the general uselessness of skirts, discarded the latter in place of jackets and trousers which they themselves had fashioned from red, brown, and gray blankets, despite the well-known eccentricities of Albanian and Montenegrin tailoring, I boldly lay claim to being quite the oddest creature in the Balkans at that moment. Since September the iron hand of circumstance had been impelling me toward this consummation. I had come out prepared only for the summer. It was now emphatically winter, and what I had brought from New York in June seemed grotesque at Ipek in December. It had not been possible to buy. I had had to forage, plucking my fig-leaves where I might. I claimed the distinction of originating the practice of wearing "Porosknit" during the Ipek winter season. It was a case of greatness thrust upon me. As for hosiery, my wardrobe contained at this date one pair of green silk socks. These I put upon my feet, and over them a pair of amorphous gray things that all too plainly had been knitted at the opera for some defenseless refugee. I thought this would do, but when I had to buy a pair of high boots three sizes too large, I saw it would not. I went into the town and secured two pairs of real Montenegrin socks. They were hand-knit of thick snow-white wool. One pair was sprinkled with embroidered red roses and green leaves. The other had a mountain-scene, with lakes, forests, rivers, and snowy peaks, very striking, if not convincing. The design was not the same on any two socks, and as I wore both pairs to fill up the boots, this was a convenience: I did not have to worry to match them.   I still had some trousers.   In the deeps of my bag, secretly hidden away against the day when I should be compelled to plunge once more into civilization, was a pair of vivid-blue summer trousers from a Broadway tailor.   They were old, but dear to my heart, and would, if cherished, I thought, serve very well in the first moment of reappearance into the world. I could not cherish them longer.   I put them on, and the combination with the socks was such that I was in a hurry to get on my boots.   First, however, I concealed their vivid blue under a pair of English refugee trousers.   These were the remnants of the suit which the ox had butchered weeks before.   They were made of brown paper-thread reinforced with stiff clay.   Over them I placed a third pair of trousers, stout, but stained, khaki, the product of a degenerate tailor in Athens.

I had only flimsy brown shirts meant for the warm weather, but I received as a gift a lovely garment of heavy gray flannel.   It was a lady's shirt, perpetrated by school-girls in some neutral land for what must have been their ideal of the fattest woman in the world.   In the neck they had allowed for ample room.   When I buttoned it, it fell away as gracefully as a hangman's-noose.   I could easily have crawled right out through the neck of the shirt. Décolleté was not *en regle* then, so I gathered the collar up like the mouth of a meal-sack and secured it with a safety-pin. This curious rosette-like bunch out of which my head emerged was all of the shirt that appeared to a cruel world, for I wore two sweaters. The first, counted from inward outward, was of white near-wool, cut like a Jersey, with no collar. The second was a heavy gray woolen coat sweater of excellent quality, but distressingly ragged.

One more touch was added to my costume before I put on the nondescript gift-coat mentioned before. Remember it was cold in Ipek, and every one knew the temperature there would not be a circumstance to what it would be on the mountain-top. In the general ransacking that preceded the transfer from carts to pack-horses, the nurses unearthed many things, some of which were showered upon me. I had four "cholera-belts." These are broad knitted bands of wool with clasps at the ends, and are intended to be fastened securely around the abdomen. They were the easiest things to take off or put on as the temperature required, so I wore them on the outside. One was deep lavender, one was orange, one was coral pink, and one was green.

I buttoned the orange one under my arms, then the others followed, overlapping one another, the lavender one being drawn about the hips like the scarfs that Spanish dancers affect. They gave me the torso of a brilliant segmented bug. At last came the coat, which flapped about my knees and enveloped my hands in long and shapeless sleeves. It had been a nice coat, it was a gift coat; never look a gift-coat in the lining.

Drawn over my head I wore a gray, crocheted "slumber-helmet." This is an affair much on the order of an aviator's cap or a medieval hood of mail. It was splendid for the ears and, in conjunction with the meal-sack shirt, kept the throat very warm. On top of it I wore my broad-brimmed felt cow-boy hat, tied with shoestrings to the back of my head. By the time I had dressed on the morning of our departure I was dizzy with trying to remember what I had on, and as for realizing just what I looked like, it was impossible. After one glance, an Irish nurse enlightened me. For the first and only time I saw her perplexed; but only for an instant did she study me as if trying to remember something.

"Oh, I know," she said; "you look like a piece of French pastry with a nut on top."

Nineteen days later, in that identical costume, but a good deal the worse for wear, my landscape socks peeping out through my toeless boots, and a four-weeks' growth on my face, I drove up one Sunday morning to a gilded Roman hotel in the Via Ludovise, and, unflinchingly stepping out of my *fiacre*, faced the obsequious liveried staff. I have not been decorated for it, but that is no proof that I do not deserve it.

In the end the horses were packed, and about nine o'clock in the morning of December first, under an entirely cloudless sky, we began to worm our way through the crowded town. Several packs were scraped off in the crush, and these delayed us almost an hour; but in the outskirts the crowd lessened and, dropping into the single-file order of march that we were to follow for many days, we passed out on the ice-covered road that led to our mountain-trail. In the edge of the town whom should I meet but the daring Peter? He embraced me with emotion, remarked apropos of nothing at all that he considered me a wonderful chauffeur, and struck me for another napoleon, if not in the same breath, at any rate with a swiftness that took mine.

. Soon we passed the place where the automobiles

had gone over, the nurses wondering at the twisted wrecks below. They were to get used to twisted wrecks in the next few days—wrecks of pack-trains dotted with human bodies. At the beginning of the trail we faced about due west up the profound crag-shadowed valley of the Lim, a rushing mountain torrent that filled the whole cañon with sound, so that it was difficult to speak. The trail led under overhanging walls of rock a thousand feet high, and beyond, through a vista of pines and gray *aiguilles,* were the high mountains in gleaming, receding ranks. There, faintly above the voice of the Lim, came the voice of the big guns. We did not know it, but we were hearing them for the last time. An hour later they came to us no longer. Those women might freeze, they might starve, bandits might get them, they might even tumble over a precipice, but they had outdistanced the Teutonic thunder.

CHAPTER· XI

OVER THE MOUNTAINS

WHEN we left the sound of the German battle-line on the Montenegrin trail it was just about six weeks since I had evacuated Valjevo with the Christitch party. Then the German army had been a good twenty or twenty-five kilometers away. In these six weeks they had fought their way through Serbia under a continual rain that turned such roads as the country possessed into ribbons of swamp worse than the fields and mountains through which they ran. With the aid of no railway, they had had to provision their troops almost entirely from Austria. They had marched through densely wooded hills and through barren mountain-passes, constructing bridges as they went. In the last part of the march they had faced terrific winter. We had marched ahead of them. There was nothing in particular detaining us except necessary rest for the weaker. Our business was to get away. After six weeks the German army had gained ten or fifteen kilometers on us. They were not farther than that

351

from Ipek. The secret of this rapid advance was superior artillery and aëroplanes. They stood safely out of range, and accurately knocked the Serbian positions to pieces. We thought, however, that the mountains would hold them for a while, and when they did come into Montenegro, it would be from Prijepolje in the north and Cattaro on the coast.

In choosing the mountains rather than the Germans, the nurses undoubtedly made as great a gamble as they ever will, no matter how near the front they go, and all were determined to go back to war as soon as they were reëquipped. They were gambling on the weather in December, on the mountains of Montenegro. If the weather remained as it was that morning, all had excellent chances of coming through. If a blizzard like the one we had faced coming into Ipek or the snowstorm we had weathered on the "Field of Blackbirds" caught them on the high precipices, only the very strongest of them had any chance, and that was very meager. It is hard to realize just how deserted and wild those mountains are, and just how slender, makeshift, and primitive are the communications between Ipek and Androvitze. Only at long intervals on the trail are there places where it is even possible to lie down. The precipices are on the one hand, the steep mountain-side out of which the path has been cut on the other. Sometimes there are trees on this slope, but frequently not. When we went over, two or three feet of snow covered the ground. It would have been utterly impossible to make a camp along the higher parts of that trail. It would have been equally impossible to go ahead on the path that was like polished glass. We could not have had a fire. The horses would certainly have fallen over the cliffs, our food would have been lost, and those who did not freeze would have starved. Strong Montenegrins might have come through it; those weakened English women would have little chance. For three days this gamble lasted. The weather we had was remarkable for that season, almost unprecedented. Had nature been in a different mood, there is no doubt at all that England would have mourned the death of all those women in a single day. Everybody appreciated the chance keenly, consequently no one mentioned it until we arrived at Androvitze. Then they looked back at the upheaved barrier which they had crossed and unanimously shuddered. "Good heavens! if winter had caught us there!" they said.

There are two routes from Ipek to Androvitze. The one we took is supposed to be shorter, steeper, and more dangerous. We took it on the advice of Nikola, for everybody else in the place said that, ice-covered as it was, it would be impassable, and many who had started that way had turned back. It is the path by way of Chakar. The other trail was being used by the army and refugees. That is why Nikola advised the shorter one for us. He was undoubtedly right. He said he would guarantee it was not impassable and where there was a great deal of danger he would lead the horses across one by one. Nikola had his nerve. He went ahead as a scout, and chose our stopping-places for the night. In the mountains he was invaluable.

A small party of nurses, including the three who had formerly been with me, accompanied by two Englishmen and some attendants, left Ipek a day earlier than we, but by the army route. They had a horrible time. On one occasion they tramped from six o'clock in the morning until two o'clock the next morning in search of shelter, and finally shared an old shed crowded with soldiers, who had built a fire. Had they stopped sooner they would have frozen to death. One of these women was well past middle age. Such things as this by such

The beginning of the mountain trail above Ipek

The two women are Russian nurses

women are not done by physical strength, but by an indomitable sporting will power. Under such conditions it is vastly easier to lie down and die.

Some French, Russian, and Norwegian nurses also faced these ordeals, but in general suffered less, I think, because they came through earlier. There were four Norwegian girls with us. The mountains were home to them, and they invariably led the pack. Only Nikola could outdistance them. They looked and felt their best climbing up or racing down steep places.

Those who took the army route saw sights more terrible than those we saw. With us mainly it was pack-horses that we looked down on, dashed to death at the foot of the precipices. The other route was full of human wreckage, with officers, soldiers, artillery, and horses jumbled together in the gorges below them, and dead refugees lying on the slopes above them. We met numerous wounded soldiers, stragglers, hardy mountain refugees, and military couriers. There were not enough to inconvenience us. We had that forbidding trail pretty much to ourselves. Trusting to Nikola, we clung to the icy thread that led always to wilder and more remote mountain refuges.

Whatever might lie before us, we considered the

present hour, and found it good as we followed the gradually ascending path that was now hunting determinedly for a way out of the gorge in order to run along the ridges above. The sun continued to beat down on us, and the snow melted a bit, ameliorating the aggravating slipperiness of our path. The exertion of climbing warmed us up, too, so that I began to regret the thoroughness with which I had dressed. At the top of a specially steep climb I stopped to wait for a group of the nurses toiling up behind me. They were part of the Irish contingent, and scrambled up the slippery incline with true Gaelic abhorrence. They had on heavy coats and sweaters and knitted hoods and thick mitts, so that all I could see of the real Irish was a small patch of face. Blowing and puffing, the foremost, and the most insuppressible, reached the top. Under her woolen helmet her forehead streamed with perspiration, and she began tearing off her thick gloves before she stopped scrambling. She looked like an Arctic explorer. "Oh, is n't the heat terrible!" she panted, and sat down in a snow-drift.

It was terrible, and grew more inconvenient as noon approached. With the afternoon, however, the chill of the mountains came on, and we were glad of our elaborate arrangements to meet it. Only once in the day-time did we suffer from cold while crossing the mountains. Then it was for the two or three hours when we were crossing the bald snow-fields of Chakar, a mountain that is swept by gales from every direction and which is on the divide between the Adriatic and the Ægean.

We never stopped for a midday meal in the mountains. We had neither the time nor the meal. As we trudged along, we gnawed on pieces of soldiers' biscuit or stale bread, and very delicious it was, too. We had got a comparatively late start, so that the ice had time to thaw a little, making it possible for the horses to keep on their feet nearly all the time. Of course half a dozen packs or so fell off just at first, but after a while each driver learned the one position in which his pack would ride, and our trouble in that direction lessened.

It was about four o'clock in the afternoon when we began to descend once more into the narrow valley. Here it was sufficiently widened out to allow the "road" to run along the morass of rounded boulders which ages of furious floods had piled there. This valley was spooky enough. The sun, disappearing behind the high peaks ahead, left blue shadows among the pines that were almost as dark as night. I crunched along on the snow, now and then stumbling when one foot would go into a crevice between the rocks. Here I met a specter. I was alone. I had forged ahead of the party, expecting to find Nikola and the camping-place soon. Intent only on watching my footing, I was startled by a cry out of the shadows on my right. *"Americano, Americano,"* it said, and then, *"Dobrun, Dobrun, Americano, Dobrun."* Out of the shadow something seized my arm, and on the instant I saw a strange Serbian soldier very much the worse for wear, ragged, emaciated, hollow-eyed, but smiling pleasantly. How on earth he had recognized and placed me I did not know, nor could he tell me very clearly, for he spoke only a little French, though he understood it fairly well. I asked him how he knew me as an American, and he pointed to my hat. None but an American could be under a hat like that. As for Dobrun, he informed that he had been there when we were, and was one of "the captain's" men. He was hurrying back from Androvitze to Ipek with despatches. He had messages for my Dobrun captain, who, he informed me, had been at Ipek several days. I was greatly disappointed that I had not seen my good friend there, but meeting this soldier

in the wilderness, and at least hearing that he was
not dead, made the whole trip more cheerful.

Nikola had made heroic efforts to get us shelter
that night and, considering the circumstances, had
succeeded very well. Where the valley spread into a little flat a quarter of a mile long and a third as
wide were two Montenegrin taverns built to house
the natives who passed that way. One at the west
end of the flat was built of stone. The ground
floor was a stable for the horses, as is always the
case in small Montenegrin inns. The second floor
was one medium-sized room, without any furniture
to speak of, and a tiny kitchen, with a stove built
into the wall. Fifty or sixty people had engaged
accommodations there for the night, and though
the landlord was perfectly willing to take us, too,
as Nikola quite seriously put it, it would be "a little
crowded." The other edifice stood at the opposite
end of the flat. Its first story was also built of
stone and used as a stable. On top of this a wooden
shack had been erected. There was one fairly
good-sized room with four windows, an old stove,
and some benches. A second room adjoined it, but
was only about a third as large, and there were two
tiny rooms like cupboards. Also there was a loft
filled with hay. By lying like sticks in a wood-

pile all the women could have slept in the big room, which Nikola had procured for their benefit. The cracks in the floor allowed the steaming air from the stable underneath to spread to the chamber above.

On the ground all about the place was deep snow, but the weather was perfectly clear. Eight of the women said they would sleep on the snow more comfortably than in the hotel, "Hôtel de l'Ecurie" we called it. Soon after we had partaken of abundant tea and coffee, and of cheese and tinned meat sparingly, I found them spreading their blankets upon the smooth snow. A hilarious mood prevailed. They were in for something which generations of their ancestors had never done. They had slept in every conceivable place and condition except right on the snow, and now they were going to do that. There was no acting; they were really hilarious. They had tramped only ten continuous hours, and had dined on what at home they would never have touched. They had only fourteen hours of march to do next day.

With their insufficient blankets spread neatly on the snow, I saw them come up to the cook's fire, where three kettles of water were now boiling. From the little rucksacks which they carried, each drew out a hot-water bottle and with the best bed-room air of comfort filled it! Side by side with my enigma of why England is not run by her women stands my enigma of the hot-water bottle. It was not the first or the last time that I saw that perform-ance. They carried hot-water bottles to bed with them when they slept as the little tinned sardines are thought to sleep; they carried them when they went to bed on the dry grass; they filled the kettles from rivulets, and heated them in the shelter of a wagon when their bed was to be in the puddles about the wagon; no harem resting-place was com-plete until the astonished old Turk had brought enough hot water to fill forty bottles. When they finally got on board ship to cross the Adriatic at its most dangerous point, while submarines were chas-ing them, they ferreted out the ship's galley, filled their hot-water bottles, lay down on deck, and slept or were sick as the case might be. No matter what happened, I never heard one of them grumble as long as she had a bottle magically warm. No mat-ter what our good luck, I never saw one satisfied when she could not have her bottle filled at bed-time. I believe if the British Government would furnish every militant suffragette with a nice, warm hot-water bottle every evening, they would be found as docile as lambs. Going to bed with three blankets on that snow, and carefully preparing a hot-water bottle, seemed to me like Jess Willard having his hair curled before a championship fight. It seemed to me fated to be about the most transient pleasure I had ever met, but if it made women like those happy, nothing under heaven was too dear to buy it.

My view of the matter amused them immensely, but they heartily disagreed with it. They said not only was a hot-water bottle a fine thing to sleep with, but in the cold mornings before the march began the water still retained enough warmth to make it agreeable for a wash. Next morning one let me try it, and what she said was true. After that lots of them wanted to lend me a bottle. They nearly all had extra ones. They had thrown away their clothing, their precious souvenirs, they could not carry as much food as they needed; but they had extra hot-water bottles!

A bell tent had been brought along in case we had to camp where there were no houses at all. It occurred to me that this, spread as a ground sheet over a lot of hay, would aid the hot-water bottles. So I searched it out. From the landlord, a stingy old codger who had charged only twenty dollars

Trackless mountains of Albania

A mountain home in Montenegro

for that stable, more than he would ordinarily make
in a year, I bought some hay, and soon had, a fairly
decent place for the eight to sleep side by side.
They at once declared it the best bed they had had
in a long while.   There appeared to be a scarcity
of fire-wood about "Hôtel de l'Ecurie," though
there was no excuse for it, because the mountains
round about were well wooded.   This had deterred
the women from having a fire at their feet.   One
does not sleep out many times without discovering
that a fire at one's feet is a luxury that should not
be missed.   While making an excursion down the
stream, I came upon a big pile of fat pine planks.
They were hidden there, with heavy rocks piled on
them.   Not wishing further to annoy the landlord,
as quietly as possible I dragged about nine tenths
of this lumber to our "camp."   Then we had a
great fire, which, so the nurses said, was the final
touch to their comfort.   But my sins came home to
roost.

On a carpenter's-table which I dragged from
the side of the inn I lay down by the side of the fire
to sleep.   What little wind there was blew the fire
away from the women toward my table.   I had
piled the most massive planks I could find along
the edge of their bed to guard against the fire

spreading there. In my position I got the warm air with but little smoke, which floated above me, and soon with the others I was asleep.

I closed my eyes on the wonderful Montenegrin sky, sprinkled with its magnificent stars, and on the glittering peaks about us. The women, I fancy, were already at home again in quiet old Edinburgh, in London, wonderful London as it was before 1914, living their wonted lives in the Scotch Highlands or amid the wild beauty of Wales. I, too, dreamed. Despite the dead slumber which fatigue brought to us, we always dreamed, mostly of home, seldom of war. I remember distinctly I had dined at an uptown restaurant. I was going to hear "Siegfried." At One Hundred and Fourth Street and Broadway I got into a taxi, and directed the chauffeur to drive as fast as possible to the Metropolitan. It was cold in the taxi. I looked to see if the windows were up. They were, but it grew colder, while Broadway became brighter and brighter. I thought I had never in my life seen the city so brilliant, animated, gay. At Sixty-sixth Street the glare seemed to hurt my eyes, and, as we rounded Columbus Circle, the illumination became a blinding flash, rising and falling, flickering, but extending everywhere. I woke up, and my

first impression was that I was much colder than
when I lay down.   Also the whole place was filled
with bright light that made the snow glisten.   In a
few seconds I took in what had happened.   The
wind had shifted away from me, had caused the
barrier to catch fire, and the edge of the women's
palet was blazing high.   Due to the snow underneath, the flame could be easily stamped out, and
when there was only smoking straw, for the first
time I became aware that not one of the women
had waked up.   The edge of the straw, the tent,
the fringes of their rugs, were burnt within six
inches of their feet.   They were sleeping as calmly
as ever.   That is what fatigue and cold mountain
air will do.

I raked the fire farther away, fixed a new barrier,
heavily plastered with snow, which, melting, would
keep it wet, and convinced that everything was all
right, I lay down again without waking any one.
I had not intended going to sleep, but after moving
my table nearer to the fire, for it was now incredibly
cold in the valley, I dozed off again.   I heard the
huge icicles that hung from an old mill-sluice near
by snapping and cracking, and the trees on the
mountain-side crackled and popped with the frost.
The women told me later they were having various

dreams with one common characteristic: in all of them their feet were delightfully comfortable—"All cozy and warm," one said.

I do not think I dreamed any more, but after a while I waked up. It was the second time in my life that I ever understood what people seem to mean when they talk of "Providence." The other time was also in Serbia. Sir Ralph Paget and I were motoring on one of the most thrilling roads in Bosnia. There was the usual tremendous precipice on one side, the lip of the road being only crumbling dirt. What looked like a horrible death came to an officer on horseback just as we passed him. Sir Ralph was in the front seat with me. For perhaps twenty seconds we both looked back, sick with the horror of what we had seen. There was a slight curve in the road just ahead, but I had not noticed this. What made me turn round again at the end of certainly not more than twenty seconds I do not know. I had not finished looking behind; I had forgotten for the time all sense of danger. But a feeling I shall never forget turned my head, as if by force, without any thought on my part, to the road ahead. There was not any road there. Over the steaming radiator I looked down, down, down on feathery treetops waving in an abyss. My radiator was hanging over the cliff. As I spun the wheel, I had not the slightest idea the car would answer; I knew my front wheels were already over. They were not. With the fountain-pen that is now writing these words the distance between my track in the crumbling dirt and the sheer drop was measured. When the butt was placed on the outer edge of that deep rut, the point jutted into space. Sir Ralph had looked round when I had spun the car.

"We were n't looking," he said, smiling quietly, and in the very best English fashion that was the end of the matter.

This same feeling now woke me up. I was not cold; there was no noise. The time had come when somebody ought to wake, and somebody did. The wind had freshened, and changed more directly toward the women. My barrier had caught fire again, and the dry hay, the canvas, and the rugs beyond it were blazing, while the wind fanned it like a furnace. Almost simultaneously with me the women awoke. Most of them were tied up in sleeping-bags which they had sewn their blankets into. All were tangled up, and the fire was simply snapping at them. This time the deep snow on which they slept undoubtedly saved them from horrible burns, if not from death. I had on high boots of heavy leather, and this fact, joined with the deep snow and my blanket as a flail, made it possible to put out the fire. It had burned the lower edges of their clothing, had destroyed their shoes, which they had removed and placed near their feet, and had burned about half their rugs. In the middle of this tangle, —smoking rugs, bags, woolen scarfs, tent canvas and straw,—out of which they could not extract themselves they sat up and laughed. Another new experience! Planning how to borrow one another's extra boots for the march in the morning, they fell asleep, but this time I had no desire to neglect that fire again.

It had not been what one would call a peaceful night for us around the fire, though those within the "hotel" were unaware of all the excitement. Just before dawn the final foray came. There was not supposed to be much danger from bandits on the route which we had chosen, especially as the Montenegrin Government had taken precautions to police it. Still, as Nikola had expressed it to me, whenever we went into camp at night, "some of those dogs would be pretty likely to be sneaking about." As I lay there looking up at the paling sky, I was startled by some rifle-shots a little way up the path by which we had come. Bullets whistled through the forest, and a rather steady *crack, crack* kept up for some time on both sides of the valley. Everybody was startled, and none knew what to expect; but the firing did not come closer, and we never discovered what was the occasion of it.

When we got under way this second day a clammy mist enshrouded everything and shut off from our path the thawing sunlight. The following four or five hours were exceedingly difficult. We began climbing out of the valley almost at once by a forty-five-degree ascent which "switch-backed" in the shortest possible distance to the ridge above. The higher up we climbed, the steeper became the path. This was most unfortunate. The leading ponies fell down and slid rapidly backward, losing their packs and knocking those behind off their feet. It was like knocking down a row of dominoes which one has stood on end. When a front pony fell hard, it was "Look out, all below! Stand from under, and get away from the precipice edge!" As many as six or eight ponies were down at once, and the contents of their packs scattered everywhere, while the rest of the bunch slipped and pawed, struggling to keep their balance. Some of the nurses helped matters by going ahead, and with butcher-knives, hatchets, and bayonets chipping the surface of the ice. Finally pieces of blankets were tied about the horses' hoofs, and this solved the problem almost completely.

Rosinante never slipped down. From Ipek to Androvitze she bore my meager luggage and much of the time invalids of the party, and she never so much as stumbled badly. I think every other horse was down at least once, but, despite the fact (which I had discovered only after I bought her) that her wind was broken, and on every slope she sounded like a second-hand street-organ, she kept on her feet. This saved me much trouble, for after the first day I led her myself, and had she slipped like some of the others, I would have been there yet, trying to put the pack on her back.

In the late afternoon we came up a narrow, heavily wooded gorge of marvelous beauty to the foot of Chakar, and there stopped for the night in a stone inn which was not large or clean, but dry and warm. Most of the snow was gone on the lower slopes of Chakar, but on top we could see the high winds blowing the snow-clouds about. One cannot skirt about the lower shoulders of this mountain or escape its highest snow-fields. The way to the sea leads squarely over its rounded summit—a way that in summer must be a delight to scramble up,

"Mon cher Capitaine"

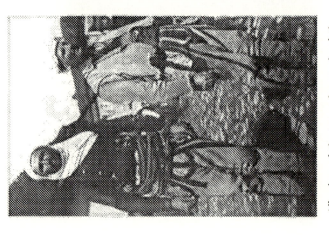

Albanians of the type who murdered the refugees

but in December was not so inviting. Nikola encouraged us with cheerful promises. Once over that summit, he said, all our way to the sea would be "down-hill." At that stage of our march, next to flying, "down-hill" represented the *summum bonum* to us. In a broad geographical sense Nikola was right. Chakar was the divide, but in a practical tracking tramp's understanding of the case, Heavens! he was a liar! He did not mention the Little Kom. If he had, I think I should have passed the winter on the Oriental side of Chakar.

Next day we crossed Chakar, but that is all we did. Like a famous nursery hero, we simply went up and came down again. That night we passed in a Montenegrin village. All that I can remember about it is that I saw here a most beautiful child, a boy of ten whose father had just been shot; that we sat around a camp-fire while the Irish girls sang songs; and that Nikola paid forty dollars for enough hay to feed twenty horses two times.

The fourth day, through mud the like of which I never want to see again, we came to Androvitze, only to find no provisions there, and to hear the glad tidings that because of a wash-out no automobiles could come up. From then on began a tramp of nine days, each day filled with hopes that the next would see us in automobiles or carts. They never came; we walked into Podgoritze.

Just as I was putting the finishing touches to Rosinante's saddle before leaving Androvitze, I felt a hand fall heavily on my shoulder and, turning around, beheld *"mon cher Capitaine,"* him of the far-off, happy Dobrun days. The captain loves his country, and so do I. After a while, when we did speak, it was of other and trivial things. We promised if possible to meet at Podgoritze, and if not there, at Scutari, and if not there, in Paris, and, as a last resort, in New York. The captain's physique and stoicism are Serb; his perfect manner, his *bonhomie,* his warm humanity are French, and the mixture makes *"mon cher Capitaine"* a very charming companion. There is nothing Teutonic about him.

The moist, warm breath of the Adriatic came up to meet us at Androvitze. We began to have mists and heavy rains, with now and then a clear day and the skies of southern Italy. The invaders and the savage mountains were behind, and somewhere down the very good road that now led on before us was the sea. During that monotonous succession of days before we came to Podgoritze, the sea and how we should get across it, became the main subject of conversation, the constant thought in our minds. For weeks the sea had been our goal, a practical goal to us, an impossible dream of escape to the starving hundred thousand at Prizrend. Rumors began to float up to us by courses we could not trace of ships that would take us to Italy. One said that all would have to go down the coast to Durazzo. Several told of an American sailing-vessel, the *Albania,* which would be waiting at San Giovanni di Medua to take off all neutrals, all women and children, and the men who were over military age. The rest would have to go to Durazzo. Still others told of British transports waiting to help the army and the refugees, and some spoke of no hope at all, saying that the Adriatic was too dangerous. The mythical sailing-vessel was the favorite, and we all believed in it more than in any other.

Then one day a young Englishman in clean, new khaki came riding up the road to meet us. He was a representative of the British Serbian Relief Fund sent out to survey the field in Montenegro. Two weeks before he had been in London, and gave us the first news of the world we had had in six weeks. He had crossed the Adriatic on a torpedo-boat, sending his luggage by a small vessel which had been torpedoed. He brought a cryptic message,

saying that Sir Ralph Paget wished all the British
to hurry to Scutari as fast as possible.   This was
encouraging.   It even seemed as if those in authority were at last taking cognizance of the fact that
there were British women who might need aid.   We
almost dared to hope it might mean a break in the
policy of *laissez-faire,* which, during the retreat, had
left the units to shift for themselves as best they
could, with the purely voluntary aid of Serbians,
who brought them out of Serbia, saw to housing
and provisioning them, and made them as safe as
possible.   The things which a British representative
might have done for them, such as going ahead and
securing what food could be had, seeing to accommodations at the places where they stopped, collect-
ing horses at Prizrend and Ipek, establishing temporary camps in the mountains at easy stages, where
on arrival the women might have found tents and
plentiful fires, and finally some semblance of system
which at least would not have allowed them to feel
utterly abandoned by their own Government were
not done at all.   The doctors and nurses recognized
early that they could stay and be captured or starve
without any apparent concern on the part of the
officials whom they had thought responsible for
them.   The English women should have been forced

to come out earlier than they did, and, to be perfectly fair, I understand that Sir Ralph Paget suggested this to them, but they refused. After they were allowed to remain, a little system, a little thought, foresight, and trouble could have alleviated immensely their hardships. By using half a dozen men and horses, fixed camps could have been established which would have rendered the mountain-trails much less arduous. Not until Scutari, where there was a British consul, did anything resembling official aid come to the British women, and here it was in a slipshod, slap-dash fashion.

Soon after leaving Androvitze we came to the Little Kom, a mountain rising some eight thousand feet, flanked on the east by a magnificent snow peak much higher. The blizzard that had struck us at Ipek had caught many refugees, soldiers, and prisoners here. Forty Bulgarians are said to have been found frozen to death in a space of a hundred yards. Snow lay deep upon its summit when we climbed it, but in the valleys below the day was like early autumn. After the Little Kom, Nikola's oft-repeated promise of a down-hill trail became more or less true. It was our last really hard climb, and I was not sorry, for going up it I fainted three times, a thing I never knew I could do before.

The weaker women rode up, but one was so afraid of horses she would not mount. I shall never forget her at the end of that day; but no one heard a word of complaint from her.

One night we stopped at a Montenegrin village of most primitive aspect. The people were all in native costume. No trace of civilization as we know it was evident. At one of the huts I applied for shelter. The peasant who came to the door to meet me was dressed in skin-tight trousers of white wool, richly ornamented in fancy designs of black braid. His shirt was yellow linen, and his short jacket of the same material as the trousers, but even more ornate. He wore upon his head a white skull-cap, and around his waist was a flaming knitted sash. His feet were clothed in brilliant socks and *opanki*. He was six feet tall at least; his black eyes flashed, and his black hair fell long and thick from under his white cap. As picturesque and primitive a model as any artist could wish! Behind him in the smoky "kitchen," on the earthen floor of which a fire burned while the smoke wandered where it would, stood a fierce Montenegrin beauty, proud, disdainful, but not inhospitable. In her arms was a young edition of the man. These wild people filled me with admiration, gave me the taste of remote, unbeaten paths which every traveler loves. Here was the real thing, a native family just as it was on that hillside four centuries ago. I made signs to my charming bandit host.

"Come in," he said. "I am from Chicago; where do you come from?"

A dozen years in Chicago had given him enough money to return to his ancestral home, buy a good farm, marry, and revert in luxury to the life of his fathers. I believe a greater percentage of Montenegrins have been to America than of any other nation. Because of my hat, they were continually hailing me, and they ruined that unbeaten-trail taste for which I sought so avidly.

Several incidents broke momentarily this part of our march, but, for the most part, it was of a sameness—day succeeding day consumed in quick marching. Every morning there was the rush to get on the road, and every waning afternoon the wonder when and where we would camp, and whether it would be grass and a fragrant wood-fire or sloppy mud and a vile inn. There was the excitement when "Sunny Jim," the bright and youthful Serbian orphan whom one of the women was bringing from the wilds of Serbia to the wilds of London, was accused of making off with an officer's pocket-book. Our indignant declarations of Jim's impeccable honesty helped not at all until a search, which inexorably extended to the accused's young skin, proved beyond doubt his innocence. Then there was the morning when just above our camp a firing-squad ended the career of two deserters, and the day when, almost starving, we came to a beautiful river and purchased a forty-pound fish, the very best fish ever caught.

So gradually we neared Podgoritze. At least from there we hoped to get conveyances for the three hours' drive to Plavnitze, on Scutari Lake, there to take a boat for Scutari. We had come to consider Podgoritze as marking the end of our troubles. Near it one morning I was leading Rosinante, who carried one of the women. She had been one of the strongest until at Jakova a Turkish dog of doubtful lineage, but undoubted fierceness, had attacked and bitten her badly. At home she designed dainty costumes for actresses. This was her first experience at roughing it, but she was enjoying everything immensely.

"I am so happy!" she said, looking down at her dress and at me. "We are going to be home just in time for the January sales!" So after a week,

King Peter and a party of refugees crossing a bridge in the Albanian Alps

a good part of it spent in resting, we came to Podgoritze.

On leaving Androvitze we had come each day more in contact with the army, for the route they had taken joined ours there. Many thousands were about Podgoritze when we arrived, and many more thousands had already reached Scutari. Looking at these filthy, ragged, starved, ill men, one wondered if it were still permissible to call them an army. How could any feeling of nationality or cohesion now be alive in this dull, horror-stricken horde? Could this frayed remnant, these hollow-eyed, harassed officers, these soldiers, as mechanical and listless as automata, be really considered a military force? Had not that rugged, surpassingly brave thing, the almost mystical *esprit de corps* which had endured a continuous and hopeless retreat for ten weeks, died when the peaks above Ipek shut off the distant Serbian plains? Had not the story of Serbia ended in death and destruction at the evacuation of Ipek?

It is true that the retreat through Albania and Montenegro was only a *tour de force* in the business of getting away. At the moment the need for armies had ceased; there was no country to defend.

It was a flight without military manœuvering, merely *sauve qui peut*.   A few thousand were able to find food and equipment sufficient to aid the Montenegrins, and in Albania about twenty thousand were actively engaged.   The sole object of all the others was to reach Scutari, where it would be "up to" the Allies to reclothe, rearm, and provision them.   From one thousand to fifteen hundred were lost in Albania by savage native attacks. Many hundreds at least must have died on both lines of march from cold, exposure, and starvation.   A good part of the smaller artillery was saved.   The soldiers, weakened as they were, went through incredible hardships to effect this.   In many places on the Montenegrin route it had been necessary to take the guns to pieces, and the men had had to carry the heavy barrels on their shoulders.   The paths were slippery with ice, the ascents long and very steep, the precipices at times dizzying, the cold severe, and there was little or no shelter.

But we did not see a disorganized, soulless mass about Podgoritze.   We saw the cream of Serbia's fighting men, the nearly superhuman residue which remained after shot and shell, disease, exhaustion, cold, and starvation had done their cruel censoring; after the savage teeth of frozen peaks had combed out all but the strongest. And the near-annihilation of their bodies only allowed to be seen more clearly the unfaltering flame of their determination and their devotion to the glorious quest, the temporary loss of which hurt them more deeply than all they had to bear. Dauntless and alone, they had fought the unequal battle, and defeat was more bitter than death.

Germany, Austria, and Bulgaria did not destroy the Serbian army, nor did it die of utter despair at Ipek, though well it might have. The Serbian army cannot die. In two months they have reorganized, reëquipped, and rested. The hundred and fifty thousand of them will not be a pleasant army to meet. Remember their position. Nearly every one of these men has left a family behind him, and that family is pretty sure to be starving. At best it is exposed to the dangers of very dangerous invaders. This may dishearten a man, but it also makes him desperate. The sufferings of that fugitive army gathered about a fugitive prince in a friendly, but foreign, country is not even half physical, however great their burden is in that direction.

To realize at all what the loss of Serbia means to the Serb, one must consider not only the separation from home and family; one must understand a little the strength and depth of the Southern Slav's desire for a free Slav nation.   One must know the extent to which this idea has permeated all his thoughts, all his literature, all his folk-songs for five hundred years.   One must have learned that it is his religion.   And to know this one must have seen what Mme. Christitch has charmingly pointed out in her comments on "The Soul of the Southern Slav," namely, how his very life is bound up in the instinct of brotherhood.

A man's brother or cousin in Serbia is more to him than his wife and children, devoted as he is to them.   The loss of a brother is the direst of all calamities, and, to the Southern Slav, all lovers of Slavic liberty are brothers.   This feeling has resulted in an idealistic patriotism that only those who have come in contact with it can realize.   It is a patriotism that is astounding in its capacity for sacrifice.   It is firmly and irrevocably resolved on the liberation or the extermination of its people.   Whether one agrees with its desires or not, its presence is undeniably there, fiercely blazing in the desolate, disease-swept camps of that exiled army.   Its sorrow is not of physical discomfort or even of personal loss.   Centuries of dogged fighting have taught the Serb to accept such things as part of the day's work. Their grief is deeper than that. It is the crushing sense of a supreme idol broken.

CHAPTER XII

PODGORITZE, a straggling white blot on the Plain of Zeta, facing fertile prairies southward as far as Lake Scutari, flanked on the north by utterly barren peaks, for many centuries has had a rugged history dotted with incidents of more than local significance. Its environs gave the great Diocletian to the Roman Empire and even at that time it stood high among the cities of Illyrium. Around it have raged many desperate conflicts between the Turks and the ever-victorious Montenegrins. To-day—or yesterday—it was the business capital of Montenegro, and but for its proximity to the Albanian border would doubtless have been the political capital also. It has been said that nowhere west of Constantinople could such colorful and astounding market-scenes be met as in Podgoritze. The color, when I saw it, was distinctly drab but the scenes were no less exciting.

To get down to intimate things: we were hungry, although at the "hotel" we made a pretense at meals

—a bit of unclassified meat, bread made of bran and sand, Turkish coffee, and crème de menthe, a whole bottle of it, which made us feel civilized beyond words. In the market-place were still a few things for sale. There were tiny fish from Scutari Lake which were peddled around by old men in incredible filth and the odor of which caressed the very stars. Also one could get—by fighting one's way to them —decayed apples, a little sausage that rivaled the fish in smell, and now and then a ham. But the hams which at this time still survived the mob-hunger were old, battle-scarred veterans which remained intact through the self-same weapon as the fish and sausage. One wonderful unsullied thing we found, many pounds of fresh *kimak,* a sort of clotted cream which in the Balkans passes muster for butter. It is very delicious and nothing could have been more tempting to us. I could scarcely believe my eyes when I saw it on a little table in the market-place, guarded by two comely peasant women. A large crowd was already around and more were gathering each minute, but no one was buying and I wondered if none of them had any money. Forcing my way through the by-standers, I found a Montenegrin policeman in violent argument with the proprietors of the popular *kimak* and with certain indignant members of the crowd. This did not worry me at all. My whole attention was centered on that cream-cheese with a concentration that would have delighted William James. Upon the table I laid ten dinars and, picking up a knife, began the attack on a large and elegant chunk. The women, the policeman, and part of the mob yelled protests and made threatening gestures, but some of the crowd cried *"dobro Amerikanske"* and evidently approved my direct method. The policeman, who was a walking museum of beautiful, barbaric arms, ancient pistols of ivory and silver, sabers and daggers thrust into a marvelous crimson sash, began addressing me in English. Of course he had been in America, everybody has in Montenegro. It is the prerequisite to possessing a small fortune, marrying, and living happily ever afterward. He said the women would not be allowed to sell any of the kimak for more than four *dinars* a kilogram, that being a fair price, no matter how much we might need it. The women insisted that in extraordinary times extraordinary prices were permissible and flatly refused to sell for less than ten *dinars*, their determination being strengthened by numerous offers from the crowd of twenty and even thirty *dinars* a kilo. Around this *impasse*

The only street in San Giovanni di Medua

The forty British women of the Stobart mission waiting for the
boat at Plavitnitze

there seemed no way. They would not sell at the legal price and they never did, I suppose. That cheese remained there all day with a ravenous crowd round it and at nightfall the women went away—most likely to meet a wealthy purchaser in some corner far removed from the somewhat uncompromising arm of the Montenegrin law.

At Podgoritze I met the Captain once more, and with elaborate courtesy he invited me to dine with a group of officers in the evening. The hour was at six but we were having such an absorbing time investigating Podgoritze and recounting experiences that we were fifteen minutes late in arriving at the dingy place where the officers had mess. I shall never forget the little scene as we entered, though why it remains so vivid I scarcely know. The commissariat of the inn had failed almost completely and what we saw was a dozen officers in bedraggled uniforms and a look in their eyes that I cannot define. It was common to all of them and had in it at once suffering and starvation, humiliated pride, and the deepest patriotic grief. It was always only from their gaze that one could tell what hell these refined and highly educated men were suffering; in their speech they were always either terse and practical, or cheerful and witty. At each end of the bare, greasy pine table was an empty wine bottle with a tallow candle stuck in it, giving the only light in the evil-smelling room. Lying on three or four heavy earthen platters were scanty stacks of almost meatless bones which the gentlemen eyed with a most ludicrous air of apology when we unexpectedly appeared. They sat there, elbows on the table, their faces resting on their hands, one or two of them smoking, all silent. To one who had known the past fastidiousness of the Serbian officer, the picture was indeed an epitome, but a wicked grin spread over the Captain's face.

"M'sieur," he said to me, "I have invited you to dine with me. On the way I have the delight and honor to exhibit my kennels!" His brother officers replied with as good as he sent, however, and after a little we went away laughing, the Captain vastly amused at having invited a guest to a dinner that did not appear. Once out in the open again under the cold Montenegrin stars, because we knew it was useless to seek a repast that night, we contented ourselves with gastronomic memories of the city of cities.

"Ah, to be on the boulevards again, to smell Paris once more!" exclaimed the Captain. "To quietly sit at a table all white and gleaming in a little café

clean as heaven, to glance at the radiant ladies—
à droite, à gauche—as one selects a civilized repast,
to see the passing crowds so great and happy whom
pleasure and not war have brought together, to live
like a human being, *mon ami*, to breathe once more
the blessed air of France!" His perfect French
turned to a shout of guttural Serbian as he hailed
a passing friend and together we sought solace in
Turkish coffee. I hope that for many years to
come he and his comrade cavaliers may live to
breathe that blessed air and carry to their indomitable, struggling country the culture and the fine
intellectual wealth of that incomparable nation.

I saw King Nikolas come riding through Podgoritze next day on a milk-white horse. He wore a
gorgeous costume with silken sashes, and gold-
embossed pistols and saber, many medals, and gold
embroidery. His gaze was very stern, and he
frowned heavily but returned our salute cordially
enough. Even then he had issued a proclamation
saying that his subjects must not be alarmed if the
court were moved from Cettinje, and preparation
for this was already under way.

After two or three days horse wagons were procured for us to go to Plavnitze to take the boat to
Scutari. It required four hours, and most of the

time we were facing a freezing wind, so that we were numb when we arrived at the large warehouses near the boat dock. The boat had been expected to be waiting for us, but it did not come until nearly noon next day. We had brought virtually no food, thinking to reach Scutari by night, so that the delay was more than inconvenient.

As night came on, the authorities were persuaded to open up one of the immense empty storehouses for us—"us" being the regular unit with the addition of eight or ten members of an English hospital that had been working in Montenegro. The roof of our abode was very high and full enough of holes to afford fine ventilation, and the floor was of concrete, so we soon had a large camp-fire going. It proved to be one of the most comfortable camps we had, the feeling that our troubles were nearing the end adding much to our content. However, we were ravenous. Some one had found two hams, which they bought without very close scrutiny, and these with a little bread were our supper. Unfortunately one of the hams was distinctly the worse for age, but some of the party were hungry enough to try the doubtful experiment of separating the good bits from the less good, and during the night more than one suffered. That evening we sat long around the fire, the Irish girls singing songs and all of us telling the biggest lies we knew, thus beguiling ourselves into forgetting for a little the things behind us.

Next morning while we waited for the boat on the pier, Lieutenant-Commander Kerr arrived with his party of marines. I have already described this plucky little band who refused to talk about their troubles, although suffering so terribly. It does, indeed, seem strange to me that with such magnificent fighting material England has so far been distinctly unfortunate. When the boat came we still delayed until the arrival of a general and his staff, who were going to cross with us. During this time we heard heavy firing down the lake from the direction of Scutari, and in a little while saw an Austrian aëroplane coming toward us, flying at a great height. There were no anti-aircraft guns about, and nothing but a few rifles to protect us if he saw fit to bomb the narrow pier, which was crowded full of Serbian soldiers, the marines, and ourselves. On nearing us he came quite low and circled about several times, but flew away without dropping a bomb, but not without causing a good deal of excitement because we were in a pretty bad position to be bombed. If he had some bombs, but re-

frained, I bow to him here; if he wished for some,
I hope he dropped into the lake.

Shortly before the boat sailed an Austrian prisoner crawled down the pier toward us. This
is not an exaggeration, certainly he apparently
crawled. Every movement showed great exhaustion, and he bent far over so that his hands almost
swept the ground. Steadfastly his face was turned
to earth, though his head oscillated with a swinging
glance from side to side. When we did catch a
glimpse of his features, we saw only a grayish bunch
of matted beard, caked and tangled with filth, which
spread up to meet shaggy locks of almost snow-
white hair. His mouth remained continually open.
Mechanically he was searching the ground for food
in a manner startlingly identical with that of a
hungry dog or a pig. On a pile of loose stones
there were some small pieces of maize bread which
had fallen as some one ate a hunk of the crumbling
concoction that the Montenegrins make. The Austrian prisoner came upon this find. While a nurse
was canvassing the crowd to see if any bread remained among us, this creature, who had ceased to
be human, searched the pile of stones through and
through, tearing them apart and, as the crumbs
ever sifted lower, scattering them with a studious

attention to the minutest particle which they hid
that seemed to me more eloquent than any frenzy.
A little bread was found for him and he managed
to get on the boat.   If he had not, he would have
died, for it takes two days for strong men to go
around the lake.

In his eyes, and in the dumb glances of how many
thousands more, we read the deep damnation of
those responsible for war, whoever they may be.
By most trustworthy estimates I know now that
more than forty-four thousand Austrian prisoners
died from starvation and exposure on that eight-
weeks retreat, and the most of them, of course,
"played out" in the mountains.   With all the sin-
cerity that I can display I want to bear witness to
the truly admirable attitude of these prisoners as I
saw them.   It is true that many thousands of them
were Austro-Serbs, whose hearts were with their
kinsmen, but in no instance did I see one of them
guilty of any brutal act, not even when they stood
in torture at the door of death.   Out of the fifty
thousand that Serbia held, six thousand came, more
dead than alive, to the sea.

At last we scrambled on board and our argosy
weighed anchor.   It was a strange, hybrid craft,
built originally for a sail-boat, but since endowed

with a reluctant gasolene motor that pushed us
leisurely through the placid water, so placid that
the mountains under the surface seemed as real and
solid as those that formed the shores. There was
scarcely more than standing-room on the entire
boat, only infrequently an opportunity to sit, and
the odor was terrific. We had a good many
wounded soldiers on board, as well as the many
uninjured ones whose condition was far from
pleasant.

In some miraculous manner (for there were
many more important who could find no room) a
wild Gipsy had sneaked on board with his battered
violin. He was merely a shambling skeleton
draped with brown skin, his jet eyes sunken deep
beneath his brows, his cheeks hollow and rough as
potato peel. As soon as we got a little way from
land he began playing weird, squeaky things that,
under the circumstances, were worse than the very
worst ghost-story I ever heard. The cruise of the
Ancient Mariner certainly knew no more grotesque
hours than those we spent in the deathly stillness
of Scutari Lake among the tottering remnants of
men who had played to the world one of its greatest
masques of human misery. The battered little ship
loaded with its desperate freight glided with

The ancient fortress at Scutari

scarcely a gurgle across the wild, silent, beautiful lake.   We on board only mumbled and mostly stood facing southward, straining our eyes toward Scutari, or now and then scanning the sky to see if the aëroplane were not returning to sink us.   Incessantly this wild, brown phantom rasped wilder music from his fiddle.   Hour after hour we stood thus until we ached in every muscle, until the stench and misery everywhere visible was enough to drive one insane.   Sometimes we were near the gray shores and cruel, barren peaks, again far enough away for distance to tone down the rugged land. We became unutterably fatigued and hungry and, as the afternoon waned, very cold, for a high wind which nearly stopped our progress swept down upon us and froze us to the bone.   We huddled even closer to each other to keep warm and looked every minute to see Scutari—where there was a British consul and food and rest and news from home, perhaps.   The sun set about five o'clock and left a cold, wind-swept sky, a sheet of orange doubled by the lake.   About eight we fought in the teeth of the wind around a sharply jutting shoulder of solid rock and came upon a cluster of lights, above which we could discern the mass of the huge ancient fortress of Scutari.

The port affords no landing facilities worth speaking of. The landing must be made in tipsy, leaky boats domineered by savage specimens, two to a boat, who doubtless would also answer to the adjective tipsy. A drove of these *farouche* boatmen wabbled out in their terrifying craft to meet us. They were like so many flitting chips on the dark, wind-tossed water. Nikola, who had been sent ahead to herald our coming, was commanding them, in strong, uncomplimentary tones that the high wind split up and bore to us in screeching fragments. But they were a stupid, unruly lot, and his admonitions continued to explode fast and furious, the expletives flying by our ears like whistling shrapnel. Upon the ship the human tangle appeared inextricable. No one could do more than face about. It seemed as if we must be shoveled off like so much coal. But the freezing, starving soldiers were far from inanimate. No sooner had the boats come near us than these soldiers began to scramble for places near the rail where rope ladders hung down to the water. The resulting confusion was like a herd of badly frightened cattle in a corral. The whole crowd was rocked this way and that, and, only because there was not room to fall, did many of the women escape being trampled. This state of affairs was aided by the darkness, which made it impossible to see how anything should be done. The crowd began to shout, Nikola and his crew took up the cry, so that the very stars knew we were landing at Scutari.

When finally the boats which Nikola had reserved for our use were brought up to the ship, most of them were on the starboard side while nearly all our party had congregated to port. It was next to impossible to cross the ship. I happened to be by the starboard rail where I had been all day, and, as an apparition from the watery confusion below, I saw Nikola ascending the rope-ladder. He cried to me to come down at once and help hold one of the boats to the side of the ship. I descended, holding by one hand, with the other grasping my rucksack that contained my films and notes. I got into a boat with an Englishman. The men had crowded their boats so close together that it was not possible for those next the ship to push off when filled, and this came near causing a complete *debâcle* for our expedition.

No sooner was I seated in the stern of the boat than soldiers began pouring over the ship's side into it, dropping several feet and landing with an impact that each time threatened disaster. In two minutes we had all we could possibly take and the water was in a few inches of overflowing the gunwales. I yelled to the boatmen to push off, but that was foolish because we were hemmed in and could not move an inch except straight down. A wave dashed us with freezing water and a good deal slopped into the bottom of the boat. Dressed as I was, I did not believe I could swim a dozen strokes and the Englishman felt likewise. The rest of us were soldiers. The women were all on the other side and we could hear sounds which told us there was trouble over there too. Seeing their comrades dropping on to the mass of boats below, the men above followed like goats going over a wall, quite unconcerned about where they hit. In spite of our imprecations, a young giant whom we knew would sink us in an instant climbed half-way over the rail and hung pendant above us. Shouting did no good. It had become a heedless stampede of men whose nerves, Heaven knows, should already have been shattered. We looked around to choose another boat into which to jump before that human sword of Damocles should drop, but all of those adjoining us were already full! I remember how I mentally bade farewell to my cherished films and note-book, and believe I would have drawn my

automatic and shot that hanging idiot if I had not
seen that he would drop then and sink us anyway.
He let himself over a little more and kicked his
bare feet right in my face as I stood up cursing him.
The reader will probably not believe it, but those
bare heels and George Bernard Shaw saved us.   I
solemnly affirm it.   In the instant that he dangled
before my eyes an incident in which the shocking
young hero of "Fanny's First Play" chases the
startling young heroine up-stairs pinching her an-
kles came vividly to me.   With all the venom I
could muster I got that man just above the heel
with my finger and thumb and there I stuck.   He
howled as if he had been ham-strung—he must
have thought somebody had knifed him—and jerked
himself back over the rail in a highly gratifying
manner.   Two more pairs of legs already threatened us, but we had found the charm.   We quickly
pinched them back on board, for the soldiers' opanki
offered no protection against our method of attack.
For fully ten minutes we maintained our rocking,
perilous neutrality until the swearing Achilles
gang above us became so ludicrous we enjoyed it.
Their opanki-sheathed extremities certainly proved
our opportunity.   Altogether it *was* a unique landing, unlike any I had ever made.

After every one of the unit had landed without any serious mishaps, though with several narrow escapes, we walked behind the crazy Albanian carts that carried our luggage, for more than half an hour through the streets of Scutari. How civilized they looked to us, those streets which to the traveler from Italy seem so primitive! Our tramp ended before the wide wooden doors of a court-yard upon which we read a placard—the first instance I had seen of official British aid for the women, except at Mitrovitze the special train that had carried a hundred and twenty of the nurses for three hours on their way to the sea under the guidance of a volunteer Serb leader. The sign read *"Mission Anglaise,"* and underneath, *"Sir Ralph Paget."* It was, indeed, pleasant for the nurses to find within even bare rooms, but somewhat clean, and spread with dry hay on which to sleep. It did not seem to me that such arrangements would have been impossible along most stages of the retreat, if some definite plan had been arranged and followed. That night a hot stew of meat and potatoes was brought to us with bread and coffee. We had had nothing but the doubtful ham and a bit of tinned mutton since leaving Podgoritze thirty-six hours before.

It was arranged that early next morning we should leave for the coast, a two days' journey, to take "an American sailing vessel, the *Albania*," which would carry only the refugees of neutral or non-military status. There was deep gloom among the young Englishmen. This meant seven days march to Durazzo over rough trails where blood-thirsty bandits hid. I was the only American in the place and as such my immunity from that march made me the recipient of much congratulation. I searched for an American consul but as yet our new diplomatic representative to the Serbian Government had not arrived at Scutari.

In a way I was sorry not to have a longer stay in Scutari. It was exciting and instructive to watch the broken Serbian Government reshaping itself there, to view the fagged army as it sank down into camps that, desolate though they were, promised—so the men vainly thought—a surcease from the suffering of the past months, a chance to rest, wash, and feed. No such thing happened, but when I was at Scutari people believed it might. "The poor devils, to think they will have to camp around here the rest of the winter with almost no wood!" one officer said mournfully to me. Not even such cold comfort as that was vouched to them.

Each clear day without fail there was an aëroplane bombardment which did small damage, but served to remind the army that their relentless enemies were hounding them still, and though balked for a moment by the mountains yet cherished hopes of reaching them. It may also have been a gentle hint to Essad Pasha of how long is the Teuton's arm and how ready it would be to strike any who offered a refuge to their prey. But whatever the Albanian ruler's faults, he showed himself not fool enough to be persuaded that a precarious capital in the hand is worth the good-will of inevitable victors.

"Will they come here, do you think?" was a question on every tongue. A winter campaign in Montenegro and Albania seemed almost incredible, yet I believe those in authority foresaw it. The great deciding factor was food and ammunition, and these the Italians seemed unable to transport in any safety across the Adriatic. The reason, however, may have been deeper than that; Italy may very well have wished only to hold Avlona and to let the war take its course with Serbia and Montenegro. The eastern littoral of the Adriatic has been for ages a diplomatic chessboard, and there is no reason to believe now that deep-laid schemes for its domination are not going forward. Whatever the causes, the results are obvious enough. The additional march from Scutari to Durazzo cost Serbia many thousands of her precious men. Deadly as the deadliest fire was that intolerable extra burden coming at the end of their miraculous retreat. As one more reason why the whole world loves France with a personal affection it should be noted here that, far removed from Corfu and fighting the "lion's share"—happy phrase—of war on the western front, France has shouldered the care of those thousands of shattered heroes who, while two of them stand together, will ever be known as the Serbian army. From San Giovanni to Durazzo, from Christmas to the middle of January, was a *via dolorosa* more terrible than shell-torn trenches full of bodies and at the end was the island of Vido about which Mr. Grouitch, under secretary of foreign affairs for Serbia, tells in an account in the "New York Evening Sun":

I went to visit the island where are the sick soldiers. The Greeks call it the island of Vido, but the Serbs call it now the Island of the Devil, or more often, the Island of Death. To that island are sent the soldiers who are suffering not from any particular disease, but are simply starved and exhausted, so that they need, not only food, to recover but care.

Food they get and very often they die as soon as they take it.   Care and nursing there is, unfortunately, none, and many die from want of it who would otherwise live.

The sights one sees there are terrible, and it would need a Dantesque pen to describe them.   The island is a small one opposite Corfu.

It has only one building which serves as a habitation for doctors and the personnel.   The rest is barren lands and ruins of old fortifications destroyed by the English before they gave the island to Greece.

As soon as I arrived near enough to have a good view of the shore, I found that the name "death" had been rightly given to the island.   A few paces from the landing was a small inclosure screened with tent sheets, behind which the corpses were piled.   A few meters away was a large boat tied to a sort of wooden jetty already full of bodies, and on the jetty two men were unloading a stretcher by simply turning it over and throwing another corpse atop the others.

And that operation was being performed regularly, one stretcher following another, corpse after corpse falling from a height of two meters into the boat until there was such a pile that no more could be taken, and the boatload with legs and arms protruding here and there, some hanging overboard, was taken to the sea which became the grave for those unfortunate people who had suffered so much and had died just as they thought they were safe.

There are one hundred buried that way every day. They die not from sickness, but simply because they are so tired, so exhausted physically, so famished, that it is only with the most careful nursing, by treating them like children, putting them in warm beds, etc., that one could save them. But tents are few and beds are fewer.

There is no wood to burn and therefore no fires are made. Some drag themselves to a tree, where they sit and sleep and do not wake again. They have starved too long and cannot support food any more.

The worst sight was under three or four tents, old, rickety, dirty, big and black, as if in harmony with the sights they covered. In each of them from forty to sixty soldiers were lying, not in beds, not on straw, not on the earth, but in the mud, because there were neither beds nor straw.

Our good intentions to get away early from Scutari were thwarted by several accidents. Assembled at the British consulate, we waited for hours before the carts that were to carry the luggage and the nurses came. Here we saw Admiral Troubridge again for a few minutes. He had arrived shortly before by way of Albania and had had to walk most of the way, but he seemed quite as debonnaire as ever; and, because he had been able to secure supplies for his men, was cheerful. When our carts did come, we filed out through interminable muddy streets to the end of the town and there a halt was called.

There was no one definitely in charge of the party, and none seemed able to tell why we had stopped. Nikola had been sent ahead, while Dr.

Čurčin had stayed behind to see about the unit's passports and money matters. The British consul was supposed to have made arrangements. For three hours we stood where the drivers had suddenly deserted us, taking ten of the carts with them. When they returned they had enough hay for the round trip of four days. Under the best conditions, it is two full days' journey by ox-cart from Scutari to Medua, but now the roads were in a frightful condition. In places the wide Bojana threatened to overflow them utterly. Everywhere was deep mud, and frequently for hundreds of yards stretched continuous ponds. So an early start was imperative if we were to reach the half-way village where Nikola hoped to secure shelter. Our being delayed brought about a series of adventures and at the last almost caused us a cruel disappointment.

It was about two o'clock when we got under way again and a cold, driving rain had set in which soaked the women, perched on top the groaning cart between those tremendous wheels, the riddle of which the bottomless mud soon explained to us. They sat upon the hay, which soon became like a sponge, making quite as uncomfortable a seat as can well be imagined.

Admiral Trowbridge speaking with English women in front of the British Consulate at Scutari

The rain continued steadily until late afternoon, when the clouds broke into a sunset of marvelous splendor that deluged the ruddy crags about Scutari with royal purple shades and splotches of yellow light, that glorified our road into a ribbon of iridescent reflection leading straight away westward to the blessed sea and rest, that transmuted the swollen Bojana to a rushing flood of gold, all echoes of the beauty of the sky. Although we were soaked to the skin and tramped in the midst of a savage wilderness at nightfall with no habitation in sight and knowing not at all where we would sleep, the scene laid its magic upon us. We were now traversing the perfectly flat bottom of the valley, covered by tall, withered grasses fragrant with the rain and bending under the breeze that raced over it. Disregarding the distant mountains, it had the quality of a windy Dutch landscape under clouds that were fading to dun and ashen, and brought a sense of isolation from the world, of having for the instant ceased to be a part of it, of watching it as from a star. Always in the mind of each of us was Serbia, the tragic manner of her death, the great beauty of her primitive heroism. Already "The Retreat" was merging into a unit of the past, into a finished experience whose memory tinged our every thought, as in fact it has continued unceasingly to do.

At Scutari grewsome accounts had come to us of what befell many refugees and weakened soldiers on the route through Albania from Prizrend. Several high officers, including a French major, had been murdered, as well as some fifteen hundred soldiers and many hundreds of civilians. Although from Durazzo, Essad Pasha was doing all in his power to succor and protect the Serbs, he was unable to control the wild northern tribesmen when once the all-pervasive unrest of war had penetrated their mountains. People had their throats slashed as they slept simply for the rings on their fingers. In narrow defiles they were cut off and shot down, and in lonely villages, stopping for the night, their huts were surrounded and all were butchered. As a consequence we did not view with too much faith and complacency the twenty-five outlandish beings who came along to drive the oxen. The Montenegrin Government sent along with us two young sergeants as guides and protectors. They were surly, ill-humored fellows, inexpressibly lazy and utterly nonchalant about everything except their own comfort. They seemed to be frightened themselves, for when night came they began to insist that we stop right where we were in the fields without shelter and roost on the carts until dawn. This did not seem to promise more safety and certainly not as much comfort as pushing on, so we refused to stop. The cloud-rack had blown away almost entirely now and a brilliant moon, just beginning to wan, rose after a while and made our traveling easier. Also the road had become firmer, and while we waded in water continuously we did not stick very much.

We tramped along for two or three hours after the moon rose. Just ahead of our party three Englishmen walked, the guards came along in the middle, and a young medical student from Edinburgh whom we had met at Podgoritze brought up the rear with me. This young man was named Bobby Burns and was half-American. Walking along in the wilderness together we amused ourselves discussing New York, books, the theater, and settled quite easily many profound social problems. Under the surface of this chatter, however, we considered with more or less interest every dark place on the road. He was very soft-spoken and polite, even to a fault, and his diction was always most polished. His gentle manner and his almost girlish face made him seem to have just stepped out from some sequestered school. As a matter of fact, he had been connected with an army division for months, had undergone terrific strain, hardship and exposure, had witnessed many horrible things while retreating with the army, about all of which he spoke with a cool detachment that I envied. No trace of the ordeal was on him, only always his thought was for the comfort and safety of the women, and his good humor unfailing. I liked to think that he was English, and I liked even more to know that he was American, too.

Between nine and ten o'clock when the drivers were just about ready to mutiny, apparently, we heard a shout ahead and Nikola came to meet us, saying that he had got us shelter for the night in a tiny village, for it would not be possible to reach the half-way station before far into the night. To stop meant that it would hardly be feasible to reach San Giovanni di Medua next day, but we knew of nothing to make us think a little further delay would matter.

The "village" consisted of a half-dozen huts. The forty women were to sleep all together in a fair-sized room in the largest house, while guards were to sleep outside the door. We men shared another room at a little distance. The head of the family village, at whose hut the women were to sleep, was a villainous old chap of amazing age, who boasted dozens of sons and dozens-times-dozens grandsons, all of whom congregated around to watch us. I couldn't imagine where they all came from. They poked around our luggage in the most naïvely inquisitive manner and had a disconcerting habit of sitting tailor-fashion and staring straight at one for ten minutes without winking an eye, stern and unsmiling. They were, indeed, a rummy crowd to descend into at ten in the evening in search of shelter. They appeared cold, haughty, and distrustful, although they committed no overt act of hostility. When we began to "feed" before turning in, the old mummy walked calmly in, sat down among us, and stared and fingered us to his heart's content, while his clan packed the porch outside. He spoke a little Serbian, but his Albanian no one of our Serbs could understand. Stepping out of this room suddenly, I found the crowd investigating our baggage which was on the porch. Their demeanor was such that I thought it best not to yell at them, but I went over and sat down on my bag, whereupon the bunch formed round me in a half-circle and stared me out of countenance, not uttering a sound, until they became for me a pack of coyotes sitting on their haunches with their tongues hanging out.

Then a curious thing happened. The old fellow came out. Nikola had evidently impressed upon him the importance of leaving English people alone, and as a matter of fact he eyed us a bit disdainfully. My cowboy hat took his eye and that meant that he had to touch it or he would die. He shuffled over, lifted it off my head, and examined it. "Engleske?" he murmured, using the Serbian word to me. "Amerikanske," I replied with a result that indeed surprised me. He and all his innumerable progeny showed the keenest interest at once, and smilingly gathered around me, saying grotesque words which I took to be kindnesses. They patted me all over, and the ancient patriarch thrusting his savage face—it was not so bad in its way—right into mine, repeated in a voice of greatest interest and cordiality, *"Amerikanske, Amerikanske— braat!"* ("American brother"), and again he began patting me until I felt like a patty-cake. He offered tobacco, and I produced some dried figs. From then on I felt their attitude had changed toward us.

It does seem strange to me that the only time in my life when American citizenship *per se* brought me the slightest consideration should have been among a clan of semi-savages in the middle of a howling Albanian wilderness. In many thousands of miles of traveling throughout western and southern Europe and in the Balkans, I have always counted myself lucky if I found my passport at par; to have it appear at a premium is an experience from which I have not yet recovered. I think through Montenegro some rumors of America as a land of wild liberty had come to them, and the Albanian loves wild liberty. Through misunderstanding my country, he liked me. That at any rate is the only explanation I can devise.

The night passed away for me in a great defensive battle with husky Albanian vermin, punctuated by a constant drip-drip of filthy raindrops that leaked through the rotten roof in such quantities it seemed impossible to escape them—all the more as one did not have a wide choice of resting-places, the floor being carpeted with prostrate natives, men, women, and children. "Sunny Jim," the little Serbian orphan boy who came along with us, found a corner near me, and in his dreams would murmur things I could not understand, but in a childish voice that was wretched enough. Once when he was very quiet and I thought at last he was fast asleep I saw tears trickling down his still babyish face. I had never suspected him of the slightest sentiment. He had seemed so wild and tough, full of high spirits, and enjoying the excitement of the march. In the horrible upheaval, confusion, and carnage of the retreat from the northern frontiers, he had lost his family—his father had been shot—and at thirteen was thrown upon his own resources in a situation that might well try the nerves of a strong man. To see him weeping silently in the night, when he thought no one was looking, gripped the throat and made one realize even more than the bodies by the roadside the real tragedy of war. I knew if I tried to console him, it would only humiliate him—he already fancied himself a man. I never intimated to him or any one that I had caught him off his guard.

Dr. May and Nikola had had a great argument as to how far we should go next day. Nikola held that it would be foolish and unnecessary to try to reach Medua in one day, but Dr. May said the unit must try it. I think it was nothing short of an inspiration on her part. She had no reason to believe that a day more would make any difference, but she held to her purpose. So at four next morning we were up and at five our twenty-five carts creaked down a swampy lane to the main road to begin the last day's march—the end of an eight weeks' jaunt for the women, during which they had tramped about three hundred and fifty miles. Full daylight found us two or three miles on our way, tracking over perfectly level ground but close to the rocky hills that border the Bojana valley. Mountain climbing was finished for most of us, but an accident gave three Englishmen, three nurses, and myself one more occasion to test our Alpine prowess. Quite by mistake we took a short-cut that led for miles by mere goat trails over the mountains, but which saved a long distance.

Several of us had pushed ahead of the carts and coming to a fork in the road confidently took the one that seemed most traveled, and led in the right direction. For a few miles this continued to be a good road, but then it climbed to a decayed village where two thirds of the houses, at least, were untenanted and tumbling to pieces. A little farther along it suddenly turned into a mountain trail. From this point the other road could be seen far across the valley below us, so that we were convinced that our path was a short-cut which would lead eventually into the main road. The nurses had taken a rest perhaps a mile behind, and it occurred to me that when they came to this spot, they would be at a loss to know whether to take the path or return many weary miles to the other way. So I returned quickly and brought them along—they were asleep under a tree—while the others went forward. For hours we climbed the steep hills and wished heartily that we had taken the longer route. Doubts began to come and we found no trace of the Englishmen.

We had no food with us and when in mid-afternoon we did emerge into the road again we had no way of knowing whether the caravan was ahead or behind. However, we could not afford to linger, so went on at once very hungry and chagrined. One of the women was so dead tired, she could scarcely walk at all. In the late afternoon we came upon some soldiers who told us that an "Engleske mission" had gone past them. This made us want to push on all the faster, but later we found out that they were mistaken.

At sunset we came to the long bridge across the Bojana at Alessio. On the other end stood the main town, and soldiers of Essad Pasha in outlandish uniforms were parading up and down the farther half of the bridge, for the river marked the boundary of Essad's doubtful sway. In the center

of the road, we spied Nikola calmly waiting for the
caravan to come along. We told him what we had
done and he said we must be several hours ahead of
the main party, and he added, as if it were nothing
at all, that San Giovanni di Medua was just one
hour of *our* walking away. A steamer, he told us,
was waiting there to take us every one to Italy!
That was all he knew. It is only after living the
life which I have tried to picture in this account,
only after doing without everything that civilization
gives to make existence less of a dog fight, that one
could get the full flavor of that announcement.
Italy ten hours away! Where there was clean,
fresh food in unlimited quantities, where one could
eat, eat, eat—that is what we thought of—to reple-
tion, then go to sleep in a *bed* until time to eat again,
and where, oh, dream of ecstasy, one could have a
boiling bath in a gleaming tub! Remember that
for four months before the retreat began, we had
been living under what we then thought terribly
primitive conditions. Add to this the swampy,
cornfield camps, the cold, the dirt and vermin, the
hunger, the limitless and continuous horror, the
anxiety which a four-months' lack of any news had
brought, and the fear that the Adriatic would at
last prove an insurmountable obstacle—then you

can see what a steamer waiting to take us all to
Italy meant.   We could smell the sea in the gentle
wind that came up the rough road to meet us, and
the widening river presaged the beach soon to come
in sight.

Night had now fallen, but an immense red moon
soon bulged over the hills which we had left behind
and stood—majestic sight—mirrored a hundred
times in the endless mud puddles through which we
splashed.   Each of us strained our eyes and ears
to be the first to hail the sea.   A small cavalcade
came splashing toward us, and soon we were halted
by a British officer who, with his comrades, was at
Medua seeing to the landing of supplies and the
like.   He asked where the rest of the party was
and upon hearing that they were far behind expressed anxiety that they would not catch the boat.
It had only come in that morning and was sailing
before midnight, so as to be somewhat out of the
torpedo zone by daylight.   There had not been a
boat for a week, and Heaven only knew when there
would be another!   This appeared strange to us,
but soon we were to see for ourselves a grewsome
explanation.

Only a few minutes after the officers rode on, we
came upon a rocky spur of hills along the face of

which the rude road twined. Looking down from this point we discovered immediately beneath us a reed-grown estuary, so untroubled, like dull-green glass, that for a moment we thought it simply an inland pond until looking westward we saw it expand into a shoreless ocean of silver, and faintly we heard a muffled lapping on the sand. After our three-hundred-and-fifty-mile promenade we had come to the sea, and how easily the smooth unbroken water carried one's thoughts endless miles home! Straight ahead only a little way, the sparse lights of San Giovanni were visible close by the beach and up on the cliffs behind. Having passed two large army camps, we came through a short defile to the little bay. An even swell lifted the water and sent soft, winding lines of shining foam along the beach, but the surface of the harbor was smooth and oily and, at first, seemed unbroken except for the small steamer riding at anchor two hundred yards from shore. Soon, however, we noticed that the bay was spotted with funnels and mast-tips that protruded a few feet above the water, and a good deal of flotsam was strewn along the sand. That brightly lighted steamer was anchored among a veritable cemetery of ships, and the wrecks' gaunt hands reached up on every side

of her.   Upon the white sand we saw a giant cigar
glistening moistly in the moonlight which, on closer
acquaintance, became a very business-like Austrian
torpedo.   Failing to explode, it had been washed
there after its venomous comrades had sent down
eleven ships within twenty minutes—ships loaded
with food, every pound of which would have saved
a life.   Such had been the fate of the last cargo
brought from Italy eight days before.   No wonder
boats did not come often, no wonder hundreds of
nurses had been waiting almost a week there, not
knowing if another boat would ever come.   Twelve
hours away was Brindisi, Italy's great naval base,
but two hours away was Cattaro and Austrian submarines.

If ever there was a perfect final scene to any
tragedy, San Giovanni di Medua was an adequate
finish to the life we had lived.   It is only a few
stone huts on the side of cliffs too rocky to support
vegetation.   There is a tiny pier and a few small
warehouses, a goat-run that does service as a street,
and that is all.   Everybody had already gone on
board when we arrived.   Early in the day Sir
Ralph had arranged for the ship to take all to
Brindisi.   In the late afternoon every one had embarked, so we found no one expecting us, appar-

ently. When Sir Ralph heard we had arrived, his secretary came ashore and told us where to get some bread, and said that all should come on board as soon as the rest arrived, or sooner, if the nurses would. Under no circumstances could the boat be held. About ten-thirty the carts began arriving and the unit started to embark without having had time for food, or scarcely to draw breath. They had been traveling steadily since four in the morning and were nearer dead than alive.

Most of the carts soon arrived, but the one carrying my pictures and notes did not come. Finally all the others came in and I was told that this particular cart had had a breakdown. It was then eleven o'clock and every one said that I should not miss the boat for there was no telling when another might come.   I was determined, however, to be left rather than abandon my records after all those weeks. At eleven-twenty it came creaking in. I had gone down the road to meet it, and snatching my bag, I raced for a rowboat, jumped in, and got on the ship just before she weighed anchor.

From her deck where there was only standing room—almost as bad as the Scutari boat—we looked back at the pier, black with a mob of refugees who clamored to get on the boat but who, for reasons I know not, were not allowed to. We had, perhaps, all we dared to carry. They shouted there, and some fought, while long lines of soldiers carried the supplies, which the ship had brought, from the shore to places of safety on the hillside, for at dawn they feared a raid by air and water. One line I especially remember seeing before I embarked. They were unloading little square wooden boxes filled with gold for the Government. Each box held two hundred thousand francs and there was wild excitement when one of them disappeared. Above the creaking of the anchor-chain, the noise of the disappointed mob came to us, and in the half-light the restless throngs dotted the white quays in ghostly groups, while the funnels of the sunken vessels admonished us not yet to be too sure of Italy. In atmosphere and composition the picture was Doré at his weirdest. To leave behind that army and that people seemed all at once like treason and desertion, and the knowledge that one could no longer be of service to them did not help much.

Our boat was the ill-fated *Brindisi* which very soon afterward was blown up just outside Medua harbor, the hundreds of Montenegrin soldiers on board shooting themselves rather than die by the enemy's hand. Had a torpedo found us, the situa-

Albanian chiefs assembled at Durazzo to aid Essad Pacha against the Austrians

tion would not have been pleasant. There were about two hundred and fifty women on board, French, Russian, and English, and hundreds of sick and wounded soldiers and civilians. They lay upon the decks so thick that it was almost impossible to move about without treading on them and, as we got into rough water on the open sea, fully nine tenths of them became violently ill—a horrible scene that even the moonlight could not tone down.

How strange it seemed to be going somewhere and not having to walk! In twelve hours we would be in Italy. In that time we moved for all practical purposes a thousand years. We came from a cold, dreary, desolate land, filled with the dying and the dead, from an atmosphere of hopeless gloom into a heaven of sunshine and golden fruit, where war seemed never to have passed, and repose and cleanliness could be known once more.

On the boat I met the three nurses whom I had not seen since Ipek, and I was indeed happy to know that they had come through without any serious mishaps. Their courage and readiness to make the best of things, I shall always remember, and I know that none of us will ever forget our vagabond days together from Trestenik to Mitrovitze, over the autumn hills and through the far-

flung wilderness of the Ibar. Sir Ralph, also, came
to me and courteously thanked me for the insignifi-
cant aid it had been in my power to render the
nurses. He said that he regretted not having been
able to aid us at Mitrovitze. He had had "to think
of the greatest good to the greatest number and so
could not remain" with us. It was scarcely his
presence that we had needed there. A word from
the official representative of the British Serbian Relief, asking that the nurses be taken with the others,
would have been more welcome than his or any
one's presence with us at that moment. However
as a lucky chance had made services which I could
render valuable enough to "persuade the unit to
take them on" and we were all right at last, I saw
no reason to pursue the subject. I still hate to
think about what those women would have suffered
if, on the eve of the terrible day on Kossovo, shelter
and food had not been assured them. I remarked
that it had been a strenuous time for all of us and
Sir Ralph heartily agreed. He told me that he
was "worn out from looking after the women," and
"that I could have no idea what a burden the care
of the units had been" to him. Subtle humor to
meet in an Englishman.

The *Brindisi* steamed in the center of a good-sized battle squadron. Because of the valuable cargo she had brought to Medua, the Italian Government had furnished a strong convoy. No sooner had we left the harbor than the lights of two boats appeared to port, and two to starboard, while one was ahead of us, and one behind. They kept at a distance varying from a quarter to a half-mile. When day dawned, we saw that there were five Italian torpedo-boat destroyers and one British cruiser, the *Weymouth*. Looking at the latter steaming near by to starboard, dull gray on the green water and the sunlight picking out her guns, one realized under the circumstances the beautiful practicability of a battle ship. I was told that thirteen more vessels were around us and that, during the night, we had been chased by submarines which the strong convoy had scared off.

On the *Brindisi* I met again Miss Eden, the head of the expedition into Bosnia, where I had been when the storm was gathering over Serbia. I had seen her faced with very grave and trying situations there which had been met in a manner that could only call forth admiration. Now she was very weak from starvation and suffering, and could hardly stand because of frozen feet, but she was already full of plans to return with full medical equipment to aid in the preservation of that army which we all admired.

It was about ten-thirty in the morning when we came to anchor in Brindisi harbor. So much red-tape had to be gone through that not until three o'clock did we get on shore and there we were kept an hour, not being permitted to enter the town. A string of police barred every street and the populace came down to stare as if we had been a circus. There was no food on the boat and most of our unit had been without anything since early morning of the preceding day—this, too, when they had made that long forced march. No food was brought to us and we were not allowed to go in search of any. From ten-thirty in the morning to four in the afternoon we could even smell the bakeries, but had to wait. Finally Sir Ralph arranged for a special train to take the whole party straight to Milan, and thence to Paris and London. It was the eighteenth of December—the nurses would get home for Christmas.

We were led in a gang to the station about an hour before the train started, and our rush on the station restaurant was a sight to see. Imagine what piles of oranges, grapes, apples, and bananas looked like to starving people who had seen nothing decent to eat for months; picture the seductiveness of lunch-counter sausages and boxes of sweets and dried fruits; think for an instant of tall cold glasses of creamy beer and delicious light wines, and put down into the midst of it all three hundred famished people. When the train came, for the moment the restaurant had become a restaurant in name only.

Enough coaches had not been procured to afford seats for more than two thirds of the party, but that mattered little to us. On board the Milan Express a weariness which even the excitement of going home could not conquer came over us all. We lay down on the corridor floors, in the vestibules, under the seats. Wrapped for the last time in our soldier-blankets, we roughed it one more night in the midst of civilization. It is indicative of my mental state that I took it for granted the train was going to Rome, and thence to Milan. I intended to stop in Rome. It never occurred to me to ask, so when a lot of people stumbled over me in the middle of the night as I lay directly in the entrance, and I distinguished shouts about changing for Rome I was appalled. I did not know whether we had passed the junction, or if that were it. My movements were merely reflex—due in part to what had happened in that restaurant—and I tumbled out of a window when I could not open the door, and sat upon my bag between some tracks, where I immediately fell asleep again. The feeling of absolute indifference as to what under the sun became of me was delicious. One train was as good as another to me, so I climbed on the first one that woke me up without worrying to make any inquiry. It happened to be a third-class train full of troops returning from the front on Christmas furlough. Some of them spoke English and they all immediately concluded that I was starving and penniless. I shall not soon forget their generous, wholehearted proffers of food and even money! When the guard came through and had the hardihood to ask me if I had a ticket or a pass they almost mobbed him. These soldiers were magnificently equipped and looked so well-cared for and happy, they made all the more startling the contrast with that other tortured army less than twenty-four hours away.

It would take many pages to record the sensations which I underwent on coming back to Rome and—a bath! I cannot even enumerate the kindnesses which were extended to me as a "refugee," especially by the charming English people and their friends in the hotel where I stopped. The trip from Albania had been so rapid that I found myself wóndering if I were not blissfully dreaming in some mountain hut. Thirty-six hours from the time that I was slopping through mire up to my knees in a heavy downpour, suffering from hunger and fatigue, with no idea when I might get away from that horror-stricken land, I was luxuriously feeding (I did not lunch or dine, I *fed* those first few days) in a perfectly appointed Rome hotel with kind people to talk to—even though I had no shoes! I had arrived on the nineteenth of December, exactly two months after I had boarded the train at Valjevo with the Christitch party to begin the Great Retreat.

Of those days following my arrival I have no notes and a very clouded memory. Just as people still feel the swaying decks beneath them after landing from a long voyage, my mind was still in a state of retreat. To all intents and purposes for a few days I continued to live the refugee life and seldom ceased to feel the cold of Kossovo, the hunger of Prizrend, the despair of the mountains. The very food that I ate sometimes seemed like murder when I thought of the dead at Scutari.

I wish I could comprehend and record the feelings of the men at Corfu and Vido to-day. Sitting around the dinner table on Christmas evening —for my new friends' hospitality had extended so far—one of them asked, "What of the soldier of the line? Does he still think that the game is worth the candle?"

My mind went back to a dark freezing dawn near Prizrend when by the road side I had found a man. He lay on a pile of soaking, rotten straw under an old cow-shed carpeted with filth, and he was wounded. A miserable fire smoldered beside him —a fire that might outlast him. To my surprise he spoke a little English and we discussed commonplaces, as is the way in desperate circumstances. Very near, the Serbian and enemy guns were booming in a lively duel.

"How far away are those guns?" I asked, expecting him to answer "an hour," or "a half-hour," as is the Serbian custom. But with difficulty, he rose on his elbow and looking somewhere beyond me he said:

"Maybe they are a hundred years nearer than they were four weeks ago, but not more than a hundred years!"

Not more than a hundred years, if any Serb be left to drive them out; and what is a hundred years to a nation that has not lost its individuality through "five hundred years of durance"?

"They do not count the cost," I answered. "They are not made that way. They only fight and hope."

As I recall it now, that seems to me the best epitome I can give of the Serbian people. For five centuries they have unflinchingly fought and hoped. To all who have intimately known them, their present misfortune is as the keenest personal sorrow. For if a calm and dignified spirit under the dreariest of skies, if unfaltering and unquenchable patriotism under tests that may well be styled supreme, if splendid bravery, and endurance that passes understanding, if simple immovable faith in a great and simple liberty, if deathless devotion to what one conceives as right and honorable, be any longer of use in the world, the land of Serbia and the national soul of the Serbs is worth preserving. They have a bright destiny to which the vast resources of their beautiful country and the blood of their innumerable heroes entitle them, and they will be allowed to work it out. This at any rate is what the Retreat taught me so clearly that never again will I doubt it.

THE END

LaVergne, TN USA
10 November 2010
204324LV00003B/8/P